# Research Design

D0988149

*Research Design* provides a practical overview of the central issues involved in the design of social and economic research. Covering both theoretical and policy research, Hakim sets out the key features, strengths and limitations of eight main types of study, with illustrations from real-life research of the kinds of questions each can best be used to answer. In addition, this book offers a more general pragmatic discussion of strategies for choosing between one design and another, and how different types of study can be successfully combined in wider ranging research programmes.

In this expanded second edition, the author has added new material on areas of contemporary significance across the social and economic sciences. Among these new additions are:

- a chapter on cross-national comparative studies
- more examples throughout the text of comparative research both within Europe and across modern societies
- discussions of student theses, advocacy research, selection effects and collaborative research.

This book will be an indispensable and accessible guide to research design for students, for professional social scientists and for those who commission and use social research.

**Catherine Hakim** is Senior Research Fellow at the London School of Economics.

# Social Research Today
## Edited by Martin Bulmer

The *Social Research Today* series provides concise and contemporary introductions to significant methodological topics in the social sciences. Covering both quantitative and qualitative methods, this new series features readable and accessible books from some of the leading names in the field and is aimed at students and professional researchers alike. This series also brings together for the first time the best titles from the old *Social Research Today* and *Contemporary Social Research* series edited by Martin Bulmer for UCL Press and Routledge.

**Martin Bulmer** is Professor of Sociology and Co-Director of the Institute of Social Research at the University of Surrey. He is also Academic Director of the Question Bank in the ESRC Centre for Applied Social Surveys, London.

Other series titles include

**Principles of Research Design in the Social Sciences**   Frank Bechhofer and Lindsay Paterson

**Social Impact Assessment**   Henk Becker

**The Turn to Biographical Methods in Social Science**   Edited by Prue Chamberlayne, Joanna Bornat and Tom Wengraf

**Quantity and Quality in Social Research**   Alan Bryman

**Research Methods and Organisational Studies**   Alan Bryman

**Field Research: A Sourcebook and Field Manual**   Robert G. Burgess

**In the Field: An Introduction to Field Research**   Robert G. Burgess

**Measuring Health and Medical Outcomes**   Edited by Crispin Jenkinson

**Methods of Criminological Research**   Victor Jupp

**Information Technology for the Social Scientist**   Edited by Raymond M. Lee

**An Introduction to the Philosophy of Social Research**   Tim May and Malcolm Williams

**Surveys in Social Research** (4th edition)   David de Vaus

**Researching the Powerful in Education**   Edited by Geoffrey Walford

# Research Design

Successful designs for social and economic research

Second edition

## Catherine Hakim

London and New York

First edition 1987 by Unwyn Hynman Ltd, London

Second edition 2000
by Routledge
11 New Fetter Lane, London EC4P 4EE

Simultaneously published in the USA and Canada
by Routledge
29 West 35th Street, New York, NY 10001

*Routledge is an imprint of the Taylor & Francis Group*

Typeset in 10/12pt Times by RefineCatch Limited, Bungay, Suffolk
Printed and bound in Great Britain by
Clays Ltd, St Ives plc

*British Library Cataloguing in Publication Data*
A catalogue record for this book is available from the British Library

*Library of Congress Cataloging in Publication Data*
A catalog record for this book has been requested

ISBN 0–415–22312–1 (hbk)
ISBN 0–415–22313–X (pbk)

For WRH

# Contents

# Preface

This book fills a gap in the social science literature, which remains partitioned into theoretical works, methods textbooks and substantive reports on empirical research, and is further partitioned by social science discipline. Research design is the point where questions raised in theoretical or policy debates are converted into feasible research projects and research programmes that provide answers to these questions. Current trends towards large research programmes, multi-disciplinary research, projects jointly funded by several different organisations, and contract research for government agencies and private sector bodies mean that the overall research design and strategy have to be worked out in some detail at the front end of a project or research programme. This task has been impeded by the paucity of general texts on research design that overcome the theoretical and methodological distinctions between the various social science disciplines and that present the options in a sufficiently non-technical manner to enable fruitful discussion and collaboration between those who do research, those who pay for it and those who will use the results. This text helps to fill this gap, providing an overview of the options and the logic of the choices to be made for three audiences.

Firstly, researchers themselves, when embarking on a study, often fail to think through the design of a project, and how it addresses substantive questions, sufficiently carefully. For professional researchers, this text should help in producing research proposals that find favour with research funders, whereas methods textbooks are about how to carry out a project once it has started. The book should be especially helpful to research teams doing cross-national comparative or multi-disciplinary research. Because the language of social science research tends to be discipline specific, communication difficulties can arise over aims and objectives. A common language of research design facilitates discussion of research aims among those engaged in multi-disciplinary and cross-national research.

A second audience consists of people in organisations that fund grant research or commission contract research who are actively involved in the research design stage of projects, even if they never themselves carry out research. They often have to choose between alternative designs addressed to the same issue, or between cheaper and more expensive designs, and guidelines for such choices are a help even if final decisions have to take extraneous factors into account, such as organisational policies. Some people responsible for research funding decisions will not have any social science training, and others will have experience only in a single discipline, or even a single type of study, so they need to understand the logic of research design regardless of disciplinary framework. Research proposals that are presented in terms of the principal design elements (and in plain English, with minimal use of disciplinary or specialist jargon) facilitate discussions between research funders and those doing research and overcome the communication gap that can so easily ruin negotiations. This text gives research funders, especially those who commission contract research, a clear idea of what they can expect to get for their money. The expectations and output of a case study, for example, will clearly differ from that of a sample survey. The example is particularly pertinent given the current emphasis, in research methods texts and elsewhere, on statistical analysis of sample survey data as the only type of research, producing a poor understanding and low evaluation of the contribution of other types of study.

The third audience is the largest: undergraduate and graduate students who have to make rapid decisions about the design of projects for their dissertations and theses, only a few of whom will go on to become professional researchers or work in organisations commissioning and/ or using social science research. Postgraduate courses in social research design and methods are increasingly multi-disciplinary, and should be, because so many students change from one discipline to another when choosing Masters courses and vocational training. This book is designed for the new, broad, multi-disciplinary graduate courses, but it is also used successfully on many undergraduate courses.

The book is organised into two sections. Part I sets out the key features, strengths and limitations of eight types of study, with illustrations of the kinds of question they can answer. Part II offers a more general discussion of strategies for choosing between, or combining, the eight types of study, and of other points that must be taken into account in the design of single projects or more complex research programmes, including cross-national comparative studies. Inevitably, a short book can provide only a broad overview of the contributions to knowledge that each type of study offers, the advantages and disadvantages that must be weighed up in choosing between them, and the gains from combining two or three studies within a project. But it should help those who ask for research and those who carry it out to achieve workable compromises, value for money and fruitful collaboration.

The discussion of strategies and choices in the design of social research is illustrated throughout with a wide range of examples from theoretical research and policy research. Examples are taken from across the social science disciplines: sociology, economics, political science, social psychology, history, geography and social anthropology. Within the policy research field, illustrative examples are chosen from research on health, education, the labour market, crime, housing, family studies, fiscal policy, income maintenance, and research on the policy process itself. Examples are taken from research across Europe, North America and other countries. The central theme of this book is not the discipline nor the research topic but the idea that empirical research is fruitful only when studies chosen for a project or research programme are appropriate to the questions addressed.

There are several important changes to this second edition. A new chapter has been added on the design, organisation and funding of cross-national comparative research. One consequence of the steady expansion of the European Union is rapid growth in the number and sophistication of comparative studies across Europe. At the same time, there is increasing interest in comparisons across the advanced economies of the OECD club. Such studies are not limited to analyses of national survey data. New sections have been added to all the chapters in Part I to show how each type of study can be used within cross-national comparative research. Many of the new research examples described in the second edition concern comparative studies, within Europe, the Americas, and across the globe.

The World Wide Web, e-mail and easy access to information technology greatly facilitate communication between members of cross-national research teams, but are also having a broader impact, changing the way research is done. The book has been updated to describe new facilities and information sources, with specific website addresses where appropriate. However, this is an area where change is ongoing, and rapid.

The entire text has been revised and updated, both in the examples described and in the recommendations for further reading at the end of each chapter. The whole text has also been revised to address the needs and interests of students more closely. A new section in Chapter 10 offers advice on choosing topics for student dissertations and theses. Students are often the most innovative in their research designs – inventing new applications and combinations of research types, and helping to maintain the dynamic element in the development of research designs.

# Key to abbreviations

| | |
|---|---|
| BCS | British Crime Survey |
| BMRB | British Market Research Bureau |
| BSAS | British Social Attitudes Survey |
| CAPI | Computer Assisted Personal Interviewing |
| CASS | Centre for Applied Social Surveys |
| CATI | Computer Assisted Telephone Interviewing |
| CHRR | Center for Human Resource Research |
| CPS | Current Population Survey (of the USA) |
| CWHS | Continuous Work History Sample (USA) |
| ESRC | Economic and Social Research Council |
| FES | Family Expenditure Survey |
| GHS | General Household Survey |
| GSS | General Social Survey (USA) |
| IALS | International Adult Literacy Survey |
| ILO | International Labour Office |
| ISSP | International Social Survey Programme |
| LFS | Labour Force Survey |
| LIS | Luxembourg Income Study |
| LS | Longitudinal Study |
| NBER | National Bureau of Economic Research (of the USA) |
| NCDS | National Child Development Study |
| NES | New Earnings Survey |
| NIT | Negative Income Tax |
| NLS | National Longitudinal Surveys of Labour Market Experience (USA) |
| NOP | National Opinion Polls |
| NORC | National Opinion Research Center |
| NOS | National Organisations Study (USA) |
| OCG | Occupational Changes in a Generation (USA) |

| OECD | Organisation for Economic Co-operation and Development* |
| ONS | Office of National Statistics (Britain) |
| OOPEC | Office for Official Publications of the European Community |
| PSI | Policy Studies Institute |
| PSID | Panel Study of Income Dynamics (USA) |
| PUS | Public Use Sample |
| SAR | Sample of Anonymised Records |
| SIME/DIME | Seattle Income Maintenance Experiment and Denver Income Maintenance Experiment |
| SOEC | Statistical Office of the European Community |
| SPSS | Statistical Package for the Social Sciences |
| SSRC | Social Science Research Council (USA) |
| TARP | Transitional Aid Research Project (USA) |
| WFS | World Fertility Survey |
| WIRS/WERS | Workplace Industrial/Employment Relations Survey |
| WVS | World Values Survey |

* By 1999, OECD membership consisted of Japan, Australia, New Zealand, Canada, the USA, Mexico, Luxembourg, the Netherlands, Belgium, France, Britain, Germany, Austria, Denmark, Finland, Norway, Sweden, Iceland, Ireland, Switzerland, Italy, Spain, Portugal, Greece and Turkey.

# 1 Introduction

Before a building of any consequence is built, there is an initial design stage. Architects are invited to present their ideas, sometimes on a competitive basis, on the shape, style and character of the building, while taking account of its functions, purpose, location and so forth. The design stage can attract substantial interest and controversy, far more interest than the actual building work. The architect who produces the design selected as the winner will then be responsible for supervising all subsequent work to implement the design, including that done by quantity surveyors, builders and other specialists who are hired in to help turn the blueprint into a reality. The architect may never lift a single brick, but famous buildings are known by the name of the architect rather than that of the construction company. Without wishing to push the analogy too far, this book is about the architect's role and design functions in relation to social research, while most methods texts are about the builder's job.

Design deals primarily with aims, uses, purposes, intentions and plans within the practical constraints of location, time, money and availability of staff. It is also very much about *style*, the architect's own preferences and ideas (whether innovative or solidly traditional) and the stylistic preferences of those who pay for the work and have to live with the final result. Methods texts are about how to produce a study, once the goal is defined or chosen, and can be very dull. I do not deal with methodological and philosophical issues (see Galtung, 1967, 1990; Sayer, 1984) or with theoretical issues, which depend heavily on the particular study, the researcher's discipline and also, arguably, national intellectual styles (Galtung, 1990).

## Rationale for a focus on research design

The design function is virtually invisible when a researcher carries out a project singlehanded and unfunded, developing and revising the initial plan as the study progresses. The design stage becomes more visible with the development of large-scale studies, contract research for central government and other organisations, studies involving multi-disciplinary teams, and research programmes that involve several studies concerned with a central topic or set of issues. Large-scale social research does not automatically rule out the muddling-through approach, but it does force design issues out into the open at an early stage, so that the design function becomes more visible – even if visibly badly done by committee.

The design role is also becoming more visible as a result of the increasing division of labour and specialisation in social research. Experts in sampling, fieldwork and data analysis are now well accepted. But the idea of a research design specialism is still resisted among social scientists.

Research design issues rarely arise in certain social science disciplines. Economists, for example, use secondary analysis of existing data (both aggregate data and survey micro-data) to such a large extent that design issues are often reduced to the choice of dataset. Experiments are the domain of psychology. Most social science disciplines use more than one type of study, however, although sociology is distinctive in regularly making use of all the research designs identified here. The term 'social research' is used here in the broadest sense to encompass all social science disciplines, and one purpose of this book is to encourage disciplines that currently use a restricted range of research designs to branch out and consider other types as well. Although the choices researchers make are inevitably constrained by resources, most people become experienced with one type of study and then stick with it, safely and unadventurously.

While sociological examples will crop up with particular frequency, given their tendency to use the widest range of research designs, this text is multi-disciplinary in orientation and is intended to be of use to all social science disciplines. Economics might benefit from the use of qualitative or experimental research, for example, and a well-focused case study should be within the repertoire of any social scientist.

There is already a vast literature on particular research techniques and methods. Despite variations in content and style, they have in common a focus on how to do research and the technical details, with occasional forays into the philosophy of knowledge. The focus here is not on *how* to do any type of research but on *when* and *why* any particular type of study should be chosen for a project: the pros and cons of each type, including the frequently overlooked factor of relative costs and the time required; how they overlap and hence present partial alternatives; and how they can be combined or linked together logically in a research programme consisting of a number of individual projects. The focus is on choices and strategies in research design, and the reader who decides to opt for any study type will need to refer to the relevant how-to-do-it methods literature for further guidance on implementation. The information needed to make informed choices and develop a research strategy differs from that needed actually to carry out a project, and often it is needed by people who will not themselves be carrying the proposal through to completion. This text offers an assessment of the key strengths and weaknesses of the eight types of study, their relative appropriateness for different research issues, their usefulness in terms of output and the product obtained.

One positive consequence of increasing competition for research funds is that people are asking sharper questions about the value of any research project. This means that we have to look more closely at what is gained from any study, at the relative merits of different types of study, and at the cost-effectiveness of research designs. There is now an even balance between grant research and contract research in research funding, producing greater emphasis on value for money and a trend towards tightly defined research designs with clearly stated objectives and timetables. This is leading to greater rigour in research design and should have positive consequences for social science research in the longer term. In the short term, a well-designed study is more likely to get funding than a confused design. This book should also help those who have to assess research proposals, sometimes from a different social science discipline, or while working in a practitioner or policy-making role.

## Theoretical research and policy research

There are substantial design differences between theoretical research and policy research. The outline that follows reiterates the distinction drawn by Scott and Shore (1979: 224–39) and Majchrzak (1984: 11–21) between knowledge for understanding and knowledge for action, and the distinction drawn by Gibbons *et al.* (1994) between Mode 1 (discipline-based) and Mode 2 (policy-oriented) knowledge production.

*Theoretical research* is concerned primarily with causal processes and explanation. The factors (or variables) considered are frequently abstract or purely theoretical constructs for which operational definitions and indicators of varying degrees of precision and validity are developed. The intended audience for theoretical research is the relevant section of the social science community (that is, academics in the main), who can all be assumed to speak the same specialist language. The long-term aim is the development of social science knowledge. Theoretical research is essentially concerned with producing knowledge for understanding, usually within the framework of a single social science discipline.

*Policy research*, in contrast, is ultimately concerned with knowledge for action, and the long-term aim is in line with the famous dictum that it is more important to change the world than to understand it. This broader objective means that policy research encompasses a more diverse variety of research, including theoretical research in many cases, but also descriptive research, which maps out the landscape of a topic, issue or problem, studies to monitor how existing policy is working, extending in some cases into formal evaluation research. A distinctive feature that differentiates it from theoretical research is a focus on *actionable* factors (or variables) either in addition to, or in preference to, theoretical constructs; and actionable variables are usually defined operationally from the very start, from the ground up rather than down from theory. The intended audience for policy research includes all the relevant groups of policy-makers, decision-takers, public pressure groups, managers of organisations, client groups, and so on. This diversity within the intended audience leads to specialist jargon being eschewed in favour of 'plain English' in reports on research results and summaries of key findings.

There is no firm dividing line between theoretical and policy research. For example, change may be brought about by (academic) research results that re-orientate the way an issue is perceived, by altering people's definition of the situation and, in due course, the way they deal with it. But the differences normally have implications for research design.

The concern with *actionable factors* can lead to quite different emphases in policy research and theoretical research on the same topic. For example, it may be that the home environment and personal characteristics are important determinants of educational attainment, but policy research would focus more on school characteristics and processes, particularly school organisation, atmosphere, leadership, curriculum goals and teacher expectations, with a view to minimising the effects of non-school factors and maximising the impact of those factors that are malleable.

Theoretical research is normally conducted within the framework of a single discipline, sometimes based on one particular approach within the discipline. As Smelser (1980: 28) notes, 'to bring theoretical explanation to bear is simultaneously to select, exclude and thereby distort the whole historical record'. So theoretical research looks 'ethnocentric' or biased from the broader perspective of policy research, which is typically *multi-disciplinary* or *transdisciplinary* (Gibbons *et al.*, 1994: 168) and is rarely anchored to a single discipline.

To a far greater extent than theoretical research, policy research is *multi-dimensional* (Majchrzak, 1984: 18). There is a greater propensity towards multi-method studies and research programmes, owing to the political pressures to get a fully rounded and balanced picture on any topic. Even single projects need to cover the conflicting interests that arise on an issue. Research designs must often be multi-level. For example, research on educational policy issues may need to address the matter at the level of the local neighbourhood or school, at the level of local or state government, and at the national level, as well as taking account of the potentially conflicting interests of teachers, parents and others who are affected by changes in policy.

The need for a comprehensive picture in policy research leads to a preference for studies that are *nationally representative*, or else permit extrapolation to the national level. In contrast, a great deal of theoretical research is carried out with small local studies, the results of which cannot readily be generalised.

Other differences between theoretical research and policy research are of a more peripheral nature, or are contingent rather than inherent distinctions. A good deal of policy research addresses respondents and informants as *role-holders* rather than as private individuals, as illustrated by interviews with employer/management representatives, trade union representatives or minority group representatives. Policy research is usually carried out within an agreed timetable, whereas theoretical research projects may run for a decade or longer before completion. In order to be accessible to all interested parties, the results of policy research must be written in 'plain English', in addition to (or instead of) specialist language, and must be presented in the context of policy options, sometimes extending into recommendations for action at the end of a report. Policy research is socially accountable and produces socially distributed knowledge (Gibbons *et al.*, 1994).

Questions about causal processes can arise in both theoretical and policy research, but those arising in policy research tend to be more complex than in theoretical research – to judge by the simple-minded presentation offered in many methods textbooks (see, for example,

Ackoff, 1953; Krausz and Miller, 1974; Miller, 1992). These and other texts tend to focus on the example of testing whether a particular antecedent is a necessary or sufficient cause of a known behaviour, attitude or other social phenomenon; the dependent variable is identified and the *antecedents*, or causes, are assessed. Some types of policy research deal instead with the *consequences* of a given social phenomenon; the consequences can be large in number and infinitely diverse, with no prior assumptions as to their nature and number. In this case there is a *single* independent variable and numerous dependent variables. Examples here would be research on the effects of putting platoons of black soldiers into white infantry companies (Stouffer, 1950), the effects of school climate on teenagers' aspirations and achievements (Coleman, 1961), the effects of natural disasters (Wright *et al.*, 1979) or the social consequences of unemployment at the individual level and the societal level (Hakim, 1982b). Sometimes a policy research study is designed to cover *both* antecedents/causes and consequences/effects of a given social phenomenon, and the resulting comprehensive reports can readily look 'descriptive' to readers unfamiliar with the broad range of issues being covered. Examples here might be the USA National Longitudinal Surveys of Labour Market Experience described in Chapter 8 or the British 1980 Women and Employment Survey discussed in Chapter 6. Also policy research addresses macro-level causal processes, which are poorly served by a methods literature that tends to use simple micro-level examples of explanatory research – such as whether fatigue and level of illumination influence performance (Krausz and Miller, 1974: 82). When policy research is required to provide answers quickly in areas that have attracted little academic interest, the answers on causal processes must inevitably be more broad-brush and imprecise than strictly desirable. In other cases, where the timetable and funds permit it, the causal analysis can be as sophisticated as the best theoretical research ever achieves – as illustrated by the guaranteed annual income experiments described in Chapter 9.

Accurate description plays a significant part in both policy research and theoretical research. In both cases the central question is often 'did X happen or not?', with the bulk of the study concerned with defining, describing and measuring X with a view to concluding that it did or did not happen. The single factor in question may be the key element of a complex theory (for example, the thesis that jobs became deskilled as a result of capitalist industrialisation, or the thesis that the working class adopted middle-class values as a result of increasing affluence), the key issue in a policy debate (for example, whether health inequalities declined as a result of the National Health Service in Britain), or both (for example, whether the sex segregation of jobs has declined, whether as a result of women's changing attitudes and increased labour force participation or due to legislation prohibiting sex discrimination). Being clear that something did, or did not, happen is a crucial first step before considering possible explanations, and it may even constitute the test of a thesis.

Another difference between theoretical and policy research is their contrasting approaches to the quantitive analysis of survey and other data. Theoretical research (and academic writing more generally) is orientated towards reporting *statistically significant* results, with a lesser emphasis on the *size and strength* of any association between the social factors studied. In contrast, policy research requires robust results on associations, the impact of any given factor and so forth. Generally, this means that results must report large and strong effects rather than small but statistically significant effects; research results should not be so dependent on (and hence possibly artefacts of) such finely tuned social measurement that they might readily disappear in a replication using less precise measurement; and results should concern factors of enduring social importance rather than trivial matters. Abstrusely technical academic conflicts over research results or social measurement sometimes reflect quite different approaches to assessing the importance of research results (as illustrated by Murphy, 1985). It also means that simple descriptive tables, which show clearly very large differences or unexpected patterns and associations, can be just as useful as complex multiple regression analyses in policy research, a point discussed by Cain and Watts (1970) and Coleman (1970). Unfortunately, the *statistical significance* of research findings (which is determined in large part by the size of the sample used for the study) is, quite wrongly, regularly confused and conflated with the *substantive* or *practical importance* of research results, which is a matter for judgment and cannot be determined mechanically by statistical techniques (Morrison and Henkel, 1970; McCloskey, 1985). When social scientists complain that 'significant' research findings are ignored by policy-makers, it is often because their results were of little or no substantive importance.

Evaluation research is a growth area in policy research, with numerous texts and journals devoted to it (Abt, 1976; Patton, 1990; Chelimsky and Shadish, 1997; Rossi and Freeman, 1999; *Evaluation Review*, *Evaluation Studies Review Annual*). Evaluations are concerned with assessing all the outcomes of a (proposed) policy, but particularly whether the policy's intended objectives were achieved. Some evaluations include before-and-after studies and can approximate to natural experiments, as noted in Chapter 9. More often, evaluations are carried out after policy implementation and are, in that sense, backward-looking.

More commonly, policy research is concerned with prediction and hence with simulation, forecasting, modelling trends and more qualitative approaches to identifying possible future developments. All these rely, ultimately, on data from one or another of the eight types of study described in Chapters 2 to 9, as shown also by Hoaglin *et al.* (1982).

The distinctions drawn here dispense with the crude distinctions sometimes offered between 'pure' and 'applied' research, based on superficial characteristics such as funding source, timescale, audience, or even whether or not it is academics who carry out a study. As Rossi has pointed out, the dividing line is a very fine one if one looks at the characteristics of the research itself (rather than at superficial factors such as who paid for it); well-designed, broad-focused policy research tends to be more useful to policy-makers as well as being of greater disciplinary interest (the benefits are not mutually exclusive); and policy research tends to demand greater technical skills because the public salience and policy uses of the results demand the highest quality (Rossi, 1980). Perceptions of policy research can be distorted by the relatively greater visibility of the utilisation phase, where controversy can arise, and political ideology and vested interests together play a rather greater role than the information produced by the research (Weiss, 1983), as illustrated by the debates that followed publication of the Coleman report (Cohen and Weiss, 1977). The trends towards academic secondary analysis of major government surveys and *collaborative research* (with the funding, design and analysis of major research projects carried out jointly by government and the academic social science community) tend to erode even further the notion that there are any necessary, clear-cut and mutually incompatible differences between policy research and theoretical research. Even where collaborative research arrangements are not set up from the start, funding and management of a study may transfer from government to the social science community (or vice versa) within the lifetime of a research programme (as in the case of the Panel Study of Income Dynamics in the USA), further eroding the idea of significant and irreconcilable distinctions (Rossi, 1980).

In sum, while there are distinctions between policy research and theoretical research that have implications for research design, the similarities and overlaps are great enough for this text to cover the design process in general and as applying to both fields.

*Advocacy research* must be distinguished from policy research proper. Advocacy research consists of collating available evidence or producing new information to support a *pre-determined* policy position. Advocacy research is commonly carried out by pressure groups, lobby groups and interest groups (such as trade unions) and, occasionally, by political parties, journalists and academics – especially those working in the social policy field. Independent research institutes and think-tanks vary: some do policy research and are in the truth and knowledge business, while others do advocacy research and are in the power and persuasion business (Denham and Garnett, 1998). The precise character of a research report (or summary of research findings) is not always self-evident, as advocacy research usually presents itself as respectable policy research that happens to lead to clear-cut conclusions. In practice, the conclusions are pre-determined, and any contrary evidence or conflicting explanations are simply ignored. Gilbert (1997) discusses one example: feminist use of advocacy research techniques to inflate rape statistics into a major social problem in the USA. Rossi (1987) describes how pressure groups for the homeless in the USA rejected a good policy research study on the extent of homelessness because it did not produce the inflated statistics they wanted. In Britain, a government survey of homeworking aroused controversy because it revealed a complex picture of homeworking very different from that promoted by feminists and pressure groups; yet subsequent studies all confirmed the first survey's findings (Hakim, 1998: 178–99). Many of the research reports published by the British Equal Opportunities Commission are designed to show women as victims rather than as winners (as illustrated by McKnight, Elias and Wilson, 1998). Unfortunately, advocacy research is often equated with policy research, thus giving it a bad name.

## A classification of study types

This text is organised into two parts. Part I identifies eight main types of study and discusses their essential features, strengths and weaknesses. Part II discusses how to choose between the types; strategies for combining them and developing research programmes; the practical issues of research funding and management; and the special features of cross-national comparative studies.

The classification of study types was developed with reference to research design issues. It differs from those used in methods textbooks, although nomenclature is variable anyway, especially across the social science disciplines. So the logic of the classification of the eight types of study needs to be set out, along with a brief outline of the types that are excluded.

Methods textbooks are concerned primarily with the researcher's tasks, the work that will have to be done, the techniques to be used and problems that may be encountered – all with a view to offering guidelines for action. Although some discussion of research design may be offered, the focus is generally on the *implementation* stage – the procedures and tasks for translating the initial idea into a plan of action. Here the focus is on the design stage, so study types are distinguished with reference to their purpose and intellectual strategy rather than the methods or techniques used. So, for example, *field research* does not feature as a study type, even though it is an important method used in case studies and some methods texts are devoted to it (Johnson, 1975; Burgess, 1982, 1984). The term *qualitative research* is used here to refer to depth interviews and focus groups rather than in its looser meaning of any research that produces non-quantitive information (Patton, 1990; Denzin and Lincoln, 1994; Miles and Huberman, 1994; Bryman and Burgess, 1999). From a research design perspective, the types of study discussed in textbooks on qualitative research can be classified as case studies (mostly), qualitative research (occasionally), and very rarely other types as well. Case studies encompass almost all research in social anthropology, many studies in comparative sociology and comparative political science, and substantial numbers of smaller studies in modern societies – especially in evaluation research. From a research design perspective, the fundamental difference between case studies and qualitative research (as the terms are used here) is that qualitative research is concerned with obtaining people's own accounts of situations and events, with reporting *their* perspectives and feelings, whereas case study research is concerned with obtaining a rounded picture of a person's life, a situation or event from the perspectives of all the persons involved, usually by using a variety of methods and sources of information. The distinction is illustrated by the differences of perspective between an autobiography and a biography of one person's life. Qualitative research can deal with causes only at the level of the intentional, self-directing and knowledgeable individual, whereas case studies can deal with a greater variety of causal processes. Similarly, distinctions are drawn between *ad hoc* surveys, regular surveys and longitudinal studies, even though they all employ quantitive methods, because they are used to address different questions.

*Censuses* are not covered, although it is debatable whether they constitute a completely separate type of study. The increasing use of sampling in population census work has tended to blur the distinction between censuses (which used always to give 100% coverage of the universe being surveyed) and interview surveys (which are normally based on sampling of some sort). Increasingly, it is the statutory obligation to participate in, or respond to, a census that distinguishes national exercises of this sort (Hakim, 1982a: 38–9) – an option not available to most researchers. Studies in which all members of a social unit are surveyed are censuses, strictly speaking, but they are more readily regarded as falling within the category of interview surveys (without the sampling) or as case studies. Ballots and referenda are not usually regarded as a type of research – although some would argue that they should be (Marsh, 1982, 1984).

*Cross-national or cross-cultural comparative studies* are becoming increasingly common and important. They are not treated as a separate category, however, because they are always based on one type of study, with secondary analysis of existing data, case studies, *ad hoc* and regular interview surveys being the most common. There are significant additional problems in carrying out the same study in two or more countries, or interpreting data collected in different countries, but they do not of themselves create a separate category of research design – as those who are aware of the problems of cross-cultural research at the sub-national level might agree. The classification of study types presented in Chapters 2 to 9 is applicable in all countries (whether industrialised or developing) and forms a common framework for research design across all social science disciplines, thus contributing to the development of multi-disciplinary research and comparative research. However, cross-national comparative studies do present additional problems of design and organisation, which are discussed in Chapter 13.

The eight main types of study identified in Part I are literature reviews, secondary analysis and meta-analysis of existing data; qualitative research (defined here as depth interviews and focus groups); research based on administrative records and documentary evidence; *ad hoc* interview surveys; regular or continuous interview surveys; case studies; longitudinal studies; and experimental social research. Each chapter outlines the key features of the type of study – its distinct, unique and specific contribution – but also notes the links, overlaps and connections with other types. This is developed further in Chapters 10 and 11, which discuss ways of combining projects and logically interlinking projects within a research programme. Examples of cross-national comparative studies are given for all eight types of study, and Chapter 13 extends this discussion.

Along with Yin (1994: 3), we reject the idea that the various research designs can be organised hierarchically. No single type of study is inherently inferior or superior to others. Each does a particular job and should be selected according to the nature of the issues or questions to be addressed; the extent of existing knowledge and previous research; the resources and time available; and the availability of suitably experienced staff to implement the design. This realistic appraisal is often missing from the research design process, where there is a temptation (perhaps for prestige reasons) to go for the biggest and most complex study people think they can get away with. Parsimony seems to be less valued in social research design than it is in other fields. It is notable that epidemiologists use the laudatory term *elegant* for research designs that manage to address a question in the simplest way possible. Similarly, in social research the aim should always be to achieve the research objectives with a design that is as simple and elegant as possible.

The sequence of presentation is roughly in terms of the complexity – hence the time and resources and overall costs – of a particular research design. The middle ground is occupied by case studies and sample surveys, currently the two dominant options in qualitative and quantitive research respectively.

## Qualitative and quantitive research

One theme running through discussions of research methods is the contrast (or even the contest) between qualitative and quantitive studies. In sociology, there has been a bias towards quantitive research, and hence towards the multivariate analysis of large survey datasets as the 'ideal' type of study for almost any research topic. This is dysfunctional, because no single study is universally appropriate for all research questions. Too often, scholars propose secondary analysis of an existing dataset, or a new survey, when the questions to be addressed require case studies or qualitative research instead. The bias against non-quantitative studies seems now to be diminishing, with renewed awareness of the unique contribution of rigorous case study research (Feagin *et al.*, 1991; Yin, 1993, 1994) and non-quantitative studies more generally (Denzin and Lincoln, 1994). However, it remains necessary to guard against the almost unthinking prejudice in favour of quantitive studies, which may seem more 'scientific' because they involve 'hard' numbers. On the other hand, case studies can be wasted opportunities if they are not conducted and analysed with proper intellectual rigour.

Ragin's (1987) thesis that there are two basic approaches to crossnational comparative research can be extended to identify two main approaches to all data analysis. As Ragin puts it, there are two ways of establishing a meaningful dialogue between ideas and evidence. The *variable-centred approach* is typically adopted by people doing analyses (or secondary analyses) of large national datasets, often covering large numbers of social groups, cultures or countries. The holistic *case-oriented approach* treats each country, person or other social unit as an integrated, complex whole, and is sensitive to complexity and historical specificity. Causation is understood conjuncturally. Ragin presents a logical procedure for analysing causal processes that differentiates between necessary and sufficient causes, identifies the multiple possible outcomes of a single cause, and identifies the multiple potential causes of a single outcome. Similarly, Yin (1994) has developed rules and procedures for the rigorous analysis of case study material. Ragin and Yin point out that the analysis of case study material follows different procedures, but can be just as rigorous and transparent as the logic of statistical data analysis. Other scholars reject the idea that there are major differences between the analysis of data from quantitive and qualitative studies.

King, Keohane and Verba (1994) argue that the logic of inferential analysis applies equally to survey data and case study data. They accept that the two styles of research differ, most obviously in data collection, but they insist that both can be systematic and scientific. They state that the goals of all good research are descriptive inference and causal inference. *Descriptive inference* is concerned with the development of *ideal types*, which identify the essential features of a social unit (such as the family) or a social process (such as a revolution). *Causal inference* is concerned with establishing causality and causal processes – as distinct from the statistical correlations identified by most multivariate analyses. Writing within a political science perspective, all their examples concern national and international political processes, but their argument extends to all the social sciences. As they and others point out, truly experimental research in natural settings is virtually impossible in the social sciences, so this is not a realistic model for most social science research. In the absence of experimental controls, rigorous analytical logic is essential for dealing with non-experimental data.

Finally, there is growing recognition of the limitations of statistical analysis and linear logics for dealing with change processes that involve qualitative change, multiple causation or multiple outcomes. Lieberson (1985) points out that the causal modelling done by many social scientists is flawed. He criticises the routine application of regression analysis to large datasets, and points out that different datasets and analyses are required for different research questions. One promising development is complexity theory, also called chaos theory (Byrne, 1999). This moves away from the linear logic underlying most multivariate analysis towards a more holistic perspective that allows emergent properties (also called 'strange attractors') and qualitative change to be identified.

Byrne also rejects variable-centred causal models in favour of more qualitative approaches to the interpretation of quantitive data, for example through cluster analysis. Complexity theory reinstates prediction as an important test of any social science theory, and it includes an explicit role for agency in change processes.

Research design is about asking questions that can answered with the data collected. In periods of rapid social change, the limitations of variable-centred statistical analysis become clearer, there is greater appreciation of the benefits of holistic case-centred approaches, and there is increased concern with prediction. In addition, the expanding power and potential of data analysis packages widens the scope for manipulating all forms of data. In this context, the dichotomy between quantitive and qualitative research may break down, with better recognition of their complementary contributions to answering important research questions.

## The presentation of study types

All types of study are presented and discussed in terms of 'ideal types', in the sense that their strengths and weaknesses are outlined with reference to good examples of their kind. Obviously, the quality of the results actually obtained from a project depends crucially on the competence, experience and interest of those who carry out the research. All the strengths of the sample survey, for example, are endangered or potentially lost if the survey agency is disorganised, makes serious mistakes, overlooks significant details of sampling or interviewer briefing, or achieves a response rate below 60%. A capable research team can wreak havoc with a good research design if they fall out with each other and refuse to co-operate. These problems are considered further in Part II. But the point needs to be emphasised because it is so often overlooked: people can acquire a pejorative image of a study type because they have come across an inadequate example that demonstrated all the weaknesses but none of the strengths. One reason for switching to an alternative design is that the researchers needed to make a success of the preferred option are not available.

The presentation of the eight study types in Part I follows a fairly standard format to cover the following aspects: definition of the type, its essential features and key strengths as well as its limitations; comparative advantages and weaknesses relative to other designs; examples of cross-national comparative studies; and practical considerations affecting feasibility, such as costs, timetables and any special expertise required. In addition, each chapter notes any *overlaps* between studies (designs that merge the characteristics of two types of study), the potential for *linking* two studies (for example, extending a survey with studies of deviant cases within it) and situations where studies can be *combined* (the linkages being logical and conceptual rather than direct).

Costs do not *automatically* increase with complexity. Complexity may arise chiefly in the theoretical issues being addressed, which are dealt with during the research design process and invisible 'thinking through' work, without necessarily increasing the costs of carrying out the study. Small-scale experimental social research can be cheaper than large-scale surveys or longitudinal studies. But by and large, secondary analysis, qualitative research and studies based on records are simpler and cheaper designs, while regular surveys, longitudinal studies and experimental social research are among the most time-consuming and costly. Hence the question of trading down to cheaper designs or trading up to more complex designs is considered in Chapter 10.

Again, complexity is only *broadly* related to the solidity and scope of a study design. There are cases when an unnecessarily complex design is used and where a simpler type of study could achieve much the same purpose. For example, time is a key variable both in regular interview surveys and in longitudinal studies, but the latter tend to be more complicated to carry out and more expensive. For some research questions, the simpler alternative of a regular survey may achieve results of equal or greater solidity and scope than a longitudinal study.

Arguably the most complex designs arise in research programmes, which are discussed separately in Chapter 11, because they involve logically interlinked projects rather than a single complex study.

The discussion is illustrated throughout with interesting examples taken from the full range of social science disciplines and the various fields of policy research. Sometimes major examples of a research design are presented in some detail. But the overriding aim has been to offer examples that illustrate the range and variety of each study type, or that illustrate particular features especially well, as a stimulus to creative thinking about how to adapt and use them. Examples are taken mainly from European and North American research, with selected examples for other areas.

The implementation of each design is discussed only in terms of foreseeable factors affecting feasibility. There is no discussion of the methods and techniques involved, and readers are referred to appropriate sources elsewhere. Becker (1998) offers useful general advice and ideas on how to do research.

## Choices, strategies and practicalities

In Part II, the focus turns to more general issues in research design, a task where the options, difficulties and possible solutions can be identified but where in the end much depends on the talents, imagination and creativity of the research designer, within the context of specific practical constraints. These four chapters are concerned with setting the abstract rules of principle for research design into a 'real-world' context of getting funds and research management in order to achieve feasible and operational research designs that will get beyond the blueprint stage to be successfully implemented.

Sometimes one may be content with doing a single study and be lucky enough to obtain sufficient resources for it. But it is helpful to be prepared for those instances where resource constraints, or other factors, force one into 'trading down' to a cheaper, or quicker, design. Equally one should be prepared to take advantage of those fortunate occasions when the research topic strikes a chord and the option is opened up of 'trading up' to a more complex design, or of combining two or more studies in order to achieve a more rounded research design. There are advantages also in taking a clear view from the start of where a study might lead, so that an initial study may eventually be developed in a logical fashion into a research programme, circumstances permitting.

Some issues in research design arise primarily in research institutes or in other organisations (such as central and local government) where there is a unit responsible for the design, commissioning and management of research projects. But, arguably, research design issues arise to an equal extent among individual researchers who work alone, such as students and lecturers – it is just that they are more easily overlooked by solo researchers.

As all professional social scientists have acknowledged, research design includes an imaginative, creative, innovative element that cannot be taught or planned. For example, one imaginative study surveyed the *children* of people who had been included in Rowntree's 1950 survey of York city, in order to study income mobility across two generations (Atkinson, Maynard and Trinder, 1983). Sometimes the imaginative element consists of devising a solution to a practical problem, such as finding a sample. For example, a study of the impact of maternity rights legislation on employers and working women in Britain was carried out by obtaining a sample of women who had recently had a baby (from maternity benefit records) and then getting a sample of employers from the women themselves (Daniel 1980, 1981). Similarly, the first national survey of employers in the USA was carried out by using the General Social Survey to produce a sample of employers' names and addresses from workers in the GSS sample (Kalleberg *et al.*, 1996). However, imagination can range more freely, and creativity is most fruitful, when the more essential aspects of research design have been tackled and got under control, if not out of the way. It is difficult to think creatively about doing a case study if one is constantly reconsidering whether a case study is the most appropriate design in the first place.

The emergence of independent research institutes and the mounting of major research programmes are changing the pattern and organisation of social science research work in the long term. Members of large research teams, and those who work on individual research projects within a wider programme, need to have a clear perspective on how their task fits into the design of the whole, even if they are directly involved in only one part of it. Research proposals that offer clearly specified and feasible research designs are becoming essential for obtaining research funds, but they also play a part in the recruitment, management and retention of research staff.

# Part I
# Types of research study

# 2 Research reviews, meta-analysis and secondary analysis

A review of the literature and existing studies is commonly part of the ground-clearing and preparatory work undertaken in the initial stages of any empirical research. But a comprehensive research review can become a research project yielding substantive information in its own right, especially if the new techniques of meta-analysis are applied to all known studies on a particular issue. At its most basic, secondary analysis consists of re-interpreting tables and statistical evidence in existing reports, and thus overlaps with the research review. But secondary analysis also extends to major studies in their own right that collate data from a variety of sources to produce substantively new findings. Research in some social science disciplines, notably economics and geography, relies almost entirely on secondary analysis of existing data, because economists and geographers rarely carry out their own data collections, relying almost exclusively on the efforts of others – in particular the large national datasets produced by government statisticians (Griliches, 1985).

Major research reviews, meta-analysis and secondary analysis are considered here together. Although they are distinct – research reviews and meta-analysis seek to consolidate knowledge on particular issues, while secondary analysis may break new ground – they all rely on existing information, and some studies combine the research review with meta-analysis (Rosenthal, 1976), or the research review with secondary analysis (Hakim, 1979; Lieberson, 1981; Guttentag and Secord, 1983), or secondary analysis with meta-analysis (Crain and Mahard, 1983).

## Research reviews

Research reviews provide a synthesis of existing knowledge on a specific question, based on an assessment of all relevant empirical research that can be found. Reviews of theoretical developments, which often merge into history of ideas essays with little concern for empirical research findings, are not considered here. Good research reviews are multi-disciplinary, in that relevant studies from any social science discipline are covered, although some questions attract greater attention within particular disciplines (Lester, 1983).

Research reviews can vary a great deal in emphasis, style and presentation. They can focus on the contemporary situation, or incorporate a historical perspective (Kessler-Harris, 1982; Reskin and Padavic, 1994; Hakim, 1996). They may seek to establish enduring patterns and relationships that are not specific to any historical period (Lester, 1983), or cross-cultural comparisons may be undertaken to establish the effects of cultural factors as well as historical factors (Milner, 1983; Hakim, 1999a).

Even when the emphasis of a research review is on the substantive knowledge gained from research to date, the different types of study need to be distinguished in order to assess the implications of research design for the type of question addressed and the nature of the information obtained (Dooley and Catalano, 1980; Hakim, 1982b).

Methodological research reviews have a specific emphasis on assessing the contributions and weaknesses of different research designs for answering the question of interest, and hence on separating fact from artefact in research results. For example, Braithwaite (1981) reviewed over 200 studies to assess whether the use of self-reported information on criminal activity (as obtained in interview surveys) instead of information obtained from official records affects research findings on the association between social class and criminal activity. Crain and Mahard (1983) reviewed 93 studies yielding 323 samples of students to assess the implications of using random-assignment experimental designs versus other designs for findings on the effects of school desegregation on black students. Walton (1966a, 1966b) reviewed 33 studies to assess the effects of the researcher's discipline, and choice of research design, on the results of community power studies.

Another option is the policy-oriented research review, which summarises current knowledge with a view to drawing out the policy implications, and requires knowledge of the policy debates as well as research expertise (Wilson, 1983; Wright, Rossi and Daly, 1983), or which summarises the current state of knowledge and practice for stakeholders (see Chapter 11), interest groups and others with direct interest or involvement in a policy area (Tomlinson, 1983). One approach for this is the focused synthesis, which draws on discussions with stakeholders, policy-makers and unpublished materials as well as a selective review of research reports (Majchrzak, 1984: 59–60). Yet another type of review addresses issues that have faded from, then re-emerged on, the policy agenda, re-capturing material from old studies as well as synthesising contemporary material (Hakim, 1982b).

Traditionally, research reviews veer towards the 'essay' style, which leaves the door open to subjective assessments and comments, partial or selective coverage, and other weaknesses. Meta-analysis is proposed as a more rigorous approach to research reviews, but it does not entirely resolve the question of partial or selective coverage. The number of studies reviewed can vary a good deal, depending partly on the topic but also on the reviewer's assiduity in tracking down relevant material. Some researchers discover over 200 relevant studies where others find only 35 (Braithwaite, 1981: 37).

## Meta-analysis

The techniques of meta-analysis were developed mainly in psychology, where the studies reviewed are typically controlled laboratory experiments that produce quantitive data, which are subjected to statistical analysis. The aim of meta-analysis is to provide an *integrated* and *quantified* summary of research results on a specific question, with particular reference to statistical significance and effect size (that is, the magnitude or strength of the impact of one factor on another). The approach consists, in essence, of treating each study in the review as a case within a sample of relevant studies, and applying statistical analysis to all the cases – for example, to assess whether the fact that one-third of all the studies reviewed found a particular (statistically significant) association is itself a statistically significant finding, or to calculate an overall effect size from those found by the studies reviewed (Rosenthal, 1984).

A good example of meta-analysis is the assessment by Rosenthal and Rubin of some 350 studies of the self-fulfilling prophecy, in particular the effects of researchers' expectations on the research results they obtain. This assessment was originally prompted by theoretical and methodological concern that the results of experimental research in laboratory settings were sometimes artefacts of the research procedures, created in whole or in part by the fact that researchers had expected these results. The practical and policy relevance of the self-fulfilling prophecy quickly became apparent, leading to further replications of these experiments in real-life settings to demonstrate the effects of teachers' expectations on children's performance and achievements in school, the effects of healers' expectations on recovery from illness, and so on (Rosenthal, 1976, 1984; Rosenthal and Rubin, 1978, 1980).

Meta-analytic procedures have also proved useful for literature reviews that are concerned with assessing the influence of research designs and methodological factors on the results obtained by different types of study on the same broad issues, such as the effect of school desegregation on the educational attainments of black children (Crain and Mahard, 1983) – a topic that has attracted a good deal of argument and controversy among social researchers as well as policy-makers (Cohen and Weiss, 1977).

Meta-analytic procedures are appropriate for research syntheses in areas where experimental and quasi-experimental research is the most common study design, or where study results are entirely quantitive. The use of meta-analysis is partly dictated by the fact that the original data from laboratory experiments are rarely available for re-analysis and by the difficulties of pooling data from a number of such experiments for secondary analysis with larger samples (Rosenthal, 1984: 103–5). The approach is not applicable to studies that produce qualitative results or where quantitive data is only one part of the complete dataset (as in case studies, for example). However, a broadly similar, but simpler, approach is suggested by Yin (1994: 121–3) for secondary analysis and research syntheses of case studies. And the review by Crain and Mahard (1983) cited above illustrates how meta-analysis can also be applied to methodological reviews and policy research.

## Secondary analysis

Secondary analysis is any re-analysis of data collected by another researcher or organisation, including the analysis of datasets collated from a variety of sources to create time series or area-based datasets. Most commonly, secondary analysis is applied to quantitive data from previous studies. But it is also feasible to carry out secondary analysis of numerous case study reports (as outlined by Yin, 1994: 119–20) or even of reports on single cases as illustrated by Moore's re-interpretation of a 50–year-old anthropological case study (Moore, 1983). The focus here is on the distinctive contributions of secondary analysis, rather than on additional analyses that extend or re-assess the findings of the main report on a study, as illustrated by the numerous re-analyses of the Coleman report (Cohen and Weiss, 1977).

The simplest approach is to use a *single dataset*, either to replicate the original researcher's results or to address entirely different questions. For example, data from the NLS and PSID studies described in Chapter 8 have been used to look at the determinants of divorce and separation. Ross and Sawhill (1975) replicated ISR analyses of PSID data to draw slightly different conclusions, although they agreed that the husband's employment difficulties and the wife's employment opportunities both increase the likelihood of marital disruption. Cherlin (1979) addressed the same question using NLS data and concluded that, other things being equal, married couples were more likely to divorce or separate if the husband had experienced more unemployment and if the wife had higher actual or potential income. In both cases, large-scale quantitive datasets provided the basis for research on a relatively rare event (divorce) that was not the original focus of the two longitudinal studies. Studies such as these have contributed to the development of theory on the relative benefits (economic, psychological and social) of marriage for men and women and rational choice theory of marriage and divorce, as well as being of practical interest in relation to the hidden social and economic costs of high unemployment.

One popular design is to merge several years' data from a regular survey (or even several years of a panel study) either to achieve a sufficiently large sample to study a minority group in the population (such as ethnic minority groups or the self-employed) or to permit the use of detailed classifications – of occupations, for example (Rose, 1999).

A second approach is to use a *single dataset that is extended by the addition of data from other sources*, thus providing a richer basis for the secondary analysis study. Hodson (1983) analysed USA Current Population Survey data, augmented by information on the companies and industries in which employees worked, in order to look at the consequences of economic segmentation for income inequality. Parcel and Mueller (1983b) extended PSID microdata with three sets of contextual data (on the industry, occupation and area of residence of persons in the sample) taken from a variety of sources (censuses; official statistics and previous academic studies) in order to evaluate the relative impact of these 'ecological' factors, compared to personal and work history characteristics, on earnings. Hakim (1998) analysed British 1991 Census microdata, enriched by adding hourly earnings data for each detailed occupation from another national survey, to show that the pay gap between men and women was smallest in sex-segregated occupations and largest in integrated occupations employing men and women together. The study thus overturned a long-standing theory that occupational segregation remained the principal cause of earnings differences between men and women.

The most complex secondary analyses use *multiple datasets* to provide an overall assessment of findings on a topic; to ascertain results that are robust enough not to depend heavily on the particular procedures used in any individual study, or its location in time; to study trends and change over a long period of time; or to carry out area-based research, cross-cultural and cross-national comparative studies.

Research on the enduring effects of education, throughout a person's life-time, on their knowledge, values and attitudes was based on secondary analysis of over 50 surveys and opinion polls carried out over the period 1949–75 (Hyman, Wright and Reed, 1975; Hyman and Wright, 1979). The secondary analyses reported in Freeman and Wise (1982) drew on some half-dozen data sources to obtain a comprehensive picture of youth unemployment and how results varied between study designs. Rindfuss *et al.* (1984) pooled data from six national fertility studies carried out in the USA between 1955 and 1976. The larger dataset thus created allowed them to assess the relative importance of historical factors, social structural factors, age and life-cycle effects on the probability and timing of women's first birth, prior to the contraceptive revolution of the 1960s.

A large proportion of economic research is based on secondary analysis of macro-level time series, which consist of a large number of national statistical indicators and measures collated from a great variety of official surveys and statistical series. But social surveys now have a sufficiently long history for it to be possible to collate data on a particular theme from opinion polls and *ad hoc* surveys spanning half a century, in order to study social change and trends at the micro-level as well. Precise comparisons in terms of question-wording and social indicators are neither feasible nor appropriate; since behaviour and attitudes change over long periods, the particular items of information used and operational definitions of the central issue addressed in the analysis will often have a *logical equivalence* rather than being exact duplicates. For this reason, it is desirable to locate the maximum number of relevant datasets with similar types of question, rather than relying on single sources for particular points in time. A good example of this approach is a study by Lipset and Schneider (1983) that documents the dramatic post-war decline in public confidence in government, business, organised labour and trade unions, the military, the press, educational and religious institutions. The study is based on trend analysis of some 200 opinion polls and surveys carried out in the USA, mainly since 1960, but with more limited data for earlier decades going back nearly half a century. Similarly, Dogan (1993, 1998) analysed Eurobarometer surveys, the World Values Survey, and International Social Survey Programme data to demonstrate a dramatic decline in public confidence in political institutions and trade unions, a sharp decline in religiosity and nationalism, and rising individualism during the post-war decades across all Western European countries. Simon (1985) combined analysis of opinion polls from 1937 to 1980 with content analysis of hundreds of magazine articles published between 1880 and 1980, to study trends in public opinion in the USA towards immigration and immigrants.

Secondary analysis of surveys for the study of trends over time is, of course, constrained by the existence and accessibility of relevant surveys. But the study of trends over even 'short' periods of one or two decades can reveal substantial amounts of unacknowledged social change, as illustrated by Ferree (1974) and Gilmartin and Rossi (1982). Access to relevant earlier surveys is improving, as the deposit of datasets, both new and old, in data archives becomes established practice (Hyman, 1972; Hakim, 1982a).

However, early survey data is simply not available on certain topics, and one has to rely on aggregate data from standard national sources, which can provide information only on net change at the aggregate level rather than on gross change at the micro-level (see Chapter 7). One solution to this problem is to construct *synthetic age cohort data* to present information, at the aggregate level, on the profile of age cohorts at periodic intervals. For example, synthetic age cohort analysis is regularly applied to population census data, which provides information, at the aggregate level, on each 10-year age cohort at 10-yearly intervals (Das Gupta, 1975; Hakim, 1979: 6–9; Lieberson, 1981; Simpson *et al.*, 1982). Synthetic age cohort analysis can also be applied to survey microdata to assess changes in attitudes, knowledge or behaviour (Ferree, 1974: 397; Hyman *et al.*, 1975; Hyman and Wright, 1979). Another option is to use information from retrospective surveys, although these will cover only survivors from earlier periods and are subject to problems of recall bias (see Chapter 8).

Secondary analysis of multi-source datasets is used to study geographical patterns and variations *within countries*, sometimes using existing compilations of area-based statistics, sometimes using datasets specially collated for towns, cities or other areas (Donnison and Soto, 1980; Bradbury *et al.*, 1982; Hakim, 1982a: 73–81). An important innovation in this field is the development of socio-economic area typologies, which provide an alternative to political geographical classifications for research on variations between *types* of area in social, economic and political behaviour and attitudes (Webber and Craig, 1978; Hakim, 1982a: 52; Craig, 1985) – an innovation that was well established in market research and social research by the 1990s.

## Population census studies

Population censuses merit separate mention because they are the oldest and largest socio-economic surveys conducted in any country, and the most frequent single source of cross-national comparative data, especially for studies covering all regions of the world.

Secondary analysis of census data is well established in the social sciences, especially demography, social geography and sociology (Hakim, 1982a). The computerisation of nineteenth-century census records and the introduction of sophisticated data analysis into historical research revolutionised historiography and produced the new specialism of cliometrics (Hakim, 1982a: 82–94). Some of the new quantitive studies overturn received wisdom and introduce a new perspective on the recent past.

*Time on the Cross*, Fogel and Engerman's study of slavery on southern USA plantations and in urban industrial enterprises, is one classic example. Contrary to the prevailing consensus that the slave economy was in decline prior to the American Civil War, they showed that slavery was profitable and efficient compared with free agriculture and with free workers in industry; that the material conditions of slaves compared favourably with those of free industrial workers; that the typical slave field hand received about 90% of the income he produced; and that the destruction of the black family was a myth: the family was the basic unit of social organisation under slavery. These unexpected findings were obtained from secondary analyses of 1850 and 1860 census records for plantations in southern USA, wills, and a wide range of other documents, described fully in a separate volume of *Evidence and Methods*. In Britain, historians at Cambridge University are re-analysing published census statistics and computerised census records for 1891 to 1921 in order to shed new light on fertility patterns, the causes of the decline in fertility, the interaction between women's child-bearing and employment in the home and in manufacturing industry (Garrett, 1996, 1998; Szreter, 1996).

Secondary analysis of contemporary census data is given a huge boost by the release of anonymised microdata. The USA and Canada have set the standards here, releasing Public Use Samples from the 1960 and 1970 Censuses onwards, in addition to computerised samples of the nineteenth-century censuses. In Britain, Samples of Anonymised Records (SARs) were first released from the 1991 Census, and the 1891 Census records were computerised in the 1990s by the Mormon Church. Practice in other European countries varies. In Germany, controversy over census confidentiality seems to rule out the release of microdata. In Italy, complete (but anonymous) census files can be obtained by academics for research analyses. The release of microdata permits secondary analysis on topics, and social groups, that attract little or no attention in government census reports. For example, Spain and Bianchi (1996) analysed microdata from the USA 1990 Census and CPS data to explore all aspects of women's lives: marriage, fertility, employment, earnings, and how these are combined. Hakim (1998) analysed the British 1991 Census SARs to look at homeworkers, small firms and the solo self-employed, part-time workers, working students, and changing patterns of occupational segregation. The census SARs also provided data for a case study of pharmacists, to illustrate the divergent work patterns of men and women even in integrated occupations.

Boserup's landmark study of *Women's Role in Economic Development* is a good example of the way in which census and related data can be re-analysed for cross-national comparative studies. For example, she showed how women's share of modern occupations is generally smaller than their share of traditional bazaar and service occupations, and that women's workrates tend also to decline with economic development (Boserup, 1970: 184).

## Cross-national comparative studies

Secondary analysis of existing data is one approach to *cross-national comparative studies*, especially for studies that cover large numbers of countries and/or trends over time. A distinction can be drawn between macro-level studies, which use aggregate national statistics for each country (from official statistics, censuses, and so forth), and those using microdata from interview surveys.

Saunders and Marsden (1981) relied on the national statistical series collated by the Statistical Office of the European Community (SOEC) to carry out comparative analyses of the distribution of earnings in six countries (Britain, Belgium, France, Germany, Italy and the Netherlands) and to study changes in earnings distributions during the 1970s. Although the focus was on describing similarities and differences between the six countries (for example, in the dispersion of individual earnings, occupation and industry differentials in pay), the analysis was sufficiently detailed to draw conclusions, for example, about the differing importance in each country of the determinants of the sex differential in pay.

Batstone (1985) compiled economic, industrial, social and political indicators from a wide variety of sources to create a dataset for 18 OECD countries covering two periods: 1960–75 and 1976–82. This dataset was analysed to test and re-assess three previous explanatory models for international variations in strike activity, and then to develop a more complete model that could account slightly better for the variation in working days lost due to strikes.

One advantage of using survey microdata for comparative studies is that the raw data can, if necessary, be re-coded and re-classified to improve comparability between the datasets used, instead of relying on the (non-comparable) classifications chosen by the original researchers. To extend a comparative study of social mobility in England, France and Sweden (Erikson, Goldthorpe and Portocarero, 1979) to the United States, Erikson and Goldthorpe found it necessary to re-classify the 1973 OCG-II study data originally analysed by Featherman and Hauser (1978). They concluded that the USA does not have exceptionally high rates of social mobility in consequence of the rapidity of change in the occupational structure, at least not during the twentieth century, a finding that raised questions about the reasons for the persistence of the American mobility ideology and the failure of socialism in the USA (Erikson and Goldthorpe, 1985).

A comparative study of the sex segregation of occupations by the International Labour Office (ILO) was based entirely on secondary analysis. In this case, the ILO created the dataset itself, by asking governments to provide the necessary statistical information on the occupational structure for three points in time: 1970, 1980 and 1990. The study eventually used data extracted from population censuses and labour force surveys for 41 countries across all regions of the world. The results overturned the assumption that western European countries, in particular Scandinavian countries, have lower levels of occupational segregation than other countries (Anker, 1998; Melkas and Anker, 1998). In fact, China had the lowest level in the world in 1990, despite a rising trend in the 1980s (Anker, 1998: 176–8, 323).

Comparative databases are sometimes compiled by academics. One example is the Luxembourg Income Study (LIS), which became feasible only after academics obtained access to microdata from government surveys through data archives. The LIS consists of 60 income and demographic variables coded to common criteria, and is derived from a variety of national datasets providing detailed data on household income in the 1980s and 1990s in 16 OECD countries. Thus the British data are extracted from the Family Expenditure Survey or the Family Resources Survey; the USA data are taken from the March CPS; the Swedish data are derived from the Swedish Income Distribution Survey; and so on. The LIS is used for comparative analyses of poverty and income distribution (Smeeding, O'Higgins and Rainwater, 1985a, 1985b, 1990; Mitchell, 1991). It also illustrates the potential for further exercises of this nature, which facilitate cross-national comparative studies based on secondary analysis.

International comparative studies are usually restricted to industrialised societies (for example, de Boer, 1977; Robinson and Kelley, 1979; Roos, 1983), but some scholars extend their secondary analyses to the more limited data typically available for late-developing countries in order to achieve more comprehensive tests of broad theories (see, for example, Robinson, 1984).

## Practical considerations

The comprehensive research review, meta-analysis and secondary analysis all offer the advantages of speed and relatively low costs compared to other types of study, and the ground to be covered can be specified fairly precisely before the project is started. The disadvantage is, of course, that the scope and depth of the study will be constrained by the material already available: particular aspects of a study may have to be dropped if unanticipated data limitations emerge during the course of a project. These studies are usually carried out by researchers who are specialists in the particular topic or issue being addressed, rather than by specialists in a particular type of study. If a secondary analysis aims only to expand on the original analyses of the data, the original research team may be best placed to do this efficiently. If the focus is on different issues and questions, an appropriate subject specialist will be better placed to exploit the available data. As a general rule, a second researcher will bring a fresh perspective to the strengths and limitations of any dataset, and be more innovative in exploiting it. Furthermore, desk-top computers and user-friendly data analysis packages make secondary analysis projects accessible to almost anyone. However, if a project needs only one or two well-defined tables from a national survey, to supplement other data, it is easier to persuade someone who is already working with a dataset to produce them for you, with the provider duly acknowledged as the source.

Cooper (1998) provides a step-by-step guide to doing a research review, with an overview of the techniques of meta-analysis as practised by psychologists. Glass *et al.* (1981), Hunter *et al.* (1982) and Rosenthal (1984) provide fuller expositions of the statistical techniques of meta-analysis. Light and Pillemer (1984) assess the merits of both qualitative and quantitive techniques for research syntheses, with particular reference to social policy research.

Library searches for published reports on a particular topic or question are hugely facilitated by the development of on-line databases on library holdings, computer-assisted library search facilities, indexing and abstracting services, the digitisation of library holdings (full-text databases), and the constant expansion of the internet. Developments in these fields are so rapid and dramatic that researchers can only be advised to contact their local library or information centre to find out what is currently available. Databases, indexes and search facilities can be very general or very specialised. They may specialise in the social sciences broadly defined; or in particular disciplines, such as economics, law or statistics; or in particular sources, such as newspapers or government publications.

Secondary analysis of survey microdata and national statistical series is facilitated by the increasing number of statistical and other compendia produced by international bodies (such as the UN, ILO and OECD) and academics (Mackie and Rose, 1982; Taylor and Jodice, 1983); the proliferation of guides to particular sources of data and their research uses (for example, Blake and Donovan, 1971; Carter, 1976; Buxton and Mackay, 1977; Taylor, 1980; Hakim, 1982a; Willigan and Lynch, 1982; Goyer and Domschke, 1983; Maunder, 1974–85; Dale and Marsh, 1993); and focused reviews of the research techniques and scales used in recent studies (Cook *et al.*, 1981; Miller, 1992: 207–460). Finally, Hyman (1972), Hakim (1982a) and Stewart (1984) provide general texts on doing secondary analysis and how to identify appropriate American and British datasets, while some archives provide their own guides to their holdings.

The establishment of national data archives, and agreements on the exchange of datasets between them, make it much easier to identify and obtain datasets. Some countries, such as the USA and Britain, now have several data archives, each with a different emphasis. For example, in Britain there is the University of Essex Data Archive for computerised datasets, the ESRC Qualitative Data Archive described in Chapter 3, and the Ethnic Minorities Data Archive at the University of Warwick Centre for Research in Ethnic Relations. The Census Microdata Unit at the University of Manchester holds microdata from the 1991 and subsequent censuses; enriches these datasets with complementary data from other sources (including area statistics and typologies); and provides documentation and research advice to users in and beyond the academic community. Hakim (1998: 251–65) describes the labour market data in these files, and Dale and Marsh (1993) provide a general guide to 1991 Census data and all outputs. The Centre for Longitudinal Studies at the University of London Institute of Education holds and updates the three British cohort studies (see Chapter 8), and acts as the research gateway to the census-based 1% Longitudinal Study described in Chapter 4. The datasets available in archives are described in Chapters 3 to 9 of this book.

Some data archives publish newsletters as well as data catalogues, and some provide advice on identifying datasets suitable for a particular study. The larger data archives have websites advertising their holdings, and most allow potential users to search their on-line catalogues in this way. It is rarely necessary to visit an archive. Datasets can be sent to users on diskette or on CD, can be downloaded over the internet, or can be accessed directly on the archive's computer via the internet. Lane in Oyen (1990: 187–202) lists the names and postal addresses of the main data archives in OECD countries. At present, most archives are in OECD countries, but this will change as more and more countries adopt the strategy of creating central data storage for social science data.

*Useful websites*

http://www.nsd.uib.no/cessda/europe.html is the CESS-DA (Centre for European Social Science Data Archives) gateway to websites for all European and North American data archives. These vary. Some are in the national language only; others are in English as well.

http://www.csv.warwick.ac.uk/fac/soc/CRER_RC/centre/nemda.html gives access to the Warwick University Centre for Research in Ethnic Relations (CRER) National Ethnic Minority Data Archive in Britain.

http://odwin.ucsd.edu/idata gives the San Diego Internet Search Engine for social science data on the net, mostly in the USA.

# 3 Qualitative research

As noted in Chapter 1, the term qualitative research is used here to refer to a specific research design rather than as a general term for non-quantitive research methods. Qualitative research is concerned with individuals' own accounts of their attitudes, motivations and behaviour. It offers richly descriptive reports of individuals' perceptions, attitudes, beliefs, views and feelings, the meanings and interpretations given to events and things, as well as their behaviour. It displays how these are put together, more or less coherently and consciously, into frameworks that make sense of their experiences, and it illuminates the motivations that connect attitudes and behaviour, the discontinuities, or even contradictions, between attitudes and behaviour, or how conflicting attitudes and motivations are resolved and particular choices made. It is especially popular in feminist research (Reinharz, 1992). Although qualitative research is about people as the central unit of account, it is not about particular individuals *per se*; reports focus rather on the various patterns, or clusters, of attitudes and related behaviour that emerge from the interviews.

Qualitative research is used for exploratory studies leading into more structured or quantitive studies; as an alternative to opinion polls; and to examine causal processes at the level of the intentional, self-directing and knowledgeable actor, who can be lost from view in the over socialised conception of man in sociology (Wrong, 1961) and in the statistical analysis of survey data. The use of qualitative research does not necessarily imply adoption of 'methodological individualism' – the view that all explanation can be reduced to accounts at the level of the self-directing individual – which is propounded by some scholars (Boudon, 1981) and rejected by others (Runciman, 1983; Sayer, 1984). But people's own definition of the situation is an important element of any social process, even if it does not provide a complete account or explanation and may include self-justificatory reports (Semin and Manstead,

1983). As noted in Chapter 8, longitudinal studies show actors' attitudes and motivations to be more important than has generally been recognised by economic or sociological theory.

## Depth interviews and focus groups

There are two main types of qualitative research: the depth interview and the group interview.

The *depth interview* is unstructured (there is an interview guide but no questionnaire), of very variable length (but may take up to five hours), and may be extended into repeat interviews at later dates (for example, to find out how individuals' perspectives change in response to some experience or event in their lives). Although the interviewer guides the discussion enough to focus on the topic of interest, the depth interview provides enough freedom for respondents also to steer the conversation, for example to bring in all sorts of tangential matters that, for them, have a bearing on the main subject. This sort of interviewing is very different from the structured interview based on a questionnaire used in large-scale surveys, and requires particular skills. A variety of specialised techniques are sometimes used to elicit aspects of respondents' views that are not directly articulated, such as the repertory grid and projective techniques (involving sentence completion, pictures, and so forth); these may be used for interviewing special groups, such as children, or for sensitive topics.

The second method is the *focus group*, which consists of a group discussion or group interview: between four and 12 people (eight being optimal) discuss the topic of concern for one to two hours with the guidance of a moderator. Focus groups produce less information on individual motivations and views than depth interviews can achieve, but they yield additional information as people react to views they disagree with, or the group as a whole develops a perspective on the subject.

Focus groups are used extensively in market research, in evaluation research where there is an identifiable client group (as in healthcare), and in social development work by the World Bank, International Labour Office and other international bodies. Depth interviews are used more extensively in academic research. Qualitative studies normally involve small numbers of respondents. In market research, where the focus is usually fairly specific (reactions to a particular product or service, or to a new policy), depth interviews with 15–25 people and/or three to four focus groups would be typical. The more diverse and diffuse topics covered by social research usually require at least 30–50 depth interviews; but some will warrant over 100 depth interviews, at which point it becomes much easier to distinguish sub-groups and specific clusters or patterns of attitudes and related behaviour. When depth interviews are used in oral history surveys, hundreds of interviews may be collected.

Depth interviews and focus groups are usually tape recorded, so that direct quotations from respondents figure largely in the eventual report, in place of the tables and statistics offered in a survey report. But, as noted later, reports on qualitative research take many forms. In market research, a short verbal report is often sufficient if the results are clear cut – for example, if the product or advertisement is disliked.

The great strength of qualitative research is the *validity* of the data obtained: individuals are interviewed in sufficient detail for the results to be taken as true, correct, complete and believable reports of their views and experiences. Its main weakness is that small numbers of respondents cannot be taken as representative, even if great care is taken to choose a fair cross-section of the type of people who are the subjects of the study. If qualitative research is dismissed as a weak alternative to a survey, this is because the validity problems in survey data are largely invisible and regularly overlooked, particularly by economists and statisticians, who routinely work with large datasets and official statistics and often make unproven assumptions about behaviour.

The other great strength of qualitative research is in the study of motivations and other connections between factors. The question 'why?' often cannot be asked, or answered, directly and may involve a variety of circumstantial and contextual factors creating links between, or choices between, apparently unrelated matters. Whether one is seeking explanations at the social-structural level, or at the level of individual choices and life styles, qualitative research is valuable for identifying patterns of associations between factors on the ground, as compared with abstract correlations between variables in the analysis of large-scale surveys and aggregate data. Depth interviews can also clarify the reasons for discrepancy between stated attitudes and behaviour.

If one is looking at the social structural determinants of people's behaviour and views at the macro-level, then designs using large-scale surveys are appropriate. But if one is looking at the way in which people respond to these external social realities at the micro-level, accommodating themselves to the inevitable, re-defining the situation until it is acceptable or comfortable, kicking against constraints, or fighting to break out of them or even to change them, then qualitative research is necessary. If surveys offer the bird's eye view, qualitative research offers the worm's eye view. Qualitative research offers substantively different and complementary information on the way in which attitudes and experiences cohere into meaningful patterns and perspectives, as illustrated by Luker's profiles of pro-choice and pro-life activists in the abortion debate in the United States (Luker, 1984). Like case studies, qualitative research adopts a holistic perspective to people and to explanation.

Qualitative research may be used for exploratory work before a larger-scale or more complex study is mounted. It is frequently used as a purely technical first step in the design of structured interview surveys (Hoinville and Jowell, 1977: 9–23). It is also used in the development of theory (Glaser and Strauss, 1967) and for theoretical research, especially by psychologists (Argyle, 1967), and can form a significant element of a research programme concerned exclusively with causal processes (for example, Brown and Harris, 1978). It is used in conjunction with other types of study to help clarify causal processes and explanations in the form of motivations, or to complement survey reports with illustrative examples and quotations on typical, minority or deviant cases.

Qualitative research tends to be used most heavily in disciplines where the emphasis is on description and explanation (such as psychology, sociology and social anthropology) rather than on prediction (as in economics). However, some economists argue for greater use of qualitative research in economics (Earl, 1983; Antonides, 1991). Because the interviewing skills required for depth interviews are not limited to social scientists, some excellent qualitative research studies have been carried out by journalists (Terkel, 1974).

Qualitative research plays an important part in policy research and evaluation studies. The studies of homeworkers and of unemployed women described below (Cragg and Dawson, 1981, 1984) were both commissioned by the British Ministry of Labour as elements of broader programmes of policy research. Explicit use of the term 'qualitative research' is best avoided in this case, being subject to confusion with 'high-quality' research among non-specialist audiences. Qualitative research can be harder to 'sell' to policy-makers because it is a less well-known type of study than large-scale quantitive research. But the results of this type of research are generally greeted with enthusiasm: the rich depth of information makes a welcome change from statistical reports, and these reports are more accessible to non-specialists (as well as to specialists in other disciplines), so that there are fewer problems of communication or misunderstanding of research results. Qualitative research offers a more direct window on the lives of constituents (for politicians) or client groups (for administrators). These features also make the results of qualitative research more accessible and attractive to special interest groups, pressure groups, the media and the public at large, so that qualitative studies can more readily contribute to public understanding and debate of policy issues – a particularly valuable feature for issues that are getting on to the agenda (as in the case of homeworking) or undergoing a process of re-definition and re-assessment (as in the case of female unemployment, or discrimination). As well as being an antidote to impersonal statistics, the persuasiveness of qualitative research reports can assist arguments for further, more quantitive studies.

## Some illustrative examples

This design is often used for exploratory research in areas where relatively little is known, as illustrated by Veevers' (1973) study of voluntarily childless wives. This is a new social phenomenon, emerging after easy access to modern, reliable forms of contraception. *Voluntary* childlessness involves a continuous stream of decisions about childbearing over an extended period of time (potentially up to the menopause), and hence complex causal processes of motivation and decision-making over different phases of the life cycle. Since the general expectation is that married women will have children, becoming a voluntarily childless wife also involves adopting a 'deviant' role and life style. All of these factors made qualitative research a particularly suitable research design. Veevers carried out the study with a volunteer non-random sample of 52 wives recruited through articles appearing in Canadian newspapers. The depth interviews averaged four hours in length and included discussion of the woman's life history, considerable detail concerning her marriage and her husband, and attitudinal and evaluative aspects of her views on the maternal role. The study enabled Veevers to distinguish two routes to voluntary childlessness, one involving repeated and prolonged postponement of childbearing until such time as it was no longer considered desirable, the other being a firm early decision to avoid the maternal role.

Relatively little was known about the new forms of white-collar homeworking that emerged in the 1980s in most industrialised countries in response to recession and new technology. Qualitative research was carried out as the first stage of a larger research programme on homeworking. This provided a descriptive account of the characteristics and working conditions of homeworkers, their reasons for choosing this relatively unusual work arrangement and the perceived need for legislation to improve their conditions, as a basis for questionnaire development for a national survey. The study also explored possible reasons for reticence about homeworking, with a view to maximising survey response rates (Cragg and Dawson, 1981). This study was based on depth interviews with 50 homeworkers, chosen to provide a fair cross-section of known homeworking occupations.

When the topic studied is not limited to a minority of the population, it may be necessary to conduct a larger-scale study in order to obtain a fair representation of the diversity and variety of circumstances. Terkel carried out around 100 depth interviews across the USA for his well-known study of people's attitudes to work, their jobs and working conditions (Terkel, 1974). In other cases, an above-average number of interviews may be warranted by the need to compare distinct sub-groups in the population studied. Depth interviews were carried out with over 100 non-working women to explore the circumstances and motivations surrounding unemployment and discouraged workers in Britain, the role of employment in women's lives and their reactions to being without paid work (Cragg and Dawson, 1984). The largest collection of qualitative data on how people live their lives and react to experiences and events was obtained by Mass Observation in the late 1930s in Britain, of which only a small proportion has been written up into published reports (Calder and Sheridan, 1984).

Very occasionally, qualitative research is used as a substitute for interview surveys and opinion polls – particularly in wartime, when sample survey procedures become impractical and even regular exercises like the population census may have to be cancelled (as happened with the 1941 Census in Britain). For example, Mass Observation reports were used by the Ministry of Information in Britain during the Second World War, and qualitative research on morale and public opinion was used both in Britain and the USA during this period.

Occasionally, some depth of information is sacrificed in order to cover larger samples. A study of benefit-claimants' attitudes to the service provided by local social security offices was based on unstructured interviews with 350 people, but the report provided a qualitative rather than quantitive treatment of results, presenting a wealth of direct quotations illustrating the variety and character of views on the provision of contributory and social welfare benefits (Ritchie and Wilson, 1979).

While most qualitative research consists of single-time studies, and concerns individuals, it is possible for this type of study to cover an extended period of time and to look at families instead of individuals. Hood's study of the changes in family roles and relationships that took place after wives returned to work provides an example with both these characteristics. She followed 16 couples living in Midwest America over a six-year period (1976–82), interviewing them at periodic intervals. Her analysis explores the contribution of attitudinal factors (such as the husband's and the wife's attachment to home and work roles), objective factors (such as the wife's relative earning power as reflected in the proportion of total family income contributed by the wife's earnings) and circumstantial or contextual factors (such as a temporary reduction in the husband's breadwinner role owing to unemployment or business difficulties) to the process of role bargaining and changing relationships between spouses. The study produced suggestions for future interview surveys, and it also provided a detailed account of the methods used for this longitudinal qualitative research study (Hood, 1983).

## Cross-national comparative studies

Focus groups and depth interviews are used extensively in market research, where cross-national comparative studies are fairly common – for example, to test reactions to a proposed advertising strategy or theme. In theoretical and policy research, comparative work currently favours surveys and quantitive designs rather than qualitative research. The potential exists for using the latter, but has so far been under-exploited. Also, there are real problems in 'translating' the outputs of national studies (framed within national cultures and taken-for-granted assumptions) into one common 'language'. Cross-national comparisons based on case studies are more common.

## Overlaps and combinations

Because of its unstructured and exploratory character, qualitative research blends easily with other types of study. There is a strong overlap with case study research, such as life histories and case studies of particular groups. Case studies are distinguished from qualitative research by their focus on analytical social units and social processes rather than on individuals in the round. If focused sampling (see Chapter 11) is used to select respondents for depth interviews (as illustrated by Cragg and Dawson, 1984), the overlap with case study designs becomes stronger. Qualitative studies that follow individuals over an extended period of time, or collect life histories, begin to overlap with longitudinal studies (as illustrated by Hood, 1983; Gerson, 1985).

Qualitative research is often linked to surveys. The qualitative study may be carried out before the survey, as an exploratory first step that paves the way as well as offering a greater depth of information to complement the quantitive survey results. Alternatively, the qualitative study may be carried out after the main survey, which can then provide a rich sampling frame for selecting particular types of respondent for depth interviews (for one example see Cragg and Dawson, 1984). This link strengthens interpretation of the survey results, and it may be possible to set the qualitative results in a statistical context by directly linking the two sets of data. One can also capitalise on the time-lag between the survey fieldwork and the subsequent depth interviews by incorporating a longitudinal focus in the topics explored. For example, the study of unemployed women was carried out seven to nine months after the national survey that provided the sampling frame; the qualitative follow-up study looked at changes in the intervening period, and was thus able to explore the circumstances surrounding labour market withdrawal and the process of becoming a discouraged worker – someone who has ceased looking for work because they perceive the chances of getting a job to be non-existent.

Qualitative research can be used in combination with virtually all other types of study, and may be a particularly fruitful element of a research programme relying primarily on quantitive studies, informing the interpretation of more impersonal statistical data. This greatly reduces the risk that invalid conclusions will be drawn from the researcher's untested assumptions about the motivations and processes underlying correlations in the quantitive data, the attitudinal factors underlying observed behavioural differences between sub-groups, or the range of factors that might affect change in behaviour over an interval of time. The idea of using control groups or comparison groups is well accepted in relation to experimental, longitudinal and other studies; the advantages of adding a qualitative (or case study) counterpart to projects otherwise based on large-scale quantitive data should not be overlooked. For example, studies like Hood's (1983) could provide a valuable contribution to longitudinal studies of female labour force participation, such as the NLS surveys described in Chapter 8.

One example of this approach comes from a research programme on the single homeless carried out for the British Department of the Environment. In this case the qualitative research consisted of six focus groups in which the single homeless explored their needs and preferences regarding accommodation and other services. The results of this study were used to inform and extend interpretation of the results of a larger scale interview survey (Drake, O'Brien and Biebuyck, 1981: 85–97).

**Practical considerations**

There are many textbooks that discuss the theoretical underpinnings of qualitative research, how to do it, and its application in academic (mainly theoretical) research, such as Miles and Huberman (1994) and the massive collections of readings compiled by Denzin and Lincoln (1994) and Bryman and Burgess (1999). These textbooks generally devote more attention to case studies than to depth interviews and focus groups, so it is better to consult specialist textbooks.

Methods for collecting, recording and analysing depth interviews, focus groups, and projective techniques are outlined in R. Walker (1985: 27–91, 101–44), along with some examples of their application in social research. Even if specialist commercial agencies are used, depth interviews and focus groups require relatively small budgets and short timetables. For policy research, it thus offers the significant advantage of a study design that can be completed very quickly (in two to four months) for low all-in costs. For theoretical research, where speed is of little import, it still offers the advantage of low costs, especially if specialist agencies are not used. Budgets will obviously be higher if the study is longitudinal or covers large numbers of respondents, but qualitative research still remains at the cheaper end of the spectrum. Many students choose depth interviews for their first research exercise.

Depth interviews rely crucially on skilled interviewing to yield their full value. These skills can be taught and learnt (see, for example, Banaka, 1971; Patton, 1990: 195–263). Many researchers think that they acquire the relevant skills purely by virtue of an interest in the subject-matter. This does work occasionally, but working as the moderator for focus groups is a specialist skill that requires training and experience. A choice must also be made as to whether or not psychologists will be used for interviewing and focus groups; if they are, the focus of the study will veer towards personality factors rather than towards social factors – for example, results may be analysed in terms of respondents' maturity and self-awareness instead of the social, economic and organisational factors that shape experiences, attitudes and behaviour (see, for example, R. Walker, 1985: 56–70, 101–21 and 130–44). When done rigorously and systematically, the analysis and interpretation of qualitative data can be time-consuming (Silverman, 1993).

As group interviews become more popular in social research, the number of textbooks and guides increases. Stewart and Shamdasani (1990) provide an excellent short guide to focus groups, including a summary of research findings on small group behaviour. However, most of their examples come from market research. They describe the skills applied by moderators to ensure that the research brief is covered and that all participants enjoy the discussion. It is customary for travel expenses to be refunded and for payment and other incentives to be offered to focus group participants, because they have to travel to and from the venue as well as giving one to two hours of their time at a time specified by the research team. A fee of $50 or £35 was typical in 1999. In addition, childminding services, meals or refreshments may be offered. The incentives offered can be far more substantial for hard-to-reach participants, such as doctors, government officials, specialists or busy company managers.

There are other types of group discussion: the nominal group technique, the Delphi technique, brainstorming, synectics, and leaderless discussion groups. All are described by Stewart and Shamdasani (1990) and contributors to Morgan (1993). Fuller discussions of the social science applications of focus groups, and guides to doing them, are given in Krueger (1994), Morgan (1993, 1997), Morgan and Krueger (1998), Greenbaum (1998) and Barbour and Kitzinger (1998). There are also guides to running focus groups in special contexts: as part of social or community development programs (Morgan, 1993: 202–21; Aubel, 1994), in health care (Morgan, 1993: 202–21), and in evaluation studies. Aubel (1994) argues that focus groups are especially useful in action research, because programme managers and staff can be involved in designing and implementing the study, and so they learn to listen to clients and to understand their perspective on proposed policies. However, this sort of *collaborative research* is not the same thing as the 'co-operative inquiry' promoted by some consultants (Heron, 1996; see also Morgan, 1993: 153–66), which is a form of group counselling that may be confused with social science research. Whatever methods are used, qualitative research is about studying people to capture the meanings people bring to their situations and activities. So-called 'co-operative inquiry' is ultimately about developing the self-knowledge and social awareness of group participants in order to help them to initiate change themselves in their own lives or jobs. It is *not* research, although the word research features heavily in these reports.

To a far greater extent than other types of study, qualitative research benefits from good writing and presentational skills for any reports. The use of quotations from respondents does not by itself demonstrate that the researcher was able to empathise with and understand their views. In this respect, journalists can often have an advantage over social scientists.

The presentation of data, analysis and findings varies a good deal. Approaches range from those where the emphasis is on the 'raw' data collected to those with an emphasis on the report-writer's conclusions. One approach is to provide highly edited and condensed transcripts of each interview, or group discussion, with the researcher's analysis and overview of the results presented in a separate section (see, for example, Terkel, 1974). Another approach is to present excerpts from interviews that display the range and variety of views on each question, within a report that presents a synthesis, overview and interpretations; the degree to which sub-groups, clusters of attitudes, associations, contradictions and the underlying logic of perspectives and behaviour are discussed will depend on the size and focus of the study. In this approach, each quotation is attributed to a respondent, who is identified by a reference number, fictitious name or other device, and a list of respondents (identified by reference numbers and so on) is supplied with minimal pen-portraits of each one (describing age, sex, occupation and any other characteristics relevant to the study), as illustrated by Cragg and Dawson (1981, 1984). Further along the continuum is a heavily interpretive and descriptive report with some use of quotations and excerpts from interviews; minimal information is supplied on the number of people interviewed and their characteristics (Scase and Goffee 1980). Finally, there is the report that gives full details of how the research was carried out, how people were selected for interview, and so forth, then proceeds to an interpretive overview of the researcher's conclusions with very occasional reference to the interviews (see, for example, Veevers, 1973).

By and large, reports by academics tend to the latter end of the spectrum, and are more likely to be framed in terms of theoretical interests and preconceptions. Those at the former end of the spectrum are more open to re-interpretation by others. But reports on qualitative research are closer to being descriptive accounts uncoloured by theory, as compared with other types of study. Theoretical research is, of its nature, heavily selective and hence offers a partial or distorted account (Smelser, 1980: 28), but qualitative research, even when theoretically informed, is the most open-ended and hence least biased type of study.

Most archives deal only with quantitive datasets. However, there are a growing number of archives that store written and tape-recorded research material, including the results of qualitative research. The earliest one is the Mass Observation archive lodged at the University of Sussex in England (Calder and Sheridan, 1984). The ESRC Qualitative Data Archival Resource Centre at the University of Essex (QUALIDATA at http://www.essex.ac.uk/qualidata) is responsible for maintaining an information database on the extent and availability of qualitative research material from most social science disciplines, whether deposited in public repositories in Britain or remaining with the researcher. It liaises with other libraries and archives holding qualitative data, and itself holds, or is acquiring, important studies, including Paul Thompsons' oral history tape-recordings. The secondary analysis of qualitative data is a growing field (Hammersley, 1997; Hinds, Vogel and Clarke-Steffen, 1997).

Software for information retrieval and analysis of qualitative data is developing rapidly. Packages include QSR NUD*IST, ATLAS/ti and WINMAX. The Computer-Assisted Qualitative Data Analysis Networking Project at the University of Surrey (CAQDAS at `http://www.soc.surrey.ac.uk/caqdas/`) is the British ESRC's national centre for qualitative data analysis software, and is currently the only centre in this field in the world. It provides information and training on all packages, offers a newsletter and telephone helpline, and runs an electronic discussion group. Denzin and Lincoln (1994: 445–62), Keller (1995) and Fielding and Lee (1998) provide helpful introductions to computer-assisted analysis of qualitative data, and review the available software.

# 4 Administrative records and documents

Vast quantities of information are collated and recorded by organisations and individuals for their own purposes, well beyond the data collected by social scientists for research purposes. Information from records and documents enters into virtually all types of study in some degree, though usually providing only a minor part of the data. The focus here is primarily on studies that use administrative records and documents as the principal source of data, and hence on the larger or more prominent collections of such information in organisations.

Administrative records are collections of documents containing mainly factual information compiled in a variety of ways (directly from those concerned, or indirectly from employers, schools, doctors and others acting as informants), which are used by organisations to record the development and implementation of decisions and activities that are central to their functions. They are typically large in number, with high content rigidity and narrow content scope, and are often available for considerable stretches of time. Examples are health service records; school records; membership records of trade unions and other voluntary associations; company accounts and personnel records; marriage, birth and death registers; electoral registers; tax and social security records; police, court and prison records.

In the past, statistical surveys were often based on data extracted from administrative records rather than on interview surveys. In industrialised countries, the importance of administrative records as a source of data for research analysis declined, as specially designed research studies were created to replace or to complement records-based data. Unemployment statistics are now more commonly obtained from regular sample surveys using personal interviews, such as the CPS and the LFS, than from government unemployment registers or unemployment benefit records. Regular interview surveys about crime provide an important complement to data obtained from police records, as noted in Chapter 7.

At the same time, the potential for research analyses of administrative records is expanding, as organisations transfer such records from manual systems of files, forms and cards to computerised systems, and hence redesign them as management information systems that can be analysed quickly and routinely to produce reports on organisational processes and policy outcomes. Computerization makes it easier to provide suitably anonymised extract tapes for social research purposes. Prior to this, the relevant information had to be extracted manually from cards, forms or files, with all the potential for copying errors and other mistakes to occur during the extraction process, quite apart from the long time it took, the cost, and any confidentiality problems raised by allowing researchers to have access to what are often confidential or private records. Datatapes for research analysis can easily be anonymised, but some organisations impose substantial additional restrictions on access, allowing them to vet and control usage, as noted below.

This facility for producing computer tapes with selective information from administrative records for research analysis means that more data of this type is finding its way into data archives. So research based on administrative records can easily be conflated with secondary analysis of research data (see Chapter 2). There is a similarity, in that any research use of information from administrative records constitutes secondary analysis, given that the primary use of the records was for administrative purposes. But the similarity ends there, because there are significant differences between data collected specifically for research purposes and information that is recorded as a by-product of an organisation's or an individual's day-to-day activities. The point needs to be emphasised because economists, for example, who routinely use data collected by others, often display little concern for the source of the information they use, its quality and limitations, and frequently fail to distinguish between data from records and specially collected research data, treating both as if they were interchangeably valid and appropriate for any research analysis (Blaug, 1980: 261–2; Sayer, 1984: 161; Griliches, 1985).

Precisely because administrative records are created and maintained by many different organisations for varied and changing purposes, it is more difficult to generalise about their characteristics, strengths and limitations, and that of any research based on them, than it is with other types of study. Collections of records and documents must be found rather than created to the researcher's specification, and their value will depend on the degree of match between the research questions addressed and the data that happen to be available. But the research potential of such date is considerable.

## Varieties of records-based research

The design of records-based studies has to be back to front. Instead of designing the study, and then collecting the necessary data, one obtains details of the contents and characteristics of a set of records and then identifies the corresponding research model. The builder, and the materials he has available, take a stronger leading role in the design than in the usual architect-designed study. Nonetheless, administrative records can provide the basis for longitudinal studies, quasi-experimental designs, historical research, area-based studies, cross-national comparisons, studies of organisations and the policy process, as well as being especially useful for research on minority groups and rare events.

Administrative records can provide information on topics or minority groups that is not available by any other means, or only at disproportionate cost. An obvious example is the documentary evidence and records used in historical research, to which are now being added the original records from early data collections, such as the nineteenth-century population censuses and other surveys deposited in public records offices or data archives. For example, Harbury and Hitchens (1979) and Rubinstein (1981) used probate records to study patterns of wealth and inheritance. A study by Furet and Ozouf (1982) used samples of marriage records to study the spread of literacy from the seventeenth century to the present day in France. Nineteenth-century census records, supplemented by marriage records, employment records, contemporary investigations and other documentary evidence, are providing the basis for a great deal of historical, social, economic and demographic research (Wrigley, 1972; Fogel and Engerman, 1974; Foster, 1974; Lawton, 1978; Bateman and Weiss, 1981; Hershberg, 1981; Hakim, 1982a: 82–94; Hareven, 1982).

Administrative records can also provide an important source of data on events or groups too small and scattered or otherwise difficult to trace for national interview surveys to be a realistic possibility. The classic example is the use of data from death registration records for research on suicide (Phillips, 1983; Wasserman, 1984), a topic that could not be studied in any other way, whatever the limitations of the records, with health service records being used to study the somewhat different phenomenon of attempted suicide (Platt and Kreitman, 1985). Administrative records also provide a ready source of data on relatively rare events such as divorce, migration (Mueller, 1982) and crime, although some large-scale regular surveys and longitudinal studies are now also providing data on such rare events.

Administrative records are used in their own right, rather than *faute de mieux*, for research on the policy process itself and in evaluation research. In this case, records and documents, albeit incomplete accounts, are part of the reality being studied, rather than being regarded as a poor substitute for data that would ideally be obtained in other ways. For example, records provide an appropriate basis for research on racial discrimination in the allocation of public housing (Parker and Dugmore, 1976) or in the treatment of employees (Chiplin, 1981; Siebert and Sloane, 1981). In the United States, job applicant and employee records are frequently a key source of evidence in legal cases on discrimination, with increasingly sophisticated techniques being employed for the analysis of such data in class actions (Ragin *et al.*, 1984).

Studies of organisational policy and decision-making processes shade into general organisational studies in which administrative records can provide an important source of data, especially if they are available for long stretches of time. This type of use is common in case studies, with the analysis of data from records complemented by other research methods, which can provide crucial information for interpreting the records data (as illustrated by Blau, 1963; Wrench and Lee, 1982; Edwards and Scullion, 1984).

When records are available for long stretches of time, they can provide the time series data needed for quasi-experimental designs, which provide 'before' and 'after' measurements without a control group (Campbell and Stanley, 1963: 37–43; Campbell, 1969; Cook and Campbell, 1979: 207–32). For example, records can be used to assess the effect of a change in divorce laws on the divorce rate. Berk and Newton (1985) used police records on wife-battering incidents for a quasi-experimental analysis of the deterrent effects of arrest. Records can also provide data for more general longitudinal studies. Personnel records in private sector corporations and in public sector organisations have been used as the basis for research on internal labour markets: patterns of recruitment, promotion, job moves, job quits, and the effects of economic conditions, affirmative action policies, organisational growth and contraction as well as human capital factors on the careers of individuals, or of entry cohorts. A study of careers in the US civil service over the period 1963 to 1977 was based on a 1% sample of personnel records for federal employees (Grandjean, 1981), while Rosenbaum (1984) used the personnel records of a large American corporation for roughly the same period, 1962–75, to study these questions. Fruin was able to analyse the personnel records of a Japanese company since its incorporation in 1918 up to the 1970s to assess variations over time in the practice of lifetime employment and seniority-based compensation (Fruin, 1978, 1980).

Data from public sector records are sometimes sufficiently extensive in scale to permit area-based studies. Stevens and Willis (1979) combined data from police records with population census statistics to compile arrest rates for whites and ethnic minority groups for police districts, and then studied the ecological correlations of arrest rates. They found a significant association between unemployment and crime among whites, but not among ethnic minority groups, despite higher levels of unemployment among blacks.

The main disadvantage of this design is that the scope and content of studies are constrained by the nature of the data available from records. Even when relevant records exist, they may not provide the particular items of information required to address the question at issue; information may be present but the definitions and classifications applied may be incompatible with those the researcher wishes to use; there may be large amounts of missing data, which may not matter for administrative purposes but which would present serious problems for a research analysis; there may be restrictions on access; or relevant data may be censored for confidentiality reasons. Whereas with secondary analysis there is a good chance that more than one appropriate dataset might be located, and some secondary analyses have used dozens of previous studies, with records-based research there is rarely any possibility of locating better alternatives to a set of records that are less than ideal for a study. The design of research based on administrative records involves a large element of knowing what is available and making the most of it. Opportunistic designs are almost a requirement.

## The nature and quality of data from administrative records

Some datasets are compiled from records specifically for research purposes, in which case special effort is devoted to ensuring that the information is complete, checking queries or anomalies, and producing documentation for the resulting database. One example is the Aberdeen maternity and neonatal databank initiated in 1948. This was laboriously compiled from hospital and other records to provide a longitudinal file with an obstetric history and related clinical and social data for each woman resident within the district; it was used extensively for social and medical research on topics related to fertility and pregnancy (Thompson *et al.*, 1981).

More commonly, researchers have to compile their own *post hoc* account of the procedures and methods used to compile and update the records on which a study is based. This account replaces the usual methodological report on how data were specially collected in other types of study, and constitutes the documentation for the dataset extracted from the records. Many of the points to note are of a quite different nature to ordinary research data.

As a general rule, information that is essential or central to the activities of an organisation will be more carefully monitored and of better quality than more peripheral items of information. So it is important to identify the primary administrative uses of the records, and which items of data are central, or peripheral, to these purposes. Although distinctions are commonly made between public sector and private sector records, there are also important differences *within* these categories, especially within the public sector, where agency functions are often defined by law. The primary use of records may be for decision-making with reference to *minima* only, such as minimum wages or minimum health and safety standards; full details will not be recorded for those cases where the minima are clearly exceeded, so the data are truncated. Records kept in the context of implementing rules, regulations or legislation with *universal applicability*, such as car registration, will contain more complete and standardised information on all cases, to ensure consistent and uniform treatment. Other records are kept in the context of *service delivery* activities, where there is no precise, or minimum, entitlement and the nature of the service depends on the individual case, so that information in the records is not standardised and may vary greatly in quantity and detail, as illustrated by social services records. The degree of standardisation, consistency and quality of information also varies between records that are routinely compiled and those compiled on a one-off basis for some special exercise or study (Hakim, 1983: 490–5).

Distinctions can also be drawn between records kept for internal use by the organisation, those kept solely to comply with regulations and legislation, and those used to produce public statements, accounts or statistics, and between items of information supplied by the individual concerned, or by an informant. For example, the quality of information on race or ethnic minority group membership can vary a great deal between record systems, according to who supplied the information and whether it was actively used within an affirmative action policy, or whether it was collected solely to comply with some regulation.

Some understanding of the nature and original purpose of any set of records is important not only with reference to the quality, consistency and completeness of the data they provide, but also for the interpretations that can be placed on the results. Similarly, it is crucial to the reading and interpretation of any documentary evidence to know what class of document it belongs to: rule-book, public statement, official record of a meeting, personal account based on recall, public speech, letter, private diary, and so forth. Formal organisational rules are often supplemented, sometimes even overwritten, by informal rules, and such practices may affect the consistency of records over a period of time, over and above any changes to the formal rules about how the records are kept or the activities to which they relate. Obtaining information on how the records were compiled and updated usually requires consultations with the people responsible for the records. This can prove fruitful even when the records are old or historical in nature, because those responsible for them may have relevant documents or an accumulated oral history on how the records have changed and developed over time.

Some researchers dismiss data from administrative records as seriously deficient, particularly for value-laden topics such as crime. But the problem varies between subjects. Administrative records provide more reliable information than interview self-reports on some topics, such as hours worked, unemployment, annual earnings and job tenure (Duncan and Mathiowetz, 1984) or visits to the doctor (Siemiatycki, 1979). Some case studies of police procedures have shown little or no bias in official crime records (Mawby, 1979; Walker, 1983). Careful comparisons of research results using self-reported criminal activity with data from official records have shown smaller discrepancies between the two types of study than is suggested by the conventional prejudice (Blumstein and Cohen, 1979; Hindelang *et al.*, 1979; Braithwaite, 1981; Thornberry and Farnworth, 1982). The British Crime Survey shows that trends in interview survey data on crime paralleled trends in police-recorded crime very closely in the 1980s and 1990s, with occasional divergences. Although the total volume of crime in Britain is roughly double the level of recorded crime, most serious crimes are reported to and recorded by the police. However, reporting and recording rates vary by type of offence (Mirlees-Black *et al.*, 1998: 17–26). Faulty analysis of data from records can produce more unjustified conclusions than the weaknesses of the data themselves (Hakim, 1983: 508–10; Walker, 1983, 1985). The problem, while real, seems to have been exaggerated, and Braithwaite suggests (1981: 46–7) that certain prejudices persist because they are ideologically attractive to both liberal and conservative researchers. So the more informed perspective is that the interpretation of data from records requires great care, and for this it is essential to have detailed knowledge and understanding of the social processes involved in the production of data in records (Walker, 1983).

## Computerisation of administrative records

The computerisation of administrative records and systems opens up new dimensions for research analysis. Datasets can be created and used in ways that could not be imagined before. Two examples give some idea of the potential for new research. This is a growth area, where rapid developments can be expected in future years. Readers are advised to enquire about new data products becoming available in their field of interest.

The British Offenders' Index is one of the largest criminal databases in Europe. It includes details of all serious convictions in England and Wales from 1963 onwards, and is updated regularly, with data for 1998 already available by mid-1999. Identifying details on each record are matched so as to produce criminal histories for about 6 million individuals. The Offenders' Index yields Janus-type surveys, which look into both the past and the future for specified samples of offenders, or for broad categories of offender. It is used extensively within the British Home Office, by the Probation Service, and by academic criminologists for policy research, including evaluations of new schemes and programmes. For example, it is the source for regular statistics on reconviction rates within two years of release from prison or any other penalty. Periodically, analyses of criminal histories for birth cohorts are published; to date, such studies have covered people born in 1953, 1958, 1963, 1968, 1973 and 1978. Such panel studies show, for example, that the majority of all court appearances are attributable to a minority (about one in five) of the offender population and a tiny minority (less than 10%) of the male population. They also show that around one-third of each male birth cohort had been convicted of at least one serious crime before the age of 40, more than four times as many as women. The Offenders' Index is in active use as a policy research tool, with outputs contributing to many policy reviews, but there is no major general report on the database and its uses (Home Office, 1991, 1995, 1999).

The New Earnings Survey (NES) has been running annually since 1970 in Britain, after an initial survey in 1968, and again is unique in Europe. The NES is a specially designed short postal enquiry that collects data from employers on the wages they pay to a 1% national sample of employees. However, the data collected is restricted to information held in employers' records for employees, which they can easily extract, such as the person's occupation, sex, hours worked, and the make-up of earnings. The NES enquiries are conducted under the Statistics of Trade Act 1947, which forbids the release of microdata, even if anonymised, thus preventing independent research analyses of a uniquely valuable database.

Computerization of the NES database enabled the creation of a series of minimally aggregated extract tapes, which could be released for research analyses of earnings by academics. Each record in the public release tapes relates to no less than three persons, who are chosen to be as alike as possible, thus preserving as much as possible of the earnings variation in the original dataset. Aggregation was organised separately for each analysis topic, resulting in hundreds of extract tapes being produced for the research project, which attracted the participation of numerous social scientists, mainly economists (Gregory and Thomson, 1990).

The new database also made it possible to create an NES panel dataset for the 1% sample of employees, which is defined by social security numbers and remains constant from year to year. For this, records from consecutive years for each individual employee are linked, to create a longitudinal file. Initially, records for one decade (1975–86) were used to produce panel data for some 350,000 individuals. Earnings records for the 1990s and beyond were then added to the database. The panel data is used to study earnings mobility over the life cycle, and reveals surprisingly large annual fluctuations in earnings (Endean and Smith in Gregory and Thomson, 1990: 444–61; Elias and Gregory, 1994; Gregory and Jukes, 1998).

## Record linkage

Distinctions between types of records, and even between specially collected research data and data from administrative records, can become obscured in datasets that link together information from records, the population census and sample surveys. This innovation is facilitated by the computerisation of administrative systems, allowing linkage to be carried out on a much larger scale than in previous studies, which were based on either manually linking together discrete records, such as marriage, divorce and birth records (Christensen, 1963), or else on *ad hoc* linkage of information from survey respondents, with data on their incomes, earnings or social security benefits from tax and social security records (Sewell and Hauser, 1975; Moylan, Millar and Davies, 1984). Record linkage is also easier to justify when most national statistical series are centralised in a single national statistical office, so that the links are made 'internally' within a single organisation rather than across government department boundaries.

At the simplest level, discrete records within a single source are linked together to create longitudinal datasets. For example, the USA Social Security Administration has for many decades maintained the Continuous Work History Sample (CWHS), which provides a longitudinal file of earnings and benefit histories for a 1% sample of social security numbers, updated annually. The CWHS is used for internal research on the characteristics of workers covered by social security and on how this population has changed with legislative changes. Until 1976, data from the CWHS was released for academic research on workforce characteristics, earnings over the lifecycle, migration, labour force participation and related topics (Traugott and Clubb, 1976: 397; Farkas, 1977; Mueller, 1982; Tanur, 1983: 52).

More complex projects merge data from different sources into a single file, either periodically or as a continuing project. The 1973 Current Population Survey–Administrative Record Exact Match Study linked data on income, earnings and benefits from tax and social security records (held by two different agencies) to the March 1973 CPS survey data to create an extremely rich dataset for a nationally representative sample of the population. The file is available for public use and has formed the basis for methodological, cross-sectional and longitudinal studies (Behrman *et al.*, 1983; Tanur, 1983: 52).

In Britain, the ONS Longitudinal Study (LS) links population census records for a 1% sample of the population with information from other records held in the National Statistical Office, such as birth and death registration and notifications of cases of cancer. So far, information on personal and household characteristics from the 1971, 1981 and 1991 censuses has been added to the file, with plans to add 2001 census data in due course. The database is used for research on health and mortality differentials, supplementing studies based on death registration records alone (Drever and Whitehead, 1997; ONS, 1998; see also Hakim, 1982a: 43, 71–2). The census data in the ONS LS is also used for a wide range of socio-economic research, sometimes to extend cross-sectional analysis of census microdata (see Chapter 2), and sometimes as a complement to other research sources (Dale and Marsh, 1993: 312–29; Hakim, 1998).

As principles and rules are evolved to deal with the legal and ethical problems of linking data from disparate record systems and agencies, and as techniques are developed for dealing with the methodological problems (such as the varying units of analysis within record systems), more record linkage projects are being designed (Tanur, 1983: 51–5).

## Documentary analysis

It is even more difficult to generalise about the research uses of individually unique documents than about records-based studies, because so much depends on the nature and contents of the documents in question and whether they are subjected to qualitative or quantitive analysis. So only a brief indication of possible research designs is given here.

Documents may be subjected to an *analytical reading,* as illustrated by analyses of political ideologies (Fielding, 1981). Readings of the population census commentaries have provided information on changing conceptions of work and employment, the underlying rationales for occupational classifications, the changing status of particular occupations, and trends in occupational segregation (Davies, 1980; Hakim, 1980).

Documents may be subjected to various forms of *content analysis,* some of them using quantitive techniques (Weber, 1990). Content analysis has been used to expose the sex role or racial stereotypes contained in children's books, to show how the professional ideologies of scientists are structured to promote and defend their claims to authority, autonomy and resources (Gieryn, 1983), and to assess degrees of bias in media coverage of the news (Glasgow University Media Group, 1976, 1982).

Some documents are subjected to *quantitive analysis* because they provide information that is itself systematic and quantifiable. For example, the USA *Dictionary of Occupational Titles* provides various measures of the content, characteristics and skill requirements of occupations, and is used as a source of data on the occupational structure, as distinct from the characteristics of workers within occupations (Cain and Treiman, 1981; Parcel and Mueller, 1983a).

## Cross-national comparative studies

Cross-national comparative studies have so far been rare. They may increase in the future, as a result of the computerisation of records.

Despite international variations in record-keeping systems, it has proved possible to carry out comparative studies of homicide, for example. Archer and Gartner (1984) compiled an enormous cross-cultural database on criminal violence (homicide, assault, robbery, theft and rape) for over 100 countries and covering the first three-quarters of the twentieth century. This formed the basis for comparative studies of the deterrent effect of the death penalty and on whether wars produce a post-war increase in rates of violent crime.

## Overlaps and combinations

For all their limitations, records-based studies permit quite a range of research designs. Many of the examples given above illustrate overlaps and links with other types of study more commonly based on specially collected research data.

One type of overlap deserves special note. Some surveys are a cross between the postal survey and data extracted from administrative records. National surveys and censuses of employers are often of this type, with self-completion questionnaires sent out to employers, who will normally have to extract the relevant data themselves from their own records – for example, on the size and characteristics of their work force, the earnings paid to their employees, or their output and exports. Although these postal enquiries appear, on the surface, to have the characteristics of specially designed research surveys, the data that can be collected are, in practice, wholly constrained by the nature of employers' personnel records and accounting systems.

## Practical considerations

Some of the anonymised datasets extracted from government records are routinely released for independent research analysis; in other cases, access has to be specially negotiated, and in yet others, laws specifically prohibit the release of such data. The rules on access may change over time, even in relation to a single dataset. For example, the American Tax Reform Act of 1976 prohibited any further release of CWHS data for public use, whereas special arrangements for improving remote access to the British ONS LS were made in the 1980s. Access to organisational records in the private sector must invariably be negotiated separately for each study, and rules to protect confidentiality may also need to be agreed.

By the 1990s, a new convention of *controlled access* had been established in Britain for several research databases produced from government records. In all these cases, the database was longitudinal and required regular updating, or else included a panel element. This meant that names, addresses and other personal identifiers had to be retained within the database so as to permit correct matching of cases each time new information was added. The government bodies responsible for each database thus created systems to check and control requests from academics and other policy researchers for special analyses of the databases, leaving control fully in their hands while providing limited outputs to *bona fide* researchers. Systems of controlled access have been instituted for the Offenders' Index, the NES database and the ONS LS described earlier. Access remains free of charge, but researchers have to submit details of their research projects for vetting prior to submitting analysis requests. In some cases, such as the ONS LS, all output is individually checked to ensure that analyses never reveal information about individuals.

Whether the required information has to be specially extracted from records or computer files, or is already available as a standard release datatape, it is essential that sufficient time and resources are allocated to the tasks of familiarisation with the contents; preparation of basic or additional documentation with reference to the specific questions addressed by the study and pertinent data items; and, in some cases, sorting out whether missing values can reliably be imputed or estimated. Perhaps the most common mistake is to think of data from records as ready-to-use research data, whereas they usually require more preparation, care and effort than an equivalent secondary analysis of a research dataset.

Hoaglin *et al.* (1982: 147–65) and Hakim (1983) review the methodology and problems of interpretation arising in research analyses of data from administrative records. But problems are often specific to a particular set of records, or to a particular intended use of them. In the absence of detailed guides to the relevant administrative record systems and the data obtained from them (for example, Walker, 1981, and other volumes in the Maunder series), consultation with those responsible for the records is frequently required, if only to check assumptions that may be wrong.

There are many general texts on content analysis and the analysis of documentary evidence (Berelson, 1952; Platt, 1981a; Plummer, 1983; Weber, 1990). Flaherty (1979) and Boruch and Cecil (1983) review the legal and ethical considerations raised by this type of study. Although quite a few records-based datasets are now held in archives, replications of the original analyses and secondary analyses remain rare (but see Bursik and Webb, 1982; Furet and Ozouf, 1982).

# 5    Case studies

If surveys are the most multi-purpose of all research designs, case studies are probably the most flexible. At the simplest level, they provide descriptive accounts of one or more cases. When used in an intellectually rigorous manner to achieve experimental isolation of selected social factors, they offer the strengths of experimental research within natural settings. In between these two extremes there is an extended range of case studies combining exploratory work, description and the testing out of hunches, hypotheses and ideas in varying combinations. The case study is the social research equivalent of the spotlight or the microscope: its value depends crucially on how well the study is focused.

Case studies take as their subject one or more *selected* examples of a social entity – such as communities, social groups, organisations, events, life histories, families, work teams, roles or relationships – which are studied using a *variety* of data collection techniques. The criteria that inform the selection of the case, or cases, for a study determine its location on the continuum between the descriptive report on an illustrative example and the rigorous test of a well-defined thesis. Using a variety of data collection techniques and methods allows a more rounded, holistic study than with any other design.

At the minimum, a case study can provide a richly detailed 'portrait' of a particular social phenomenon, such as McGovern's (1982) account of the lynching of Claude Neal in October 1934, its antecedents and its aftermath, or Lacey's (1970) account of the social structure of the grammar school. *Descriptive case studies* may be exploratory, if relatively little previous research exists on the topic, or they may be illustrative 'portraits' of social entities or patterns thought to be typical, representative or average. Sometimes both elements are combined in a single study, with the most detailed account being presented for the case, or cases, that are most typical. For example, Lein studied 23 two-earner families with young children, but provides the most detailed accounts for four families that illustrate her fourfold typology of ideology and practice in relation to the wife's paid work (Lein, 1984). In policy research, descriptive case studies are used to present examples of 'good practice'.

After a body of research evidence has accumulated on a topic, *selective case studies* can focus on particular aspects, or issues, to refine knowledge. For example, case studies can be used to provide a more richly detailed and precise account of the processes at work within particular types of case that are highlighted by surveys, whether typical or anomalous; they can also be used to substantiate or refine causal processes thought to underlie observed patterns and correlations. One example is Fagin and Little's study of changes in mental and physical health within families in the period following the husband's unemployment; this was based on 22 families that met a number of criteria chosen to isolate most clearly the effects of the breadwinner's unemployment, and was informed by a substantial body of previous research, much of it based on the analysis of aggregate data and time series. The case studies addressed the question of whether unemployment was the cause or the consequence of ill-health, and the circumstances surrounding each process (Fagin and Little, 1984).

At the most rigorous level, case studies are designed to achieve *experimental isolation* of selected social factors or processes within a real-life context, so as to provide a strong test of prevailing explanations and ideas. Experimental isolation is the alternative to randomised assignment to treatments, which is commonly presented as the only model of experimental research (see Chapter 9). Randomisation purports to control an infinite number of variables and rival explanations without specifying what any of them are; in contrast, experimental isolation specifies the factors to be excluded or included and identifies one or more social settings in which they are present or absent, as required, for a case study (Campbell and Stanley, 1963: 37–43; Yin, 1994, see especially Campbell's Foreword). One variant of this design is the 'critical case', or 'strategic' case study, which assesses the evidence for a conclusion or explanation by looking at the *most favourable* illustration of it. Alternatively, a general explanation may be tested by looking at a 'deviant' case, which suggests that the *exception dis*proves the rule, or at least proves that the general rule needs to be re-defined as applying only in certain circumstances. The factors that are included (as relevant to the explanation to be tested) in or excluded (as irrelevant) from the selection criteria for the case study will depend on prevailing ideas; later, in retrospect, it may be seen that other controls were needed as well, or that the factors were not defined clearly enough. One example of the critical case study design is Goldthorpe *et al.*'s (1969) study of the affluent worker's life style and social and political values and attitudes, which aimed to test the thesis of working-class *embourgeoisement*. The deviant case study is best illustrated by *Union Democracy* (Lipset *et al.*, 1956), a study of the highly democratic International Typographical Union, which seemed to disprove Michels's 'iron law of oligarchy'. The study described and analysed the distinctive characteristics of the union – its history, organisation, occupational culture and membership – which explained its internal government being democratic rather than oligarchic. Strategic case studies are one example of focused sampling (see Chapter 10).

This diversity of case study designs is further compounded by the variety of methods used, whether the focus is a single case or multiple cases.

Case studies are typically based on two or more methods of data collection. Well before Denzin formalised the logic of multiple triangulation (see Chapter 11), the use of multiple sources of evidence allowed case studies to present more rounded and complete accounts of social issues and processes. Whether the case study is descriptive or explanatory, or is concerned with rigorous tests of received ideas, the use of multiple sources of evidence and, very often, multiple investigators makes the case study one of the most powerful research designs. The fieldwork for case studies may incorporate the analysis of administrative records and other documents, depth interviews, larger-scale structured surveys (either personal interview or postal surveys), participant and non-participant observation and collecting virtually any type of evidence that is relevant and available. Even single-time studies may cover an extended period of time (for example Lacey, 1970; Kagan, 1978; Martin, 1980), and case studies can be prolonged into longitudinal studies covering decades, either on a continuous basis (for example, Jefferys and Sachs, 1983) or with periodic follow-ups (for example, Caplow *et al.*, 1982; Rogers and Chung, 1983). As noted above, the experimental isolation design offers the strengths of experimental research. So case studies potentially overlap with virtually all other research designs, offering their combined and complementary strengths.

Another source of flexibility and diversity lies in the option of focusing on a single case or else covering multiple cases. A single example often forms the basis for research on typical, deviant or critical cases. Multiple case designs can be limited to two or three settings or extend to dozens of cases, either to achieve replication of the same study in different settings or to compare and contrast different cases.

Designs based on a large number of case studies are especially appropriate for topics that are too complex and involve too many actors to be addressed by interview surveys – as is the case when organisations, roles, interactions or events are the subject of the enquiry. So multiple case studies provide an important alternative to the sample survey for certain research questions where there is a need to provide broad generalisation as well as to take account of the complexity of the subject-matter. Sudman notes that confidence in the general significance and robustness of research findings increases with the number of sites in which a survey is conducted, although the largest single gain occurs when the number of sites is increased from one to two (Sudman, 1976: 26). Similarly, confidence in the generalisability of the results of a case study design increases with the number of cases covered, with the greatest proportional gains being achieved when the number of cases is increased from one to two, three, or more. When the number of cases remains small, there is an advantage in selecting them so as to cover the known range and variation, perhaps starting with both extremes. As the number of cases increases to substantial figures (over 100), the logic of statistical inference begins to complement, and even replace, the logic of analytical inference from a small number of carefully selected cases (Yin, 1994: 38–51; see also Glaser and Strauss, 1967; Mitchell, 1983).

The enormous variation in case study designs makes it difficult to summarise their key strengths and weaknesses; so much depends on the degree of fit between the questions to be addressed and the particular case, or cases, selected for the study. Some degree of prior knowledge may be necessary for suitable cases to be selected, especially if focused sampling is used (see Chapter 11). Sometimes a client or sponsor can supply relevant background information on possible cases; another solution is to do case studies as a follow-up to a survey – using the survey either as a general sampling frame, or to select deviant or strategic cases, or simply to identify the types of cases of particular interest for more intensive study. As a general rule, the greatest amount of prior knowledge is required by case studies that test causal propositions by experimental isolation in real-life settings (see, for example, Lipset, 1964). If appropriate cases cannot be identified, or access problems and other practical difficulties prevent the study being implemented, then the rationale of the design must be altered and re-oriented to somewhat different questions that can be tackled with reference to available or accessible cases, because convenience samples are not acceptable in case study research. For example, Blau changed his original design for comparative case studies of work teams in a public sector bureaucracy and a private sector bureaucracy to a design based on *replication* of the same study in two public sector bureaucracies (Blau, 1963). But if the fit is good, case studies can offer the strengths of the research programme on a smaller scale, combining different types of complementary evidence and, potentially, the advantages of a multi-disciplinary approach as well.

The principal weakness of case studies is that results can be shaped strongly by the interests and perspective of the researcher. There are innumerable examples of case studies whose conclusions are flatly contradicted by a subsequent re-study by another researcher with a different perspective on the subject. Just one example is Flanders' (1964) study of productivity bargaining in a British oil refinery, which reported immediate benefits from a new approach to pay bargaining. A follow-up study 20 years later by Ahlstrand (1990) challenged many of the earlier study's findings.

The flexible character of the case study design makes for very diverse types of study. Probably the most widely used classification distinguishes between individual case histories, community studies, studies of social groups, studies of organisations and institutions, and those concerned with specific events, roles, relationships and interactions. The five types may be used both for theoretical and policy research, as is indicated by the examples offered below. A quite different classification is used by Yin (1994: 38–51), but he too identifies exemplary cases and critical (strategic) cases as two main types (Yin, 1993: 11–12, 34, 1994: 38–40).

## Individual case histories

Individual case histories provide an enormously detailed and substantiated account of one person's 'history' with reference to some specific personal characteristic or series of events they have experienced. The alternative term of *life histories* is misleading in suggesting that all aspects of a person's life are explored equally, rather than particular aspects. Even studies claiming to have attempted a 'complete' life history will inevitably have been selective in what is covered. To date, case histories have most commonly been used to study minority groups, which are not easily located for larger-scale studies and whose experiences are more distinctive or uncommon and hence less well known than those of members of majority groups. Individual case histories of delinquents and criminals are used in criminological research; case histories of members of deviant sub-cultures (such as drug users or sexual deviants) play a part in sociological research. But this type of case study can be used for a wider range of topics, such as the experiences and changing attitudes of immigrants; the process of socialisation into and disengagement from organisational roles and cultures; the processes and experiences leading to a change of religion or (re)entry into a religious group (Barker, 1984), and so on.

Individual case histories focus *post hoc* on the antecedents, contextual factors, perceptions and attitudes preceding a known outcome (such as the fact of being an immigrant, born-again Christian or delinquent). Their principal use is in providing an unusually detailed exploration of all possible causes, determinants, pathways, processes and experiences that might have contributed, directly or indirectly, to the known outcome; this aspect makes them useful as illustrative or exploratory material for research on causal processes. Another use is simply to provide richly detailed explorations of individuals' own perceptions and accounts of their experiences for research on the interaction between attitudes and behaviour, or on the discrepancies between popular stereotypes of minority group members and their own views on their situation. Case histories can provide an obvious complement to larger-scale longitudinal studies, focusing, for example, on anomalous cases such as people who do well at school or achieve occupational success despite coming from 'deprived' backgrounds (Pilling, 1990), or vice versa. Although case histories explore social-structural determinants of the given outcome, they provide some balance to perspectives that overstress these factors (as in the oversocialised view of man noted by Wrong, 1961) because they are less likely to overlook the personal decisions and ambitions that also come into play in any process or sequence of events. Hence case histories are especially useful in disciplines and professions (such as psychology, or social work) where the focus is on the individual's capacity for change. Case histories also offer an appropriate research design for policy research and multi-disciplinary research on topics linked to professional work where the focus is on individual cases – such as law, psychiatry, the health services and the criminal justice system.

There are relatively few recent examples of case histories, and the classic studies of this type come from the work of the Chicago School of Sociology in the 1930s. Bogdan and Taylor (1975), Denzin (1978a: 214–55), Faraday and Plummer (1979), Burgess (1982), Runyan (1982) and Plummer (1983) describe notable examples of this type of study, old and new, in their reviews of the nature, value and methods of case histories (or life histories as they are often termed). Perhaps the best-known example is Shaw's study of a teenage 'jack-roller' (a person who mugged drunks and other vulnerable people), which was originally published in 1930, re-issued in 1966, and later extended by a follow-up study carried out in the 1970s (Shaw, 1966; The Jack-Roller and Snodgrass, 1982).

By definition, the individual case history covers a single person, who is interviewed in some depth over an extended period of time. To extend and substantiate this personal account, the researcher will refer to a variety of other sources of evidence, such as interviews with other people (family, friends, and professionals who have had contact with the subject), documentary sources and records, (non)participant observation of relevant social settings and events, and virtually any other relevant source of evidence. The focus on a single person does not mean that his or her account alone is used, or taken at face value. In this way, the case study is different from depth interviews discussed in Chapter 3. Unfortunately, the two designs are discussed as a single research method in some textbooks, such as Plummer (1983).

The individual case history design can be extended and modified to cover more than one case, but almost invariably with a concomitant decline in the breadth and detail and in the amount of additional substantiating evidence obtained from other sources to check each individual's account.

## Community studies

Community studies are case studies of a single local community or town that seek to describe and analyse the pattern of, and relationships between, the main aspects of community life: politics, religious activities, family life, work, leisure, community activities, and so forth. The term sociography is sometimes used for such studies to denote the *social* mapping out of the community's institutions, structure and patterns of relationships. This type of case study is heavily used in social anthropology for research on non-industrialised societies, but it is also used to study towns and communities in industrialised societies, as illustrated by studies of Banbury in Britain (Stacey, 1960; Stacey *et al.*, 1975), Marienthal in Austria (Jahoda, Lazarsfeld and Zeisel, 1972) and Middletown in the USA (Lynd and Lynd, 1929), which was the subject of a follow-up study in the mid-1970s (Caplow *et al.*, 1982).

Community studies commonly provide a great deal of descriptive material on the particular community and the pattern of social life in it, but they may also address specific questions and issues. The study of Marienthal was concerned with the impact of unemployment on the community as a whole as well as on families within it; the first study of Banbury was concerned with the impact of the introduction of large-scale industry. Even where the focus is a broad one, such as the 'life cycle' of neighbourhoods, the case study may be structured around selected community characteristics; for example, Taub *et al.* (1984) focused on crime, racial stability and property value appreciation as strategic dimensions of neighbourhood change. Community studies may focus even more specifically on policy issues or theoretical questions, such as patterns of residential segregation, the role of pressure groups, the implementation of a regional plan, public sector housing policy, or conflict arising from the competition for territory (Cox and Johnson, 1982). The wide range of topics that can be addressed at the level of the local community allows this type of case study to be used not only by social anthropologists but also by social geographers, sociologists, political scientists, economists and even historians (Hareven, 1982; Smith, 1982).

While most studies focus on a single location, the strongest designs involve the comparative study of two or more communities. For example, Taub *et al*:'s (1984) study of neighbourhood change was based on eight Chicago neighbourhoods selected to offer variation on three strategic dimensions of neighbourhood change in order to test theories about the relationships between these and other factors.

Community studies, like all types of case study, can potentially be designed within a multi-disciplinary framework. But they are often conducted within the framework of a single social science discipline, and this can so constrain the questions asked and the choice of methods and techniques as to determine the results obtained. A review of case studies of community power carried out variously by political scientists and sociologists noted how the disciplinary orientation conditioned the methods used and hence the results obtained (Walton, 1966a, 1966b).

Community case studies can also be used for cross-national comparative research, as shown below.

## Case studies of social groups

Case studies have obvious advantages for research on social groups, both small groups in direct contact with each other (such as families or work teams) and larger groups with a shared identity, common activities or interests (such as occupational groups or national pressure groups). Again, the focus may be on relatively stable patterns of relationships and activities in social groups selected as typical, deviant or strategically different on some criteria, or else on processes of change surrounding an event, such as a change of status, or in response to changes in the surrounding environment. For example, Pahl (1983) reviewed numerous case studies to identify four types of family money management system and Salaff (1981) relied on 10 cases to explore the impact of a working daughter on Chinese family roles, relationships and ideology in Hong Kong.

Following Blau's (1963) well-known, if flawed, study of work teams in two public sector bureaucracies carried out in the late 1940s, case studies have been widely used for research on particular aspects of work groups – such as the organisational, legislative and social factors that affect the work team, or the way in which operational rules devised by work teams can transform the original objectives of management or government policy – as illustrated by studies of police work groups (Punch, 1979; Holdaway, 1982; Smith and Gray, 1983), social services teams (Black *et al.*, 1983), ambulance service crews (Metz, 1981) or bread roundsmen (Ditton, 1977). This type of case study often involves *participant* observation carried out (covertly or openly) by people doing research while actually working as a member of the team, as distinct from non-participant observation, interviews and other methods used by a non-involved researcher. The advantages and disadvantages of each approach are obvious. Although ethical problems can arise in and affect the results of all types of case study, they are potentially most pronounced in case studies of work teams. The participant researcher's study is also open to the accusation that he or she became incorporated into the work team's culture (whether accepting it or rejecting it) and hence lost a sense of objectivity and possibly even lost sight of the study's purpose. On the other hand, the non-participant researcher's study is open to the criticism that they failed to observe, or take account of, all relevant factors and produced a partial (hence unpersuasive or biased) account.

Although case study designs are particularly attractive to the lone researcher, there are strong arguments for using multiple researchers as well as a variety of data collection techniques. One alternative is for the research design to provide an opportunity for the informants and subjects to review and comment on the draft report, as a validating procedure (Yin, 1994: 144–6). *Street Corner Society* has become a classic case study of the street corner gang, partly because it describes a subculture, but partly because the results have broader relevance to small group processes (such as the way individual performance is affected by group structure) and the way local groups are related to the larger social structure of the community. The case study was based largely on participant observation but, as the detailed methodological appendix added to the second edition makes clear (Whyte, 1955: 279–358), the study relied crucially on one key informant, Doc, who also commented in detail on drafts of the case study report (Whyte, 1955: 341).

## Case studies of organisations and institutions

Case studies are a useful design for research on organisations and institutions in both the private and public sectors, and encompass studies of firms (including very small firms), workplaces, schools, trade unions, bureaucracies, studies of 'best practice', policy implementation and evaluation, industrial relations, management and organisation issues, organisational cultures, processes of change and adaptation, extending to comparative studies of nations, governments and multi-nationals.

One excellent example of this type (albeit one that offers only a broad outline of how it was carried out) is Heclo and Wildavsky's study of Whitehall in the early 1970s. They used a case study of the expenditure process as a spotlight for illuminating the characteristic practices of British central government, as well as offering a description of the process as it actually operated (a process that had remained hidden by custom), noting that the expenditure process provided 'an immense window into the reality of British political administration'. Heclo and Wildavsky are political scientists specialising in public administration, and their introduction to the book presents a model approach to doing research on organisations. They reject the 'us versus them' mentality that sometimes underlies researchers' attitudes towards the subjects of a study and can create conflict over the resulting published report (see Chapter 12). Instead they emphasise that the research was only possible because they showed themselves to be trustworthy in respecting the confidentiality of information and respondents' need for anonymity (even if this entailed special efforts on their part in relation to the final report); they state their respect and admiration for their informants, who are the invisible 'co-authors' of the book, underline the similarities between the approaches of officials and scholars to their subject-matter, while noting key differences in their purpose and perspective, which means that social scientists, by taking a broader perspective, can offer a view that is both different and valid. They devoted some effort to doing enough homework so as to present an informed perspective on the subject-matter of interviews and hence also to offer a more egalitarian and stimulating discussion to their respondents; and they state clearly that their values and judgments pervade their research report, from obvious declarations to the more subtle arrangement of material and choice of emphasis. Their research report (which cuts across the theoretical/policy research divide) is detailed, well informed and extremely well written, and has become a classic case study, reprinted seven years later with an additional section updating and re-assessing their original conclusions in the light of subsequent developments (Heclo and Wildavsky, 1981).

Another successful case study is a longitudinal study of primary medical care carried out over a period of 12 years (Jefferys and Sachs, 1983). The consequences of the re-organisation of primary medical care by local doctors were assessed by a comparative study of two multiple-doctor partnerships with different practice philosophies who moved together to a new medical centre, and three other small practices (solo or two-person partnerships) who did not participate in the medical centre move but who worked in the same area of London. The report analyses the implications of the re-organised system, as compared with the old, for professional relationships between medical workers, for relationships between doctors and patients, and for service delivery generally; it also presents a detailed description of the methods used for the study.

In a similar vein, but using different methods, Rogers and Chung (1983) carried out a follow-up study to an earlier study to assess the consequences of the decentralisation of the administration of New York City schools, using case studies of eight of the 36 de-centralised school districts.

Sometimes investigators take up employment in an organisation in order to conduct a case study of some particular policy or facet of the organisation's activities. One example is Kagan's study of the implementation of the Nixon administration's 1971 wage-price freeze, which used participant observation and a quantitive analysis of a sample of case decisions (Kagan, 1978). Many case studies of schools involve the researcher working as a teacher within the school (Lacey, 1970).

One type of organisational case study that is exclusive to policy research is the best practice case study, which is used to illustrate, and thereby promote and encourage, organisational policies and practices that are seen as successful or exemplary. For example, six exemplary, but quite different, high schools are described by Lightfoot (1983).

The case study design also lends itself to historical research. For example, Littler used two contrasting case studies, a labour intensive hosiery company and a capital intensive engineering company, for his research on the changing organisation and management of labour in Britain in the 1930s and worker resistance to it. Information for the case studies was obtained from documents and records in the archives of the Bedaux company, supplemented by contemporary newspaper accounts of major strikes in the two companies and the events surrounding them, and interviews with people who had been union leaders at the time and involved in these events (Littler, 1982: 117–45).

## Case studies of events, roles and relationships

A more diffuse fifth category of case studies, which overlaps partially with the previous two, deals with specific events, roles and relationships. Strong and Davis (1977) observed over 1,000 paediatric consultations in a variety of medical contexts in Britain and the United States to study interaction between doctor and patient, resulting in a classification of four main role-formats for this type of interaction. Content analysis (Weber, 1990), and the newer techniques of conversation analysis (Hutchby and Wooffitt, 1998), are especially useful in case studies of roles and relationships (Torode, 1984; Kollock, Blumstein and Schwartz, 1985). Women's entry into sex-atypical occupations stimulated case studies looking at the role stereotypes, role conflicts and role adaptations connected with women taking up stereotypically male jobs (Martin, 1980; Heller, 1982; Epstein, 1983). Williams (1989) contrasted the problems of women entering the USA Marines with those of men entering nursing, and Williams (1993) studied men working in typically female occupations. Sykes and Brent (1983) collected data on thousands of police–civilian encounters in one city to study the nature of ordinary, everyday, interaction between authority-holding officers and civilians. A case study of the New York City Police Department focused on four critical incidents to document the two sub-cultures within the organisation and conflict between them (Reuss-Ianni, 1983). Yin (1993, 1994) reviews many classic case studies of the policy-making and implementation process. Levi (1981) takes a specific type of white-collar crime, long-firm fraud, as the subject of a criminological case study that is both historical and sociological in its perspective and draws on a great variety of research evidence. Finally, Elias (1983) offers an example of a case study in historical sociology, focusing on Louis XIV and his court in relation to French society to present a study of the court society as a historically important type of social formation.

The diversity and flexibility of the case study design enables it to be used by all social science disciplines, both for theoretical research and policy research. However, special effort is required to achieve the intellectual rigour of an explanatory study, and case studies can all too easily slip back into being descriptive and exploratory in the main.

Precisely because they are flexible, they are open to sloppy use, with the objectives achieved only partially at the implementation phase, particularly if the aims are left vaguely defined or repeatedly altered.

## Cross-national comparative studies

The flexibility of the case study design means that it is used almost as often as the interview survey for cross-national comparative studies. For example, Littler's study of the organisation and management of labour in Britain described above was complemented by briefer comparative studies of developments in Japan and the USA (Littler, 1982: 146–85), and subsequently extended by a fuller set of comparative case studies of employers' labour policies in the United States, Britain, Germany and Japan (Gospel and Littler, 1983). Comparative case studies are a well-established design for research on local and national governments and the policy process (see, for example, Heclo, 1974; Cooper, 1983).

A good example of a comparative study based on community case studies is Gallie's study of social inequality and class ideology in Britain and France (Gallie, 1978, 1984). This is based on a design that provides carefully selected similarities and differences between the four communities studied, and also places them in a national context by using opinion poll data. The research covered the employees of an oil refinery company working in four plants located in an English and a Scottish community and in a northern and southern French community. Eurobarometer and other opinion poll data were used to gauge the probable representativeness of the interview data collected in the four communities (Gallie, 1984).

In other cases, the comparative element is obtained by drawing together case studies with the same focus carried out independently by different scholars. Miers and Kopytoff (1977) and Leach and Leach (1983) provide two examples from social anthropology. Similarly, a comparative study of women national leaders was based on separate studies of nine cases, including Golda Meir, Indira Gandhi and Margaret Thatcher, all brought together in one comparative volume (Genovese, 1993). The only common feature of the nine cases was a strong bond with their father and education in separate women's colleges.

A particularly well-designed study of cohabitation as an alternative to marriage was based on comparisons of four social groups: a Dutch sample of 50 randomly selected cohabiting couples with a matched sample of 50 married couples, and two similarly selected groups of 32 cohabiting couples and 32 matched married couples in the United States (Wiersma, 1983). The use of matched samples within each country, and the replication of the same study in two different countries, allowed for a very strong test of the idea that cohabiting couples are distinctively different in terms of personal characteristics, attitudes and values, roles and behaviour within the couple.

Cross-national comparisons can be based on secondary analysis of case study information in archives, such as the Yale University Human Relations Area Files. Whyte (1978) used this database and other case studies of pre-industrial societies for a systematic comparative study of how and why women's status varies across societies and cultures, in particular to test the thesis that there are no known societies in which women dominated public positions of power and authority. He found patriarchy to be almost universal, with rare cases of rough equality between men and women (Whyte, 1978: 57, 90–93).

Case studies are also useful for exploratory research, as illustrated by studies of doctors' strikes throughout history and across the world, to consider how professional dominance and autonomy are eroded in the path toward proletarianisation (Antonovsky in Kohn, 1989).

## Overlaps and combinations

As noted earlier, case studies typically use a variety of methods and types of evidence, whereas most other research designs rely on a single type of evidence. Case studies therefore overlap with and are readily linked to all other types of study, as is evident in the examples given above.

## Practical considerations

It should be clear from the diversity of case study designs described that they can range from small projects carried out by a single researcher in three to four months on a self-funded basis to larger and more costly projects carried out by a team of researchers, occasionally over periods of up to 15 years. The number of cases studied can range from only one to hundreds. The type and quantity of data collected and analysed can vary enormously, and one of the objectives of a pilot study would be to ascertain the nature of any available records, documents, descriptive material and other sources of evidence that might be drawn upon in addition to information created by new data collection exercises such as interview surveys, informant interviews and observation. The costs and timetables for case study designs thus vary enormously. It does not always follow that a study proposal can be trimmed to fit into a con-strained budget, because essential parts of the relevant evidence may be omitted and the results produced may be much weaker and open to criticism.

One significant practical difficulty with case studies is the choice of research staff with appropriate experience and skills. Most researchers tend to specialise in particular types of work, whereas case studies tend to demand a wider range of skills: interviewing, the analysis and interpretation of information held in documents and records, the design and analysis of structured surveys, extended periods of obser-vation as well as the usual literature surveys and drafting skills for research reports. The fact that research staff are willing to 'have a go' at types of data collection or data analysis of which they have no experience is not sufficient: some additional training (whether formal or on-the-job) may be a necessary additional cost for the project to be carried out properly.

Case studies often involve specialised interviewing of informants, professionals and organisational or public role-holders, which is quite different in nature from standard research interviewing. The discussion takes place on a basis of equality (or even of researcher inferiority). Such interviews often require the interviewer to demonstrate a good deal of prior knowledge of the subject, to treat the interviewee as an informant as well as a respondent, to display sensitivity to the fact that views offered by organisational and other role-holders may not be coterminous with their private opinions. The best guides to this kind of interviewing have been written by political scientists (Dexter, 1970; Moyser and Wagstaffe, 1987). Sociologists exhibit ambivalence and confusion over role-holder interviewing, which is context-bound, rarely completely anonymous, and makes heavy demands on the interviewer (Deutscher, 1972; Platt, 1981b; Bechhofer *et al.*, 1984). Plummer (1983) discusses the extended interviewing required for life histories, and shows how theoretical perspectives (implicit or explicit) structure the entire study.

Another practical problem is that the analysis and presentation of case study data requires more skill than reports based on a single type of evidence. Two common errors are to present an indigestible mass of detailed evidence in the report, or to report only the researcher's con-clusions, instead of presenting carefully selected robust and central items of data in combination with the various questions and issues addressed by the study.

When the case study is carried out by an active participant (in a social group or an organisation, for example), ethical issues may arise, and there may be practical difficulties in combining the sometimes conflict-ing roles of team member and researcher. Two accounts of the strengths and limitations of this approach are given by Dalton (1964) and Lacey (1976).

Yin (1994) provides an excellent review of, and guide to, all aspects of case study research: design, selection of cases, implementation and management, analysis and reporting results, with numerous examples presented throughout. His book covers the full range of case study designs, as used in theoretical and policy research, with examples taken from all social science disciplines. Yin (1993) includes a longer discussion of the role of theory in doing case studies, and shows how case study research is carried out, with examples from educational research, management studies, community studies and evaluation.

More limited considerations of case study designs, their implementation and the analysis of non-quantitive data produced by this type of study are also provided within the framework of particular research fields or social science disciplines: sociology and anthropology (Goode and Hatt, 1952: 330–40; Blaxter, 1979; Mitchell, 1983; Feagin, Orum and Sjoberg, 1991), political science (Eckstein, 1975), educational research (Lacey, 1976; Simons, 1980; Hammersley, 1984, 1985), organisational research (Lipset, 1964; Van Maanen, 1979; Kimberly *et al.*, 1980), industrial relations (Whitfield and Strauss, 1998) and evaluation research (Patton, 1990; Miles and Huberman, 1994). There are also numerous textbooks on the methodological and practical problems of doing case study fieldwork (see, for example, Johnson, 1975; Van Maanen, 1979; Burgess, 1982, 1984). Douglas (1976) is one of the few textbooks to deal explicitly with *team field research*, but the book cannot otherwise be recommended because the author displays contempt for issues of privacy and confidentiality, and proposes that lies, fraud, deceit, deception and blackmail constitute reasonable techniques for social research.

Sieber (1973) offers a general assessment of the relative merits and complementarity of case studies and surveys, while Spenner (1983) offers a more detailed assessment with reference to one particular issue (the thesis that occupations are de-skilled by the process of industrial development).

Some case studies collect or compile quantitive data of the sort that may be deposited in data archives. But such data is inevitably only one part of the complete case study database. Yin (1994: 94–8) outlines how the case study database should be compiled and indexed so that the material can be stored and retrieved for further analysis or to allow another researcher to check the interpretations offered in the final report against the evidence collected. One example of a case study data bank is the Human Relations Area Files at Yale University, which store the data for numerous ethnographic studies of different cultural groups that are used extensively for cross-cultural or international comparative studies. Udy (1964) describes how he developed a cross-cultural study of work organisation in non-industrial societies based on secondary analysis of a sample of 150 cases drawn from this source. Yin (1994: 121–3) also describes a method of carrying out secondary analysis of upwards of 200 case studies using items of data extracted from the final reports on each study, an approach that falls somewhere between the more traditional literature review and secondary analysis of quantified datasets. Two examples of more theoretically oriented secondary analysis of case study material are provided by Champagne (1983) and Hammersley (1985).

# 6 *Ad hoc* sample surveys

The development of sampling theory and techniques in the early part of the twentieth century led to the sample survey becoming one of the most widely used methods of data collection in social research. Interview surveys based on a sample of the members of an organisation, occupation or local community often constitute one source of information for case studies, and sample surveys are frequently used as the main element of longitudinal studies, or of experimental research designs. Sampling alone as a research technique has even wider usage; for example, non-random sampling may be used to select people for qualitative research, and sampling techniques are often used in studies based on administrative records. However, sample surveys can constitute a research design in their own right, and it is in this capacity that we consider them here.

The *ad hoc* sample survey offers a multi-purpose research design with many advantages for both policy research and theoretical research. The application of sampling allows the production of descriptive statistics that are representative (on a national, regional or state basis) of the whole study population but at a much lower cost than with a census of every member of the population in question. Sample surveys also allow associations between factors to be mapped and measured. For example, they can show not only what proportions of working men and women are in professional occupations, but also what proportions of those in professional occupations have appropriate qualifications and what proportions of those holding such qualifications also hold professional jobs. Even without going into causal analysis to ascertain the reasons for such relationships, the bare fact of such associations, whether strong or weak, can be useful information. Thirdly, sample survey designs can be used to study causal processes, to develop and test explanations for particular associations or social patterns. This use of the survey has been facilitated and extended by the development of complex and sophisticated analysis techniques that are readily accessible in packages such as SPSS.

In developing countries, *ad hoc* sample surveys are frequently used to provide descriptive national or local statistics, especially on topics not covered by the population census. In industrialised countries, this function has largely been overtaken by the institution of a large number of regular sample surveys (and, occasionally, censuses) covering topics of continuing concern to central and local government, business and other large institutions (see Chapter 7). So, increasingly, the single-time sample survey is used for more specialised purposes: to complement and extend the information from regular surveys by more detailed investigation of particular topics or populations, and to study causal processes. Part and parcel of this trend is the continuous development of the methods and techniques of survey data collection and data analysis, for example: methods of sampling minority population groups (such as ethnic minorities or political extremists), techniques of measuring subjective factors (such as attitudes and values) as well as behavioural variables (such as criminal activity), increasing sophistication in the definition and classification of social categories (such as unemployment, discouraged workers or underemployment) and substantial developments in the data analysis techniques relevant to the study of causal processes (particularly in the field of multivariate analysis).

Another key advantage of the survey design is that studies can readily be repeated in different locations at the same time, or in the same location at intervals of time. It thus facilitates replications (see Chapter 10) and cross-national comparative studies.

One of the main attractions of the sample survey design (both for policy research and theoretical research) is its *transparency* or *accountability* – the fact that the methods and procedures used can be made visible and accessible to other parties (be they professional colleagues, clients, or the public audience for the study report), so that the implementation, as well as the overall research design, can be assessed. In contrast, many of the methods used by other research designs remain hidden, or not easily accessible. (For example, readers of research reports cannot readily have access to the tape recordings of depth interviews, to a case study database or to the administrative records used for a study.) With surveys, a standardised language has been developed to describe most of the procedures involved (such as sampling), and numerous documents can be obtained or even included in the research report: introductory letters, the survey questionnaire, the codebook, analysis of non-response, and so forth. The deposit of survey datasets in archives increases this accountability yet further by making the raw data and associated documentation available for re-analysis by others, who can become 'auditors' of the original researcher's work. Furthermore, the evidence from which conclusions are drawn can be presented 'visibly' in tables within a report, so that a reader can consider whether they are well founded and whether alternative interpretations were overlooked or too readily dismissed. Research reports based on sample surveys that provide no information on the questions asked, with coding frames unspecified, few or no tables on the results obtained and which are generally ambiguous or uninformative on key aspects of survey implementation, immediately lay themselves open to the charge of unprofessionalism, bias or dishonesty.

This transparency and accountability make survey research far more open to detailed criticism and debate than is the case with many other research designs. But it makes the sample survey a very 'democratic' study design, in that the results are accessible to non-specialists and specialists in other disciplines. For example, the reader or client can look at the questions asked and take a view on whether they were liable to be interpreted differently by different types of respondent, or whether the questions were ambiguously worded or biased in favour of one type of response. The transparency of surveys also facilitates systematic refinement of survey methods and techniques, and the development of theoretical work. Survey results can be re-analysed with different theoretical perspectives, or subtle but significant flaws in an earlier analysis can be exposed, both of which facilitate the cumulative development of social scientific knowledge and methods.

The principal weakness of the sample survey is that it normally involves the use of a structured questionnaire (be it self-completion or administered by a trained interviewer), which necessarily obtains a lesser depth and quality of information than a depth interview. However, the depth and breadth of interviewing varies enormously between surveys, as is implied by the fact that the duration of an interview in an opinion poll may be only five minutes, while some surveys involve interviews lasting one to two hours. Similarly, postal survey questionnaires vary from those with one or two pages of tick-box questions to 30-page questionnaires that might take an hour to complete. While a structured questionnaire does mean some loss of sensitivity and quality as compared with depth interviews, the degree of loss depends very much on how a survey is carried out. The counterbalancing gain is standardised measurement that is consistent across all respondents, so that the responses of different groups can be analysed on a reasonably comparable basis and (if the sampling is adequate) conclusions drawn about the entire study population sampled.

Surveys are multi-purpose in that the design can be adapted to almost all social science disciplines and research topics. Surveys are widely used by sociologists, social psychologists and political scientists (Barnes *et al.*, 1979; Hofstede, 1980, 1991; Aberbach, Putnam and Rockman, 1981; Apostle *et al.* 1983), but are also used by geographers (Fischer, 1982) and even by historians to collect data on times past (Dexter, 1970). Although oral histories of individuals, small groups or communities would constitute case studies, it is also possible to carry out oral history surveys with nationally representative samples to collect purely retrospective data on an earlier period from people still living (Thompson, 1975: 2–8). What is less well recognised is that the survey design can be used to study not only individuals but also social roles and networks and organisations.

## Surveys of individuals

The focus on individuals as the unit of analysis as well as for data collection is well illustrated by opinion polls. But opinion polls generally represent the most shallow extreme of interview surveys and thus the weakest form of this research design (Marsh, 1982: 125–46).

Good examples of surveys focused on the individual are the 1980 Women and Employment Survey (WES) and the 1982 survey of ethnic minorities in Britain. The former covered women of working age in Great Britain, using a nationally representative sample of 5,600 women in order to allow detailed analysis of sub-groups. The principal focus was behaviour and attitudes surrounding labour force participation, with a substantial amount of contextual information also collected (for example, on the domestic division of labour among married couples and employers' policies towards their female workforce), enabling analyses to relate work orientations, sex role attitudes, employment and unemployment behaviour and attitudes, contextual factors within the family and contextual factors at the workplace (Martin and Roberts, 1984a, 1984b).

Bench-mark national surveys of this kind are typically funded by central government, but may also be carried out by independent research institutes. The Policy Studies Institute obtained government and non-government funding for the 1982 national survey of ethnic minorities, based on a sample of 5,000 adults. This considered the extent and reasons for 'racial disadvantage' (the term used to cover the results of both direct and indirect discrimination) in relation to residential segregation, housing, education and qualifications, employment and unemployment, income support and health care, in addition to providing descriptive information on ethnic groups. The survey also collected data on attitudes to race relations in Britain, perceptions of racial discrimination and reports of racial attacks (Brown, 1984).

Both of these *ad hoc* surveys explored topics in unusual depth and detail. To set the results in context, both designs incorporated comparative surveys carried out in parallel with the main survey but using smaller samples. The 1980 WES incorporated a comparison survey of 800 husbands (as a partial substitute for a survey of all males of working age), and the 1982 ethnic minorities survey incorporated a comparison survey of 2,300 white adults. Sometimes the need for additional comparative surveys (which substantially increase the overall cost of the project) can be side-stepped by relying on existing national surveys for context-setting data. This approach was used in the 1981 National Homeworking Survey, which was based on a sample of 1,300 home-based workers in England and Wales. Many of the questions asked in the survey were taken from the General Household Survey, so that the GHS provided comparative national data on the labour force, job satisfaction, household composition and income. This greatly facilitated interpretation of the survey results for the minority group of home-based workers (Hakim, 1987).

As the *ad hoc* survey is used increasingly for highly focused studies of particular social groups or of narrowly defined issues, procedures for identifying and sampling minority groups become an integral part of survey design. The term 'minority group' is used here to refer to any target population for a survey that is relatively rare because it has very specific characteristics or experiences and constitutes only a small proportion of the whole population (such as one-parent families). Some minority groups may also be geographically dispersed, with uneven patterns of concentration in particular areas, as in the case of ethnic minorities. The design of what are variously termed 'sift surveys' or 'screening surveys', which are used initially to identify the target study population for the main survey (with interviews carried out with all those identified, or with a sample of them) is developing rapidly, particularly in relation to the use of telephone screening (Hedges, 1978; Tourangeau and Smith, 1985).

One example is an American study that sought to estimate the costs that natural hazards inflict upon households and to examine how such costs are distributed among the victims. In this case, a large-scale national telephone screening survey was conducted to identify households that had experienced household fires, floods, tornadoes, hurricanes and earthquakes during the 11-year period 1970–80, with a follow-up postal survey. To set the impact of natural hazards in context, the survey collected comparative data on households' experience of other 'noxious events' such as personal bankruptcy, unemployment, arrest and marital dissolutions. The report by Rossi *et al.* (1983a) provides a detailed discussion of the technical problems encountered in this type of project.

In the case of the national survey of ethnic minorities noted earlier, a new method of focused enumeration was developed to identify representative samples of the black and white adult populations (Brown and Ritchie, 1981; Brown, 1984: 7–12), and the method has since been used in other surveys (Smith, 1983a: 234). In essence, focused enumeration consists of interviewers visiting every fifth (or tenth) address in an area and enquiring whether anyone of Asian or West Indian origin is living there, and whether any people of Asian or West Indian origin are living in the five (or 10) houses to the right of that property and in the five (or 10) houses to the left. The method offers a cost-effective way of identifying ethnic minorities, which constitute less than 10% of the population in Britain.

Another option is to use regular surveys as sampling frames for *ad hoc* surveys of particular groups, sometimes by adding special screening questions to identify the target population, as noted in Chapter 7. Omnibus surveys (see below) make this an option for everyone.

When surveys are used to study causal processes, to develop and test explanations, small samples may be used instead of national samples, particularly in the early stages of the work. For reasons of convenience and cost, this often means that survey samples have to be obtained within a limited geographical area. Apostle *et al.* (1983) used survey data from several San Francisco Bay area samples to isolate 11 types of 'explanatory model' that people employ to interpret perceived racial differences and to explore their correlates and relationships with racial policy preferences. Brown and Harris (1978) used data from a sample survey of one area in London (in addition to a variety of case studies) to assess the contribution of life events and other social factors to the onset of clinical depression among women.

Surveys can obtain very varied types of information, but there are limits to the information that respondents and informants can supply on some topics, even if the interview is long and detailed. Most typically, surveys seek information about the respondent's own behaviour and experiences, values and attitudes, personal characteristics and social circumstances. But surveys often seek information that goes beyond the individual, extending to their relationships, interactions or activities with other people (members of the family or household, colleagues at the workplace, fellow members of groups or organisations they belong to), and extending yet further to supplying information about social contexts, groups, neighbourhoods and events of which they have experience. The second type of information is often of particular interest in social research, but presents greater problems of reliability and quality and hence of interpretation. Surveys can also seek information about the past, the present or the anticipated future. While the special difficulties of information about anticipated futures are readily recognised, the particular problems of people's recollections of the past, or present-day interpretations of past events and reasons for them, are more easily overlooked. Finally, there are substantive differences between surveys that address the interviewee as a private individual (in the setting of their own home, for example) and those that address the interviewee as a role-holder (as indicated by the fact that the interview takes place in a public setting such as an office, factory or other non-private location). Role-holder interviews are particularly likely to address people as informants who can supply information about social units, events and processes that go beyond the individual interviewee, but they also seek information from the individual acting in role (Dexter, 1970; Moyser and Wagstaffe, 1987).

When information on attitudes is collected, a clear distinction must be made between asking people what they think personally, or prefer for their own lives, and asking them to report what is desirable for society generally. The two types of question produce different results. The distinction between approval and choice, between public opinion and personal preference, is often overlooked in textbooks. Public opinion polls are necessarily concerned with collective norms, as perceived by respondents. Most other social surveys are concerned with the link between attitudes and behaviour at the micro-level, so they need to collect information on *personal* beliefs and preferences. The wording of attitude statements and questions changes subtly as a result of these differing objectives (Hofstede, 1980: 21).

The data obtained from a survey can be extended by incorporating information from other, more reliable sources, such as tax records, state benefit records or arrest records. Information from school records (on test scores, examination results or absences from school) may be added to student interview data; data from health records may be added to individuals' accounts of their health problems and health service usage. Statistics for local areas from the population census and other sources can provide a variety of social, economic and political indicators on the local neighbourhood, local labour market, parliamentary constituency, school intake area, or 'market' for a particular social service, according to the focus of the study (Hakim, 1982a: 79–81). Data from company records or annual reports can supply additional information on the characteristics of the firm's work force, turnover and profits, management policy and the incidence of accidents and absenteeism. Sometimes national statistics can be used to check the reliability and representativeness of parts of the survey data. This supplementary data may be obtained before or after the survey is carried out, but the decision to incorporate such additional information will affect the design and content of the survey and needs to be mapped out at an early stage (for example, to ensure a good match between the two types of information and to ensure that there are no significant gaps in the overall information).

In a survey designed explicitly as a study of roles and relationships, or of organisations, the individual ceases to be the main unit of analysis, even though the data is still collected from interviews. This usually entails interviewing at least two, often many more, persons within every social unit covered by the study, to ensure that the information obtained is more complete and accurate.

## Survey research on roles and relationships

One excellent example of survey research on roles and relationships comes from a research programme on relations between the police force and the community it serves, carried out in London for the Metropolitan Police by the Policy Studies Institute. Two surveys were carried out and the results drawn together in a comparative analysis of both sides of police–public encounters, paying particular attention to interactions between ethnic minority groups and an almost exclusively white police force. The first, a survey of the general public, obtained information on interactions with the police as victims of crime, as suspects stopped or interviewed by the police, as offenders arrested by the police, as members of the public seeking advice or as witnesses giving information to the police. The survey also enquired about views on police practice and standards of conduct and general attitudes towards the police. The second, a survey of police officers, was concerned with their role and career as law-enforcement officers, obtaining information on their work activities and interactions with the public in various contexts, and their views on police practice and standards of conduct. Comparative analysis of the two surveys allowed cross-checking of the two accounts for consistency at the aggregate level, thus increasing confidence that the surveys had obtained a representative picture of interactions. It also allowed the researchers to identify those areas where the views and assessments of the police and of the public were in disagreement, or where the general public did not support current police practice (Smith, 1983b: 76–111, 181–7; Smith and Gray, 1983: 318–37).

Another option for studies of roles and relationships is to use a single sample and do separate interviews with both parties to the interaction. This allows the respective accounts to be compared and contrasted at the micro-level as well as at the aggregate level, as in the previous example. In practice, however, even when this design is used, it is more common for the two survey datasets to be analysed in the aggregate (and very often separately), partly because the logic and techniques of survey analysis are not geared to the cross-analysis of two perceptions of the same event or situation or to dyadic relationships as the unit of analysis. As noted above, the 1980 Women and Employment Survey included a comparison survey of one in four of the husbands of married women in the main sample. Although the design permitted analysis of patterns of consensus or disagreement *within* couples (for example on sex roles and the domestic division of labour), in practice the report mainly presented the views of husbands and wives separately (Martin and Roberts, 1984a, Chapters 8 and 12, but see Table 8.21, p.108). This design is not necessarily limited to cases where there is a close relationship. A 1977 study of relationships between general practice physicians and their patients in the British National Health Service used an interview survey of 836 patients and a postal survey of 365 of their doctors (Cartwright and Anderson, 1981). Maternity rights studies have interviewed a sample of mothers of newborns, asked them for the names and addresses of their employers, and then done a survey of their employers in order to obtain the employers' experience of the new laws on maternity rights (Daniel, 1980, 1981; Callender *et al.*, 1997; Forth *et al.*, 1997).

One of the most ambitious studies of roles and relationships was the Comparative Elites Project described in Chapter 10. This looked at the nature of the roles of politician and senior government administrator, and the relationships between the two roles, in seven democracies: the USA and six western European countries. It also demonstrated that large-scale surveys can be based on loosely structured and open-ended interviews (rather than a structured and pre-coded questionnaire), although this substantially increases the survey costs (in time and money): coding the interview data from these surveys took two years (Aberbach, Putnam and Rockman, 1981: 24–36). Open-ended interview questions are thought to be more appropriate than questions with pre-determined response categories for research on elites, for specialised interviewing (for example, on patterns of thinking and ideology) and also for cross-national survey research, where fixed-choice questions can impose a spurious comparability of response (Dexter, 1970; Moyser and Wagstaffe, 1987).

## Survey research on organisations

Multiple interviews are also the norm for studies of households, schools and other organisations, but in this case the number of persons interviewed in any one social unit can stretch into hundreds if the organisation is a large one, such as a school or firm. Also, the analysis will necessarily be concerned with the organisation as the main unit of analysis, with sub-units, roles, groups and individuals within it being additional units of analysis when multi-level analysis is carried out.

Some household surveys seek to interview all adult members of the household, and the analysis considers the characteristics of individual members, the characteristics of the whole household, and the relationship between the two. One example is a national survey of living standards carried out in 1968 by Townsend (1979). The housewife, husband and other adult earners in the household were interviewed to collect information on household income from all sources, on living standards (with particular reference to a relative deprivation scale compiled by Townsend himself) and related attitudes. This design allowed the causes of household poverty to be analysed in terms of household characteristics (such as the number of dependent children), or at the level of individual members (such as the main breadwinner's low earnings or recent unemployment). Regular surveys, such as the General Household Survey and the Family Expenditure Survey (see Chapter 7), are even more thorough in collecting information from all adult members (aged 16 and over) of each household, thus offering great flexibility in multi-level analysis of individuals, families, tax units or the household as a single unit.

A good example of a survey designed to study the social structure, social climate and culture of organisations is Coleman's study of schools, *The Adolescent Society* (1961). Strictly speaking, this study uses a case study design, since it is based on 10 schools carefully selected to offer contrasts on various criteria. However, the study was based entirely on four surveys, rather than the more complex mixture of methods that is typical of case studies. The four surveys comprised two surveys (at the beginning and end of the school year) of a representative sample of students in all grades of each school, a postal survey of these students' parents (to obtain information on local community values) and a self-completion questionnaire survey of teachers in the 10 schools. Information from the two student surveys was extended by adding data extracted from school records on each pupil's grades, test scores, absences, and so on. The surveys provided the basis for an analysis of roles, role models and status systems within the high school, the various sources of these status systems (including local community values and the importance of family background) and the consequences of the school's informal status system for scholastic achievement. As Coleman noted later, schools constitute just one example of the general class of social institutions with a captive membership within which informal social structures develop alongside the formal hierarchy of roles, so the research design could also be applied to other organisations, such as prisons, mental hospitals, summer camps and factories (Coleman, 1964: 208).

The effects of schools on their pupils has attracted a greater volume of research than the effects of other social institutions on their members, largely owing to the policy relevance of the subject. Since school attendance is obligatory, research has focused more precisely on whether *differences* between schools have any impact on educational attainment (after allowance has been made for other factors, such as the child's ability and family influences). Large-scale survey designs are often used (Coleman *et al.*, 1966; McDill and Rigsby, 1973), but case study designs have sometimes been used to achieve more precise measures of school climates and characteristics (for example, Rutter *et al.*, 1979). It has been claimed that the results of case studies reveal that the school climate has a significant impact, while surveys show that the type of school attended has a negligible impact. In this case, the apparently conflicting conclusions derive not from the choice of research design but from the different criteria of 'significance' appropriate to policy research and to theoretical research (Murphy, 1985) noted in Chapter 1.

## Cross-national comparative studies

The transparency of the survey method and its application to many research topics have made it the most common research design for cross-national comparative studies. Survey questionnaires can be translated into other languages, usually with an emphasis on the functional equivalence of questions rather than on literal translations. This standardisation of research instruments greatly facilitates comparisons across countries, even though problems of interpretation often remain to perplex scholars, as noted in Chapter 13.

Some studies are theory driven. One example is Wright's comparative study of social stratification and social class, which eventually included 15 countries and took 17 years to complete (Wright, 1985, 1997; see also Marshall *et al.*, 1991). The project was based on national surveys in each participating country, starting with the USA and Italy, and extending eventually to eight European and seven other countries. As the research progressed, Wright's class theory was progressively refined and developed. The final report identified three distinct sources or dimensions of inequality: capital and property, authority within formal organisations, and skills and credentials.

Other studies are policy driven. One example is the 12-year (1972–84) World Fertility Survey (WFS), designed and organised by the International Statistical Institute with financial support from the United Nations and the British and American governments. The WFS was prompted by the realisation that something had to be done to curb rapid population growth. The project involved comparable national surveys of women of childbearing age in 41 developing countries and 20 developed countries. Sample sizes ranged from 1,800 to 10,000. All surveys contained a common module with 'core' questions, plus a variable number of additional modules, according to local interests. There was a massive research output from the project, including several comparative summaries and final assessments of the enterprise (Cleland and Hobcraft, 1985; Cleland and Scott, 1987). The project had substantial policy impacts, but also generated a large volume of theoretical and methodological outputs from the specialists involved.

The rich datasets from these two comparative projects have been extensively re-used in secondary analyses by other social scientists concerned with different topics (for example Cain, 1993; Baxter and Kane, 1995). Other comparative surveys produce more specialised results. In 1998/99, comparative national surveys of religious attitudes and practices were carried out in 11 European countries (Norway, Sweden, Finland, Denmark, Britain, Ireland, Belgium, Poland, Hungary, Italy and Portugal) to assess the importance of religion in modern society (Barker, 2001; Jagodzinski, 2001). The International Adult Literacy Survey (IALS) was carried out in the USA, Canada, Britain and several other countries in 1994. Subsequently, a second wave of IALS was implemented in OECD countries in all parts of the world. This survey project was unusual in combining the usual standard survey questionnaire with educational testing carried out in the privacy of people's homes rather than a classroom setting. Translation of the literacy tests had to be sensitive to cultural differences (OECD, 1995, 1997).

## Overlaps and combinations

Although *ad hoc* surveys are designed and carried out on a 'one-off' basis, they can nevertheless be repeated at irregular intervals of time, thus offering some of the advantages of regular surveys for measuring change over time. As the design and content will be updated at each *ad hoc* repeat, to take account of contemporary issues and survey techniques, the results of each survey will not offer precise comparisons but can nonetheless indicate changing trends. Three of the national surveys described above were repeats (in broad conception) of surveys carried out at least once previously, at intervals ranging from eight to 15 years, and the reports all provide comparisons with the earlier surveys where possible (Cartwright and Anderson, 1981; Brown, 1984; Martin and Roberts, 1984a).

Some survey designs incorporate a 'follow-up' re-interview at a later date with the same sample of respondents. These two-stage surveys incorporate some of the strengths of longitudinal designs for measuring changes in behaviour or attitudes. For example, White's two-stage survey of the long-term unemployed was able to address questions about the relationship between unemployment and health, the incidence of discouraged workers, recurrent unemployment and occupational downgrading (White, 1983).

As noted above, survey data can be supplemented by the addition of information from administrative records, official statistics and other sources, and this may extend into secondary analysis of these other sources. Hofstede's comparative study of work-related values in 40 industrialised societies was based mainly on a survey among the employees of a large multi-national company, supplemented with demographic, economic and social indicators for each of the countries (Hofstede, 1980, 1991).

Surveys are easily linked to qualitative research and provide an excellent sampling frame for linked case studies that examine particular situations, groups or processes in greater depth. Alternatively, case studies may be carried out in combination with surveys, linked only by the issues addressed. The two surveys described above on relations between police and the public were part of a research programme that included two parallel case studies: a study of young black people in a self-help group hostel carried out over six months with covert participant observation (which fortuitously included the researcher's direct experience of arrest), and a case study of the police force itself, the structure of the organisation, methods of management, the formation of policy and the day-to-day activities of the police on different shifts and in different jobs. Both case studies were reported separately (Small, 1983; Smith and Gray, 1983) but were also used to inform interpretation of the two surveys.

## Practical considerations

With the exception of omnibus surveys (see below), it is impossible to carry out *ad hoc* surveys on any scale single handed, so that teamwork is inevitable, usually with some degree of division of labour and special-isation in responsibility for the various stages of implementation (sam-pling, interviewing, coding, data analysis and report-writing), and the concomitant need for good research management to co-ordinate and integrate the research effort as a whole. Because of this, large-scale national surveys have tended to become the province of research insti-tutes and other large research bureaux, where an 'organisational' model of research replaces the 'craft' model that is traditional within smaller academic research teams and is appropriate to smaller-scale projects such as case studies (Form, 1971: 10). However, the large-scale, or national, survey becomes accessible to researchers in all locations (including universities and very small research units) by decomposing the work involved into those parts that are mainly intellectual (or pro-fessional) in character – survey design and analysis – and those that are mainly administrative (or bureaucratic) in character – sampling, data collection and coding – and subcontracting the latter to commercial or non-profit research agencies (Haug, 1971: 200; Rossi, 1971: 165). This solution can itself raise new problems of communication between the two research bodies or teams and of integration of the research project as a whole (Payne, 1979; Harrop, 1980).

By the end of the twentieth century, there was at least one *omnibus survey* in almost all modern societies. An omnibus is an interview survey that is run weekly or monthly, on a routine basis, with a nationally representative sample, by one of the large opinion poll and market research companies. Some government research agencies also run omnibus surveys that are available for use by government bodies and academics, such as the ONS omnibus in Britain and the Statistics Sweden omnibus. Customers 'buy into' the survey, paying a fixed amount for each question they insert; the price varyies according to the question's complexity, the quality of the omnibus and the size of the sample. The fixed price covers all survey costs up to delivery of the dataset on diskette, including a fixed number of classificatory variables on personal and household characteristics. Typical sample sizes are 1,000 or 2,000 persons per week or per month, which are large enough to provide nationally representative data for a country of any size. Omnibus surveys vary a good deal in quality, size and price. Some use random samples; most use quota samples. Some use face-to-face interviews; many use telephone interviews. Almost all use CAPI or CATI (see below) and are thus able to deliver the resulting coded and edited data to customers within a matter of days or weeks. Some provide advice on question-wording and related matters; others leave this entirely to the client, acting solely as data-collection and data-processing agencies. The international survey company networks (such as NOP, Gallup, Euroquest (BMRB in Britain), Taylor-Nelson-Sofra, the Walker CSM network) can arrange for a particular module of questions to be inserted in omnibus surveys across Europe, or even across the world, in addition to the home country, thus facilitating cross-national comparative work. The creation of regular omnibus surveys in most modern countries, and in many late developing countries, now puts the national sample survey within the reach of the researcher working alone. Omnibus surveys also permit survey work to be carried out within weeks, which is a far shorter timescale than if a survey has to be organised from scratch. Most important, they allow researchers to run a small number of questions (even just one or two) in national surveys. Omnibus surveys can be used as *sift surveys* to identify a sample with particular characteristics for a subsequent survey, to test alternative wordings of survey questions, and for methodological work where a national sample is preferred. For example, the ONS omnibus was used to develop a new social class classification for use in official data collections in Britain in the 1990s (Rose, 1997). If a large number of questions is required, it is usually more efficient, and cheaper, to carry out a specially designed survey.

Surveys are used to collect 'factual' information on characteristics of the person, household or company; information on behaviour, activities and events; and information on attitudes and values. The survey method has also been extended to include a variety of specialised data collection techniques, such as vignettes (Finch, 1987); literacy tests; blood pressure tests and the collection of blood samples (for health surveys); and diaries. Although the question and answer technique is most common, it is not the only one. Inviting respondents to complete diaries, over a period ranging from one day to two weeks, is one of the most flexible extensions. Diaries can be used to collect information on personal and household expenditure; journeys and methods of transport (in the British National Travel Survey); health and illness; diet and nutrition; children's behaviour; crime behaviour; alcohol consumption and drug use; TV viewing and sexual behaviour. Time-use budgets (or diaries) are the latest addition, following the pioneering work of Szalai *et al.* (1972). Professor Jay Gershuny at the University of Essex, England, has collected some 40 *ad hoc* time budget surveys from 19 countries in broadly comparable format; these provide a different approach to studying social trends (Gershuny, 1993; Gershuny and Sullivan, 1998). Media companies use time-use surveys to find out how TV-viewing and radio-listening fit into daily life (BBC, 1984). In the late 1990s, the British ONS decided to institute a new, regular Time-Use Survey to provide data on unpaid household work to complement GNP statistics on market work.

Guidelines for commissioning surveys are provided in a number of textbooks, which give practical advice on the detailed specification of sample surveys and describe the various options and criteria for choosing those most appropriate to the research topic and available resources. Two books are particularly helpful for those who would be designers or users of survey research. Fowler (1984) offers an excellent outline of survey methods that provides not only an overview for those who are considering purchasing or commissioning a survey but also a general introduction for social scientists. Although there is no detailed discussion of the uses of surveys, he offers clear advice on the many practical questions that arise, such as the choice of sample size and type; procedures for telephone, postal and personal interview surveys; questionnaire design; and data coding. Hoinville and Jowell (1977) offer another, more detailed, handbook on survey research, which covers the same ground as well as unstructured design work and the organisation of fieldwork; it also includes examples of a depth interview guide, a personal interview schedule and a postal survey questionnaire. These texts provide more practical advice, for example on the choice of sample size, than can be found in textbooks written by statisticians. The latter outline the statistical theory underlying sampling, which, while theoretically valid, is of little use in the real-world context in which most surveys are carried out. Compare, for example, the helpful advice in Hoinville and Jowell (1977: 61) and Fowler (1984: 41) with the presentation in Goode and Hatt (1952: 229), Sudman (1976: 85–105) or Oppenheim (1992). Tanur (1983) provides a concise non-technical overview of survey methods, while Robson (1993) provides a guide to carrying out a small survey.

When surveys are focused on a well-defined group (rather than the general population), the identification of a suitable sampling frame often poses problems, particularly if the group of interest is small or widely scattered. Administrative records are sometimes used as sampling frames (for example, the unemployment register is used to obtain samples of the unemployed), but limitations in their coverage must be assessed and taken into account in the interpretation of the eventual survey results. The cost of sift surveys (to identify the particular group of interest for a survey) is greatly reduced by the use of telephone screening, with sampling based on Random Digit Dialling (Frey, 1983: 57–85). Omnibus surveys are also useful for sift surveys.

Increasing telephone coverage makes telephone interview surveys a more viable alternative for certain research topics. Postal surveys and telephone interview surveys can both cost roughly half as much as surveys using personal interviews, but telephone surveys have the additional advantage of greater speed. The comparative advantages and disadvantages of postal surveys, telephone surveys and face-to-face personal interview surveys are well established from methodological work on their practical aspects (such as costs and response rates) and on the types of question and survey topics that attract good-quality response in each of the three formats. Dillman (1978) compares mail and telephone surveys, Groves and Kahn (1979) compare telephone surveys with a personal interview survey, while Siemiatycki (1979) compares all three types. Miller (1983) and McCann *et al.* (1984) review the research findings with particular reference to political science and sociological research. A comprehensive review of research findings on the comparative advantages of all three types of survey is provided by Frey (1983: 27–55).

The relative costs, speed and efficiency of face-to-face interviews and telephone interviewing are affected by the adoption of Computer Assisted Personal Interviewing (CAPI) and Computer Assisted Telephone Interviewing (CATI) systems in most large survey organisations. CAPI and CATI systems combine interviewing and data entry into a single operation, based on portable laptop computers and desktop computers respectively. Coding, routing, edit and logic checks are carried out as the interview progresses, resulting in a higher quality of data. For example, interviewers cannot forget to ask questions, so there is less missing data. Responses to open-ended questions can be typed in directly. CAPI and CATI require a substantial investment in appropriate computers, the necessary software, and interviewer training, so they are most often used for omnibus surveys and for large regular and continuous surveys, rather than for small one-off surveys. But usage is constantly expanding. Compared with paper and pencil questionnaires, CAPI and CATI surveys greatly reduce the time lag between data collection and data analysis; however there is a larger time lag between finalising a questionnaire and data collection. The systems are less flexible than traditional paper surveys (Frey, 1983: 143–9; Saris, 1991; Couper *et al.*, 1999). CAPI software currently available include

BLAISE, QUANCEPT, BV Solo and MICROTAB. There is evidence that CAPI raises response rates. For example the British Crime Survey obtained a response rate of 83%, the highest it had ever achieved, after switching to CAPI in 1996. Telephone surveys, including CATI surveys, generally obtain lower response rates than surveys using face-to-face interviews. One disadvantage of CAPI and CATI is that they so completely transform the data collection process that there is no longer a printed survey questionnaire containing all information (on routing, possible responses, sequence checks, etc.) that can be used as a reference document by data analysts. This makes things harder for secondary analysts and also for analysts within the original research team, who may not have been involved in the data collection exercise.

Another development is electronic surveys using e-mail. Like telephone surveys, e-mail surveys obtain responses that display a smaller bias towards socially desirable replies, and responses can be more extreme. Open-ended responses are relatively long and self-disclosing. Factors such as age, sex and race are less intrusive in the interaction, although e-mail surveys can never be anonymous. Their use is constrained by the limited population of e-mail users.

As a general rule, a response rate of 80% is desirable, and this can be achieved by a good survey using face-to-face interviews. Postal and telephone surveys, and surveys making heavy demands on respondents, generally get lower response rates, in the region of 60%–80%. Surveys with a response rate below 50% are effectively worthless: more people refused to participate than did participate, so the dataset cannot be representative of the population aimed for. Such datasets can be used only for exploratory analyses.

There is a long-term trend of declining response rates to social surveys. Response rates vary greatly between personal, telephone and postal surveys, but they also vary by topic. For example, attitude surveys are the hardest to 'sell' to respondents, and they generally get lower response rates. Various techniques are used to maximise response rates. Paying respondents and informants is one of the most effective, and it may become more common in the future, thus raising survey costs. Offering payments and incentives has so far been resisted, on the grounds that they can introduce bias in response rates, but also, obviously, because they raise survey costs. Payment is, however, often appropriate when surveys make heavy demands on respondents. For example, the FES (see Chapter 7) obtains a response rate of around 70%–75% with payments to co-operating families, compared with response rates in the region of 35%–55% when payments were not offered. In developing countries, and/or with relatively poor groups, payment, or a small gift, may be regarded as appropriate for people co-operating with research of any kind.

There are numerous general texts on the design and analysis of sample surveys (for example, Hyman, 1967; Rosenberg, 1968; Moser and Kalton, 1971; Hirschi and Selvin, 1973; Warwick and Lininger, 1975; Hoinville and Jowell, 1977; Rossi *et al.*, 1983b; Fowler, 1984; Hellevik, 1984; Oppenheim, 1992; Robson, 1993). Marsh (1982) and Miller (1983) provide an overview and assessment of survey research in political and social research, while Bateson (1984) discusses procedures for assessing the quality of survey data. Zeisel (1985) provides an excellent introduction to causal analysis with survey data that is accessible to people who are not mathematically inclined. Stacey (1969), Warwick and Osherson (1973), Peil (1982) and Bulmer and Warwick (1983) consider survey procedures within the broader context of social research in developing countries.

Because they yield quantitive data, surveys are routinely deposited in data archives, and *ad hoc* surveys probably constitute the largest number of archive datasets. Those that constitute a series of repeats of earlier *ad hoc* surveys (and thus begin to offer the strengths of regular surveys) tend to attract a greater volume of secondary analysis (such as the series of British Election Surveys reviewed by Miller, 1983). The routine archive deposit of *ad hoc* surveys also means that data archives provide a large body of information on the development of surveys over time, and a ready source of accumulated experience on techniques, procedures and question-wording for those wishing to design new *ad hoc* surveys.

# 7  Regular surveys

Relatively few people are likely to have the experience of designing a new regular survey from scratch, but many more will have occasion to comment on possible revision to the design of an existing survey, to make a case for repeating a successful one-off survey on a regular or periodic basis, or to specify topics that might be included, on a one-off or permanent basis, in an existing regular survey. Regular surveys are, for the most part, existing and unalterable elements in the social research repertoire. However, it is necessary to be clear about their strengths and limitations as compared with other types of study, in order to assess the merits of, say, carrying out a secondary analysis of existing data from a regular survey or opting for another type of study altogether. The introduction of omnibus surveys (see Chapter 6) makes it easier to conduct regular surveys by inserting a module on a new topic into one of the many commercial or other omnibus surveys.

Surveys that are repeated at regular intervals, or carried out on a continuous basis, exhibit as much variation in depth and breadth of the information obtained as *ad hoc* surveys (see Chapter 6). For example, the basic Current Population Survey (CPS) interview takes 10 to 15 minutes, while General Household Survey interviews (which are carried out with all adult members of the sampled households, rather than accepting proxy informants as in the CPS) take about one hour. Like *ad hoc* surveys, they may focus on attitudes (as in the American General Social Survey, the British Social Attitude Survey and the European Union's Eurobarometer Survey), or on behaviour and experiences (as in most labour force surveys), or both (as in the British Crime Survey). Most existing surveys focus on individuals or households, but regular surveys may also focus on roles and relationships or on social groups and organisations, as illustrated by the British Workplace Industrial (or Employee) Relations Surveys, which interview several people at each address (including a sample of workers in 1998) to obtain information on the workplace as a social unit (Millward *et al.*, 1992; Cully *et al.*, 1999). Because they are repeated at periodic intervals, regular surveys can achieve continuous improvements in survey procedures, well beyond those obtained from piloting an *ad hoc* survey. Small changes, and more substantive updating of survey questions and other procedures, entail some discontinuity in comparisons across time in exchange for improved data quality and relevance.

Unlike *ad hoc* surveys, regular surveys are often *multi-purpose within their specified field of interest*. There will usually be a set of 'core' topics or questions included in all sweeps, plus a number of additional topics included on an *ad hoc* basis in a single sweep or rotated in and out of the survey at less frequent intervals. Regular surveys are flexible data collections within the boundaries set by their primary focus. Additional or new topics are only ruled out automatically if they do not conform to the existing logic and framework of the survey design. For example, questions on attitudes would not be appropriate for a survey of organisations unless the individual respondent was addressed as a role-holder in the organisation who was reporting on organisational policies, attitudes and perspectives (Namenwirth *et al.*, 1981). Suggestions for new topics to be included in two or more sweeps need to demonstrate awareness of the special characteristics and uses of regular surveys – as well as the long timetables usually required to plan and test new questions in major national data collections. Because of its broad scope, and the fact that all members of a household aged 16 and over are interviewed personally, the General Household Survey (GHS) is one of the most popular vehicles in Britain for inserting special topics on a periodic basis. Burglary, voluntary work, occupational pensions, contraceptive use, smoking and drinking are just some of the topics included.

## Gross and net change

Most regular surveys use a fresh sample for each sweep and provide information on net change over time, thus falling half-way between single-time cross-sectional surveys and longitudinal surveys. For many purposes, information on net change at the aggregate level is sufficient. If information on gross changes at the micro-level or on causal processes is needed, then some type of longitudinal study must be carried out instead. In the special case of rotating sample designs, described below, information on both gross and net changes can be obtained.

For example, a project that aims to find out whether public opinion *overall* has shifted to the 'right' or the 'left' on an issue, or whether the *overall* level of unemployment is rising or falling, only needs data on net change over time, and can rely on a regular survey using a fresh sample at each point in time. *Net change at the aggregate level* is the product of all movements, swings and changes at the individual level, some of them in opposite directions and hence cancelling each other out. In situations that approximate to two-person zero-sum games, the net change will often be sufficient information, even though it does not indicate whether the net change is the result of large, or small, amounts of *gross change* in opposite directions at the *micro-level*.

When the situation being studied is more complex, the net change figures conceal more than they reveal and additional information on gross changes (or flows) at the individual level is required just to see what is going on, let alone to explain it. For example, in a political system with three major parties, net swings in support for the three main parties can be the result of no less than six inter-party swings, each of which might be small or substantial. Similarly, as women's labour force participation rises to substantial levels in industrialised countries, net changes in levels of unemployment and employment cease to be very informative – as is underlined by the fact of unemployment and employment both rising simultaneously in some countries. The need for information on gross flows between all three labour market statuses (employment, unemployment and economic inactivity), as well as better estimates of net change, underlies the choice of rotating sample designs for regular national labour force surveys in the USA and Britain (Flaim and Hogue, 1985).

It is possible for the aggregate picture to show no net change at all, because all changes at the micro-level cancel out, so that the picture at the macro-level is one of stability, although micro-level analyses reveal substantial change. For example, cross-sectional surveys in the USA have repeatedly found that the proportions and the characteristics of the welfare population do not differ much from year to year. This led many to believe that there is an unchanging group of people who are continuously dependent on public welfare. In fact, there is a large turnover in the welfare population from year to year, with only about 2% of the US population *continuously* dependent on public welfare over a 10-year period, with others flowing in and out of the category for limited periods of time (Duncan, 1984). This sort of inconsistency between the pictures at the macro-level and the micro-level is even more likely in the volatile areas of attitudes and voting preferences (Lievesley and Waterton, 1985: 186–90). The failure to make the distinction is the source of many misunderstandings between social science disciplines, or between researchers and research users, when the amount of 'change' in the abstract is being discussed – especially as some disciplines almost invariably study net change (as in macro-economics) while other disciplines almost invariably study gross change at the micro-level (as in psychology). The failure to distinguish between net and gross measures of change in social research is perhaps the time series equivalent of the well-known ecological fallacy (Robinson, 1950).

The design of a study has to be clear about whether the aim is to measure net change only (in which case a piggy-back on a regular survey will suffice) or gross change, turnover and flows (in which case a longitudinal study will be needed). If both are of interest, it will be necessary to use a rotating sample design or to incorporate a panel element within a regular survey – two options discussed below.

## Types of regular survey

Many regular surveys are carried out at a particular point in time at pre-determined intervals: quarterly, annually or biennially. Omnibus surveys are carried out weekly or monthly. National opinion polls are carried out periodically within each year; the Eurobarometer surveys are carried out twice yearly in European Union member states. Annual surveys are carried out by some states and local government; probably the best known of these is the Detroit Area Study, carried out annually since 1951, originally as a collaborative exercise by the University of Michigan and the local community/government, latterly as a student training exercise. The NORC General Social Survey, which collects attitudinal data for research analysis by academic social scientists, was carried out annually from 1972 to 1978 and then biennially (Davis, 1977; Glenn *et al.*, 1978). The equivalent Social Attitudes Survey initiated in Britain in 1983 is carried out annually, allowing a wider range of topics to be rotated into the survey at periodic intervals (Jowell and Airey, 1984; Brook *et al.*, 1992; Jowell *et al.*, 1998).

Some survey series are conducted at periodic intervals without the precise dates being pre-determined. This is the approach with two British survey series, and will sometimes be inevitable when research funds are constrained. The Workplace Industrial/Employee Relations Survey series was initiated with a first survey in 1980 and a second survey in 1984, then had longer gaps with surveys in 1990 and 1998 (Cully *et al.*, 1999). The British Crime Survey series was initiated with a first survey in 1982 and a second survey in 1984, with further surveys in 1988, 1992, 1994, 1996 and 1998 (Mirlees-Black *et al.*, 1998). In 2000, the first Time-Use Survey was carried out in Britain, to collect new data on unpaid household work to supplement national accounts.

A few regular surveys are carried out on a *continuous* basis, that is, with interviews spread out evenly across the calendar year so that the data are not affected by seasonal variations. A long-established example is the Indian National Sample Survey, a multi-purpose continuous survey with permanent staffing carried out from 1950 onwards (Murthy and Roy in Bulmer and Warwick, 1983: 109–23). Public sector examples in Britain include the multi-purpose General Household Survey, the Family Expenditure Survey (which focuses on expenditure patterns and incorporates the National Food Survey from the 1990s onwards), the Family Resources Survey (collecting data on income from all sources, and housing costs, to model social welfare benefit entitlement), the Health Survey (dealing with ill-health and use of medical services), the International Passenger Survey (providing data on emigration and immigration), the Housing Survey, the National Travel Survey (collecting data on travel to work patterns and other travel) and the Labour Force Survey (Hakim, 1982a). Commercial examples include the National Readership Survey and the Target Group Index – two broad consumer surveys in Britain that collect data on life style, attitudes and consumption patterns. In these cases, a fresh sample is used for each year of the survey. A more complicated alternative is to use a rotating sample design.

*Rotating sample designs* drop some proportion of the original sample from each subsequent interview sweep and replace it with a new sample of equal size, so that the complete sample is eventually replaced with new members, but the process is gradual rather than a complete change to a fresh sample at each sweep. If one quarter of the full sample is replaced at each quarterly survey, each section of the sample will be interviewed four times before finally being dropped from the survey, as illustrated in Figure 1. The frequency of the survey, and the proportion of the sample that is replaced at each sweep, can both be altered to determine the number of times each member of the sample will be interviewed. For example, the American National Crime Survey interviews households seven times over a period of three years (Garofalo and Hindelang, 1977). In some designs, sample members are rotated back in again at a later date. For example, the Current Population Survey (CPS) in the USA uses a 4–8–4 rotation system for sample households: they are in the sample for four consecutive months, are dropped for eight months, and then return for the same four calendar months of the following year. The procedure means that 75% of the sample is common from month to month and 50% from year to year. Although the CPS is generally described as covering a sample of households, it is, in fact, based on a sample of addresses, and the

| | Sample | Time 1 | Time 2 | Time 3 | Time 4 | Time 5 | Time 6 | Time 7 | Time 8 |
|---|---|---|---|---|---|---|---|---|---|
| Repeated | 1 | × | | | | | | | |
| cross- | 2 | | × | | | | | | |
| sectional | 3 | | | × | | | | | |
| survey | 4 | | | | × | | | | |
| | 5 | | | | | × | | | |
| | 6 | | | | | | × | | |
| | 7 | | | | | | | × | |
| | 8 | | | | | | | | × |
| Rotating | 1 | × | | | | | | | |
| sample | 2 | × | × | | | | | | |
| survey | 3 | × | × | × | | | | | |
| | 4 | × | × | × | × | | | | |
| | 5 | | × | × | × | × | | | |
| | 6 | | | × | × | × | × | | |
| | 7 | | | | × | × | × | × | |
| | 8 | | | | | × | × | × | × |
| | 9 | | | | | | × | × | × |
| | 10 | | | | | | | × | × |
| | 11 | | | | | | | | × |
| Longitudinal study | 1 | × | × | × | × | × | × | × | × |

Figure 1  Survey designs for measuring change.

*Note*: Each cross represents an inteview sweep with sample units (which may be persons, households, addresses, organisations and so on).

household living at the address is interviewed, even if it has changed, in whole or in part, since the previous interview (Kalachek, 1978; Flaim and Hogue, 1985). The CPS is reputed to have the highest response rates of all continuous surveys, with percentage participation rates in the high 90s routinely achieved.

As Figure 1 indicates, surveys using rotating samples fall half-way between regular cross-sectional surveys and longitudinal studies based on a single sample interviewed at periodic intervals. Net change can be assessed by comparisons of the whole survey results at each point in time; gross changes can be assessed by looking at the results for individual members of the sample and seeing how they change across time. Labour Force Surveys using this design produce panel data as well as cross-sectional data.

Whatever type of sample is used, the extent and speed of change in the subject of study will determine the frequency of interview sweeps in a survey series, although costs and resources will also need to be taken into account. The decision to re-design the British Labour Force Survey, switching from a biennial cross-sectional survey (up to 1983) to a continuous survey with a rotating sample (and booster samples in the spring) from 1984 onwards, was due to an awareness of considerable change taking place in the labour force and its composition, in contrast with earlier experience of steadier trends (Department of Employment, 1983). Opinion polls are taken at fairly frequent intervals during the year, owing to their focus on relatively volatile political attitudes and opinions. However, the General Social Survey in the USA was switched from an annual survey in the 1970s to a biennial survey in the 1980s, owing to fairly small year-on-year changes in the broader social values and attitudes that it addressed, although resource constraints were also a factor.

Regular surveys conducted in industrialised countries, and equivalent multi-purpose household surveys in developing countries, tend for the most part to be designed and carried out as *national statistical surveys*, whose main function is to provide trend data rather than to study causal processes and achieve explanatory accounts. They also inform the development and timing of more highly focused explanatory research on particular issues and questions that are revealed, but not fully explored, by the regular surveys. For this reason, analyses of regular surveys often need to be complemented with other research evidence. However, patchy information from several regular surveys can be combined to develop a rounded picture of a topic that has only recently come into the limelight, as noted in Chapter 2.

Regular surveys can be complex. National crime surveys, or, more precisely, victim surveys, are carried out in Australia, Canada, Germany, Holland and Sweden, *inter alia*, following the example set by the United States National Crime Survey – a continuous victim survey running since 1973 (Garofalo and Hindelang, 1977; Block, 1983). But the British Crime Survey (BCS) series is especially complex (Mirlees-Black *et al.*, 1998). In addition to fear of crime, people's experiences as victims of crime and levels of victimisation for a wide range of specific crimes, surveys also cover contact with the police; patterns of behaviour and lifestyle factors affecting the risk of becoming the victim of crime; self-reported offending (in order partly to fill the gap in information on victimless crimes and undetected crimes); attitudes to punishment and sentencing; public perception of the relative seriousness of offences; attitudes to community vigilance and victim support schemes. A complex design combines several elements in a single data collection: a *screening* survey of 15,000 interviews establishes whether respondents had been the victims of crime within the previous year; a survey of *victimisation incidents* obtains information on each incident occurring within the specified recall period (its characteristics, consequences for the victim, and whether reported to the police); and surveys of 'non-core' topics are addressed to sub-sets of the main sample. In addition, there are three self-completion questionnaires administered using lap-top computers handed to respondents, which collect data on drug use, for example, and self-reported offending. In all sweeps of the BCS, inner-city areas are over sampled by a factor of two. In addition, some sweeps have an ethnic minority booster sample to permit separate analyses, for example on racially motivated crime (Percy, 1998). The classifications used to code the data on victimisation incidents are comparable with those used in official crime statistics, so that the survey can clarify how the propensity to report crimes to the police affects the recorded crime rates. Social area classifications based on population census indicators (see Chapter 2) are used to stratify the sample to carry out sub-national analyses by type of area of residence and to test ecological hypotheses about crime rates. The national survey provides the model for equivalent crime surveys by local government, replicating and extending the survey with reference to local concerns, and using the national survey to set local results in context (Mayhew and Hough, 1982; Chambers and Tombs, 1984; Southgate, 1984).

The size and scope of the BCS is such that initial reports provide only an overview of key findings, and a team of criminological specialists is involved in fully analysing all the topics covered by the survey (Hope, 1984). Although the survey is funded and carried out entirely by the Home Office, the research unit responsible for the survey consults widely with specialists in Britain, the USA and other countries on the design and implementation of the survey, and they are also brought in as consultants to analyse particular sections of the survey data (as illustrated by Gottfredson, 1984). The BCS is thus rather more open to inputs from outside central government than are many regular surveys.

## Cross-national comparative studies

Regular surveys provide the largest number of cross-national comparative studies. A few are intentionally designed from the start as comparative projects. More often, cross-national comparability is achieved gradually over time within existing regular surveys, some of them with differing original aims.

Inglehart's World Values Survey (WVS) series is a good example of theoretical research that was intended to be comparative from the start.

His first survey series covered six European countries in 1970: Britain, France, West Germany, Belgium, Holland and Italy (Inglehart, 1977). Inglehart's thesis is that as societies and people become affluent and have greater security (in part due to the welfare state), their values change from a materialist emphasis on economic efficiency, bureaucratic authority and scientific rationality towards a post-materialist or post-modern emphasis on individual autonomy, diversity, self-expression and individual choice of life style. As social scientists in other countries became interested in testing this thesis in their own country, the WVS series gradually expanded: 24 countries participated in 1981, and the 1990 survey involved 43 countries, with a similar number in 1996 (Inglehart, 1990, 1997; Inglehart *et al.*, 1998). An equivalent survey in the field of policy research is the Eurobarometer series of attitude surveys carried out twice a year for the European Commission (Reif and Inglehart, 1991). These are used to monitor attitudes to the European Community/Union and to collect data on EU policy issues, such as equal opportunities for women in the labour market or genetically modified foods. In both these survey series there is a single questionnaire applied in all participating countries (after translation), facilitating comparative analysis as well as the analysis of trends over time.

Another model is for a specially designed module of questions to be inserted in independent national surveys so as to produce comparative data. The prime example here is the International Social Survey Programme (ISSP) initiated in 1985 by four countries: Britain, West Germany, the USA and Australia. By 1999, the ISSP had expanded to a global club of 31 countries, including Bangladesh, Chile, Israel, Japan, the Philippines and South Africa, as well as an expanding number of OECD countries (Jowell *et al.*, 1998: xiv, 191–216). This extension of an attitude survey designed for modern industrialised societies with a relatively homogeneous western culture to societies with markedly different cultures and economies prompted some debate about the limitations of comparative attitude surveys (Jowell, 1998; Kuechler, 1998).

Perhaps the most common route to cross-national comparative series is the periodic harmonisation of national surveys on the same subject. One example is the harmonisation of Labour Force Surveys in the EU. These differ a good deal, but all countries are required to send Eurostat an extract tape with a specified list of variables coded to common EU concepts and classifications, so that Eurostat can compile comparative statistics and produce research analyses, which are published regularly in the EC's annual report, *Employment in Europe*, and in Eurostat reports.

Another example is the series of crime surveys (or victim surveys) carried out in the USA, Britain, the Netherlands and several other

OECD countries. Crime survey researchers often borrow ideas from each other on methods of data collection and analysis. The resulting datasets thus offer scope for comparative analyses. From the 1980s onwards, national research agencies organised systematically comparable surveys through the International Crime Survey series carried out in some 20 OECD and Eastern European countries, using the same questionnaire. In the 1990s, the survey was extended to over 40 developing countries, usually in the form of city surveys, with the sponsorship of the Netherlands. Surveys were carried out in 1989, 1992, 1996 and 2000 (Van Dijk *et al.*, 1990, 1993, 1998).

Sometimes a new type of survey is developed in one country, spawning imitations in other countries. The technical and public success of the first British Industrial/Employee Relations Surveys in the 1980s inspired governments and researchers in other countries to conduct broadly similar inquiries. By 1999, similar surveys had been completed in Australia, France, Finland and Norway, and preparations were underway for similar surveys in Canada and Ireland. In the USA, the closest equivalent is the much smaller 1991 National Organisations Study (NOS), based on telephone interviews with the employers of respondents to the 1991 General Social Survey (because of the absence of any national sampling frame for employers in the USA due to the federal structure). The final NOS report presented analyses of both linked datasets (Kalleberg *et al.*, 1996).

A final category consists of comparative datasets extracted from surveys with somewhat different purposes. The classic example is the Luxembourg Income Study (LIS), created by coding 60 summary variables on income from all sources and personal and household characteristics from national datasets for 16 OECD countries to produce a consistent comparative dataset. So far this has been done using data for 1980, 1985 and 1990. Inevitably, there are weaknesses in the final dataset, due to gaps in the source data, differences in the way the data were collected or coded (for example, the treatment of zero or negative disposable incomes) and the variable underreporting of income in sources. However, the resulting LIS dataset has permitted substantial new analyses of income distribution and redistribution in welfare states (Smeeding *et al.*, 1985a, 1985b, 1990; Mitchell, 1991).

This last type of comparative study begins to overlap with secondary analysis (see Chapter 2). As such, there is obviously potential for other exercises of this sort. For example, the United Nations promotes the development of regular household surveys in developing countries using a common set of core classificatory variables. A 1978 OECD report reviews progress at that date. The Living Standards Measurement Study of the World Bank seeks to establish surveys that monitor welfare levels, and the impact of policies, using a standardised questionnaire. In Britain, a government initiative in the 1990s sought to standardise, or at least harmonise, the most common concepts, questions and classificatory variables used in government surveys. Policies of this nature increase the potential for comparative research across countries as well as across datasets within a single country.

Given the growing interest in comparative data, rapid developments can be expected in this field in future decades.

## Overlaps and combinations

Links between regular surveys and *ad hoc* surveys are now common practice. Since regular surveys usually contain both 'core' topics and a variety of special topics, it is fairly straightforward to design *ad hoc* surveys that hitch a ride on the questionnaire for a regular survey. The costs of the *ad hoc* survey are greatly reduced, and there is the advantage of having access to all the other contextual information collected in the same survey, which can be used in analysis. In essence, this is what omnibus surveys do, with the core topics reduced to basic classificatory variables.

The Current Population Survey in the United States provided the vehicle for the 1962 Occupational Changes in a Generation (OCG) survey and for a 1973 replication (Blau and Duncan, 1967; Featherman and Hauser, 1978). In each case a short supplementary questionnaire was added to the basic CPS interview, in much the same way as other non-core topics are rotated in and out of the CPS; the difference here was that the CPS ran the OCG supplements for independent academic studies of occupational mobility.

Another popular option is to use regular surveys as sampling frames for *ad hoc* surveys, sometimes by adding special screening questions to identify the target population. Given the wide subject matter in the British General Household Survey, it has become the vehicle for a range of *ad hoc* surveys, for example on poverty, rent subsidies and attitudes to the hospital service (Hakim, 1982a: 104). National labour force surveys provide suitable sampling frames for separate surveys on labour market minorities and labour market issues, with the additional option of using the follow-up survey to collect information on any changes between the time of the main survey and the *ad hoc* survey (see, for example, Hakim, 1987).

Rotating samples were originally designed to provide more reliable estimates of net change over time, rather than panel data for micro-level longitudinal analysis. Smaller samples are sufficient to measure change if the same panel of respondents is re-interviewed. But limited longitudinal data can be obtained from such surveys for analyses of gross changes, although they are not an adequate basis for research on causal processes. The main limitation arises from the fact that labour force surveys using this design also obtain data from *proxy informants*, which is known to be of lower quality (Freeman and Medoff, 1982; Martin and Butcher, 1982) and which removes the option of collecting any information on plans, motivations and attitudes. Another limitation is that sample designs currently used in the CPS and the LFS provide panel data on changes only over a 12-month period; this is a shorter period than in most longitudinal studies, although it is sufficient for the CPS matched sample to be used to compile worklife estimates (Smith, 1985). The third limitation is that owing to people moving house, deaths, refusals at re-interview, and so on, panel data (also termed *matched sample* data) from rotating sample surveys can be obtained for only about 70% of the original sample (Job, 1979; Flaim and Hogue, 1985). This is not, in practice, very different from the 70%–80% response rate obtained by specially designed surveys that re-interview people one year later (see, for example, White, 1983: 12–14, 287–8), although a systematic 30% non-response/non-matching rate could be significant for some topics.

Regular surveys may also provide longitudinal data by adding a specially designed panel component, so that change can be studied both at the micro-level (with the small panel sample) and at the aggregate level (with the cross-sectional samples). A panel element was added as an experimental extension to the British Social Attitudes Survey (Lievesley and Waterton, 1985). The Workplace Industrial/Employment Relations Survey includes a small panel element in the sample, usually analysed separately (Millward, Bryson and Forth, 2000). In this case, bankruptcies and closures of the sampled workplaces replace deaths and job movers as sources of sample attrition.

Regular surveys are never combined with small-scale intensive projects, such as qualitative research and case studies, largely because they are designed as multi-purpose statistical sources.

## Practical considerations

Most regular surveys collect data through questionnaires, very often using CAPI or CATI systems (see Chapter 6). Crime surveys sometimes use Computer-Aided Self-completion Interviews (CASI) systems, for example to collect self-report information on drug use. However, specialised surveys often require additional procedures to improve, check and extend the information that survey respondents supply. The Family Expenditure Survey requires all adults in a household to complete expenditure diaries over a two-week period. Time-use surveys ask people to complete time-use diaries for one day, one week or longer periods. The British Health Survey employs qualified nurses alongside interviewers to collect blood samples, do blood pressure tests and take weight, height and other measurements. The technique of bounded recall is used in surveys enquiring about relatively infrequent events, which are subject to recall bias and telescoping (the tendency to report events as happening more recently than they actually did). Bounded recall requires an initial interview to collect information on earlier events; at the start of the second and any subsequent interviews, respondents are reminded of what they have previously reported and asked what has occurred since those events (Garofalo and Hindelang, 1977: 28–31; Tanur, 1983: 10–12). This technique is used in crime surveys and in labour force surveys that reinterview people to find out whether their work status changes over time. Additional data collection procedures are expensive, but feasible. Less obviously, they also add to data analysis costs and timetables.

Almost all regular surveys publish at least one general report on each survey in the series, providing basic information on principal objectives; methodology; organisation and funding of the research effort; timetables for data collection, analysis and publications; as well as a summary of the main results. Information on costs (in money and manpower), however, is rarely provided. More detailed information on the survey design and methods is sometimes available in separate reports published at the start of a new series, as an adjunct to the general report, or at periodic intervals after the survey series has been running for some time (for example, Davis, 1977; Garofalo and Hindelang, 1977; Hanson, 1978; Kemsley *et al.*, 1980; Brook *et al.*, 1992). A report by the OECD (1978) reviewed regular multi-purpose household surveys in developing countries.

Some surveys publish short separate summaries of key findings from each sweep in free booklets or leaflets, which can be used for publicity purposes and which also advertise the full book report (which may be expensive). When such summaries are published early, they can have a valuable public relations function. One example is the booklet of *First Findings*, published within months of fieldwork for the WERS surveys (Cully *et al.*, 1998). Copies are sent to all the employers and trade unions that participate in the survey, as feedback and a thank you, and to others who assist in the research process.

Significant factors in the implementation of a regular survey series are long-term funding, a secure organisational base and some continuity in research staff, especially at the start, without which the necessary infrastructure cannot be built up and maintained with provision for continuous monitoring and updating of research procedures. One solution is to obtain co-funding from a variety of sources, if necessary with a combination of grant-funding and contract-funding (see Chapter 12). For example, the British Workplace Employee Relations Surveys, Social Attitudes Surveys and the Time-Use Survey are all funded from a combination of government and other sources.

The size and composition of permanent research teams vary with their functions. In some cases, the team will be responsible only for data collection, coding and processing through to the production of a fully edited computer tape, with analysis and report-production left to a separate 'customer' research team (as in the case of the Family Expenditure Survey, where fieldwork and analysis functions are split between ONS and the Department of Employment), or with the tape released immediately into the public domain for analysis by interested researchers and/or for teaching purposes (as in the case of the General Social Survey). In other cases, the main research team will produce a general report with overall results, but this can vary from an initial analysis of key topics (as in the case of the British Crime Surveys and British Social Attitudes Surveys) or an initial overview analysis supplemented by more focused analysis of particular topics in the current sweep (as in the case of the General Household Surveys) to a fairly detailed analysis of the survey results (as in the case of the Workplace Industrial Relations Surveys).

The Centre for Applied Social Surveys (CASS) in Britain provides courses in the design and analysis of surveys, and maintains an on-line social survey Question Bank, which contains questionnaire examples from all the main regular surveys of households and of individuals in Britain from about 1991 onwards. The CASS Question Bank web address is http://www.natcen.ac.uk/CASS/. The Question Bank is useful for researchers designing surveys of particular groups or areas that aim to be comparable with the regular statistical surveys, and for those planning to do secondary analysis of regular national surveys.

The full value of the information obtained from a regular survey series will be tapped only after the survey has been running for some time, so that analyses of trends over time become feasible and the series provides comparative data for earlier points in time on topics that have only recently attracted public or academic interest. All significant survey series are deposited in data archives, and they attract the highest levels of secondary analysis.

# 8  Longitudinal studies

Regular surveys and longitudinal studies are the two designs that most explicitly focus on social change processes, but they do so in different and complementary ways. Regular surveys provide information on net change at the macro-level, while longitudinal studies provide information on the much larger volume of gross changes (or flows) at the micro-level (see Chapter 7). Longitudinal studies are often initiated when regular surveys or other sources reveal new trends that they cannot fully describe or explain (especially if they do not contain a panel element). The longitudinal study is unique in its ability to answer questions about causes and consequences and hence to provide a basis for substantiated explanatory theory.

The *prospective longitudinal study* takes a single sample or group and follows it up, with repeated data collections, over a long period of time (see Figure 1). Strictly speaking, the term longitudinal study refers only to prospective studies. The retrospective study, which is quicker and cheaper, is considered below as a quasi-longitudinal design. Longitudinal studies cover a 'long' period of time, although what is considered a long period of observation depends on the subject-matter and context, and the issues addressed. Studies of people experiencing a spell of unemployment may continue for only one or two years, while studies of human growth and maturation may continue for 30 years or longer. Generally, there are numerous data collections in order to collect information on changes as they are happening. At the very minimum (and on the borderline between the single-time study and the true longitudinal study) there is only a single follow-up after the first data collection.

The focus here is on national or large-scale studies, which are intended to provide data that is nationally representative of the type of group studied and can hence provide incidence (or prevalence) rates for a given behaviour, attitude or event as well as information for analyses of its causes or consequences. Small-scale longitudinal studies are effectively case studies, as illustrated by the longitudinal case studies described in Chapter 6, and can employ a great diversity of data collection methods. National studies rely on some combination of three methods: interview surveys of the study sample; data extracted from administrative records (to obtain information on the sample members themselves and/or on the organisations where they are located); and surveys of informants (such as teachers, parents, doctors, or others who have direct knowledge of sample members). Studies of children generally rely on the latter two methods, while studies of adults typically rely on the first two. Studies with health and psychological components often incorporate tests or assessments of some kind (such as a medical examination, IQ test or psychological test administered as part of an interview).

In prolonged studies, the methods of data collection may change over time, to take account of maturation and ageing. For example, children may be interviewed directly as they reach maturity, whereas personal interviews pose greater problems as people reach old age. The passage of time may also bring about changes in the nature and content of relevant information in administrative records, in the roles or incumbents of informant sources, affecting the comparability (and possibly also the quality) of information obtained over time from these sources. Changes in research staff are also more likely in prolonged studies and may produce discontinuities in the approach or methods adopted for the study. Thus, although longitudinal studies set out to study change and causation at the micro-level (which usually means the individual), there are major practical impediments to achieving this aim in prolonged studies, because the research effort itself will be subject to change in the course of the study.

In addition, there are substantial practical problems in conducting any longitudinal study, the most notable ones being sample attrition and non-response. The failure to trace sample members at each subsequent wave of the study, and their inclination to drop out of it, are likely to increase over time, so that the sub-group that is successfully covered up to completion of the study may no longer be fully representative, which weakens the value of any findings. However, sample attrition due to deaths, imprisonment, hospitalisation, and so on can be treated as substantive events if appropriate information is collected. Finally, there is the danger that the questions addressed at the start of the study are overtaken by events, are dealt with by the results of other studies completed in the meantime, or simply cease to attract the same degree of interest.

Perhaps the greatest danger is the failure to design the study fully before it gets under way. As one review of longitudinal studies notes:

> all too often longitudinal studies have been planned without any clear aims or hypotheses in mind, have involved a mindless collection of large amounts of data which are never adequately analysed, and which continue over so many years that by the end the original measures are hopelessly inappropriate for the purposes for which they are being used
>
> (Rutter, 1981: 334)

Hirschi and Gottfredson (1983) have criticised criminologists for wasting longitudinal studies by using them simply to describe invariant age effects. The inherent attractions of longitudinal studies led to early projects being initiated without adequate attention to the precise causal issues to be addressed and to the very substantial implementation difficulties presented by this type of study. They became, in effect, exploratory studies, or pilot studies, for the more carefully designed studies carried out in recent years.

*Ad hoc* surveys provide single snapshots, and regular surveys provide a series of snapshots for particular moments in time. In contrast, longitudinal projects provide a motion picture study, and require a substantively different approach in terms of both theoretical perspectives and methodology. Very often, researchers apply purely cross-sectional analysis to longitudinal datasets. The most recent sweep is analysed with the benefit of work history and life history information that was collected contemporaneously and is thus not affected by recall bias or by memory loss. One example is Joshi and Paci's (1998) study of the correlates of women's lower relative earnings in the 1990s based on the NCDS cohort study described below. Truly longitudinal theories and methodologies have been developed very slowly (Bielby *et al.*, 1979: 91). Arguably, appropriate theoretical perspectives already exist: life cycle and developmental perspectives are central to economic, sociological and psychological theories, and most longitudinal studies also collect data on relevant social structural, economic and environmental factors. In any case, additional area-based or time-series data can be added to datasets at later stages if area coding is done and dates are given, as illustrated by Parcel and Mueller (1983b), Dex (1984a) and Joshi (1984). One problem is that longitudinal studies almost inevitably have to adopt a multi-disciplinary approach to studying causal processes and social change, and the quasi-tribalistic organisation of the academic social science community impedes multi-disciplinary research, as noted in Chapter 11. Event history analysis consists of regression-like models in which the dependent variable is the rate or hazard of the occurrence of some event, such as births, divorces, arrests, job changes and the like (Blossfeld and Rohwer, 1995). Event history analysis exploits longitudinal data more fully, but techniques that focus on transitions are not suitable for all research topics and can produce very fragmented results.

Although the design of any study will obviously be affected by the issues to be addressed and the resources available, certain features seem to increase the chances of success. Studies of shorter durations are generally preferable because technical and practical problems often increase and multiply with longer durations. Several overlapping samples (as illustrated below by the National Longitudinal Surveys) are thus preferable to a single sample followed up for a much longer period. Longitudinal studies should not focus on 'fashionable' topics (interest in which may not last long) but should use robust measures of attitudes and behaviour that are broad enough to be used over the full duration of the project. If suitable measures do not already exist (for example, from regular surveys), they need to be tested separately before inclusion in a long-term study. At the same time, *parts* (but not the whole) of any longitudinal study may break new ground, and these should be clearly identified as being more exploratory in character (and hence requiring further replication, or supporting evidence from other sources, before being taken at face value in any interpretation of results). However, most longitudinal studies yield surprises and serendipitous discoveries, by virtue of their unique ability to identify *sleeper effects*: connections between events that are widely separated in time, such as adolescent ambitions and outcomes in adult life.

The design of a longitudinal study needs to have some regard to the difficulties of distinguishing between age, cohort and period effects in eventual analyses of the data. *Age effects* are those attributable to the ageing process. *Period effects* are those attributable to events in the historical period during which the study is conducted (such as war, recession, changes in legislation or the political climate). *Cohort effects* are those explained by similarities among individuals born during the same time, including those connected with the size of the age cohort. For example, large 'baby boom' cohorts experience more competition for jobs when entering the labour market, whereas small birth cohorts generally experience more favourable life chances in terms of occupational and economic attainment. The three types of effect overlap (see, for example, Martin and Roberts, 1984a: 117–20), and they cannot reliably be differentiated by purely statistical techniques (Ryder, 1965;

Glenn, 1976, 1977, 1981). However, for many purposes it is sufficient to distinguish age and historical effects, which is feasible when broad age bands are sampled (but not with single-year age cohorts), as illustrated by Shapiro and Mott (1983) and Shaw (1985) using USA National Longitudinal Survey data. From the perspective of *social* research, age effects can be taken as broadly constant, so that the focus of longitudinal research will be on explanations relating to social-structural, economic and motivational factors as well as period effects.

Most early studies dealt with physical growth and intellectual development, maturation and ageing, physical and mental health, morbidity and mortality (Wall and Williams, 1970; Mednick and Baert, 1981; Eichorn *et al.*, 1982; Berkman and Breslow, 1983; Schaie, 1983). Many early texts implicitly define this life-course perspective as the only type of longitudinal study (see, for example, Wall and Williams, 1970; Goldstein, 1979), but prospective longitudinal studies have now been carried out on a wide range of topics, such as work orientations, educational and work histories (Parnes, 1975; Psacharopoulos, 1981; Sproat *et al.*, 1985), delinquency and criminal careers (West, 1969; Wolfgang *et al.*, 1972, 1985; West and Farrington, 1973, 1977; Thompson *et al.*, 1981; see also Thornberry and Christenson, 1984), the experience of unemployment (White, 1983; Moylan, Millar and Davies, 1984; Daniel, 1986), individual earnings and family income (Duncan, 1984) and political orientations and behaviour (Jennings and Niemi, 1974, 1981; Himmelweit *et al.*, 1981). The approach could potentially be applied to studying migration histories, housing histories and other topics as well. To date, most studies have been concerned with individuals as the unit of analysis, but longitudinal studies can also be concerned with households or families (as illustrated by the USA Panel Study of Income Dynamics discussed below), with organisations (Kimberly *et al.*, 1980) or with larger social units such as nations (Lieberson and Hansen, 1974).

Longitudinal studies vary in duration, and there is also great diversity in the size of studies. When the same group, or panel, of respondents is interviewed repeatedly, a smaller sample is sufficient to measure change than is needed for regular surveys using fresh samples at each interview wave. However, most national longitudinal studies use relatively large samples to allow for separate analysis of sub-groups of special interest. Sample sizes for studies that are multi-purpose within their chosen field of interest range from 5,000 to 15,000; studies of more narrowly defined issues or groups use smaller samples ranging from 1,500 to 4,000. Very occasionally, studies use samples as large as half a million persons, as illustrated by Project TALENT carried out in the 1960s in the United States (Rossi *et al.*, 1976) and by the 1% British Longitudinal Study based on tracing data for a 1% sample of the population across several censuses, as described in Chapter 4. When a panel study is combined with a national cross-sectional survey, the longitudinal sample may be well under 1,000 cases, as illustrated by Himmelweit *et al.* (1981), Lievesley and Waterton (1985) for surveys of individuals and by Cully *et al.* (1999: 216–50) and Millward, Bryson and Forth (2000) for organisational change.

## Multi-purpose studies: panels and cohorts

Some studies are *multi-purpose* within their chosen field of enquiry, and hence multi-disciplinary and sufficiently large in scale to permit separate analysis of sub-groups, using the rest of the sample as the comparison (or control) group. Two types of sample can be used: panel studies and cohort studies.

*Panel studies* take as their basis a nationally representative sample of the group of interest, which may be individuals, households, establishments, organisations, or any other social unit. Probably the best known and most successful study of this type is the Panel Study of Income Dynamics (PSID) being carried out by the Institute for Social Research (ISR) at the University of Michigan.

Initiated in the mid-1960s, the PSID has continued to interview a representative panel of over 5,000 families each year since the first survey in 1966. The PSID has what might be called a 'self-regenerating' or 'non-wasting' design, in that any members of a family in the sample who move away (for example, to form a separate household) continue to be included in the sample. The split-offs largely compensate for attrition of the original panel, and ensure that the age structure of the families, and of their members, remains representative. Despite 28% attrition in the original sample over the first 10 years, 1966–76, the addition of split-offs meant that there were some 5,860 families in the panel by 1976 (more than the original number). The design has ensured that the panel study continues to provide a general purpose source of data on the structure and sources of family income, the causes and consequences of changes in income, low-income families, changes in family composition and the number of earners, government income support measures, sickness, unemployment and retirement. Apart from the results presented in a series of ISR annual reports, *Five Thousand American Families: Patterns of Economic Progress* edited by Duncan and Morgan, and periodic overviews (Duncan, 1984), the panel study is widely used by other scholars, sometimes to replicate the ISR's own analyses, sometimes for quite different purposes. The contextual information on factors related to family income is sometimes analysed in its own right, for example to study patterns of unemployment and to compare cross-sectional and longitudinal pictures on the distribution of unemployment (Hill and Corcoran, 1979), fertility (Hofferth, 1983), sex and race differentials in labour supply and earnings (Lloyd and Niemi, 1979; Parcel and Mueller, 1983b), the work disincentive effects of unemployment insurance benefits (Capen *et al.*, 1985), the trade union mark-up on earnings (Chowdhury and Nickell, 1985), or the causes of marital breakdown (Ross and Sawhill, 1975). Elder's (1985) collection demonstrates the variety of topics studied with PSID data, and includes two introductory chapters on the PSID. By 1989, children of the original PSID sample were aged 20 to 38, prompting numerous studies examining intergenerational correlations in income, welfare usage and economic status. Some scholars argue that the analysis of intergenerational relationships became the main strength of the PSID in the 1990s.

*Cohort studies* take as their basis a particular cohort of people, and either the entire cohort or a nationally representative sample of them is followed up over a period of time. A cohort is a group of people who have some characteristic or experience in common: the same date of birth or marriage, entry to an institution (such as school or hospital) or having the same experience (such as a spell of unemployment, military service or imprisonment) at roughly the same time. When they are not otherwise defined, cohort studies are concerned with age/birth cohorts.

Age cohorts may be defined broadly (for example, people born in the 1970s) or narrowly (for example, people born in a single year, or one week of a single year). Perhaps the best-known example is the National Child Development Study (NCDS), which takes as its subjects all persons living in Great Britain who were born between 3 and 9 March 1958. After the perinatal study in 1958 (which covered the full cohort of 17,000 children), data collections were carried out in 1965 (at age 7), in 1969 (at age 11), in 1974 (at age 16), in 1981 (at age 23), in 1991 (at age 33) and in 2000 (at age 42). Up to age 16, data was collected from school and medical records, from interviews with the mother (carried out by medical and other staff) and from postal surveys of teachers, doctors and other informants with direct knowledge of cohort members, to obtain information on the health, educational, social and economic circumstances of surviving members. At age 23, a personal interview survey of cohort members was carried out to obtain information on their educational and work histories since age 16, marital and family formation histories, their current circumstances, health, activities and attitudes. By this time, about 10% of the cohort members were known to have died or emigrated, and some could not be traced, but an excellent response rate of 93% among those traced yielded data for 12,500 adult cohort members. In 1991, 86% of the target sample of 15,666 were traced to their current address, and response rates of over 80% were achieved on the personal interview, self-completion questionnaire and other instruments, producing data for 11,400 people at age 33 years, with only a small bias towards high achievers.

The NCDS has provided the basis for research on child development and health, the incidence of family poverty and its impact on the child, educational attainment and the impact of the type of school attended, the transition from school to work and youth unemployment, as well as studies of particular sub-groups (such as children in one-parent families, those with physical disabilities and children with an unemployed father), which rely on the rest of the sample for control groups and comparative data (Fogelman and Wedge, 1981; Fogelman, 1983). From the 1980s onwards, the NCDS has been used to study all aspects of labour market participation, family formation, housing careers, income and health, with the benefit of life history data not contaminated by recall bias or missing data (see for example Ferri, 1993; Dale and Egerton, 1997; Joshi and Paci, 1998; Hakim, 2000: Chapter 5). From 1991 onwards, data on the children of the NCDS cohort was collected.

Studies of age cohorts can potentially follow the cohort throughout life to become cradle to grave, or sperm to worm studies. So far, this has never happened, but the NCDS is likely to be the first to do so. Some argue that overlapping samples are more efficient than age cohorts, which confound age and period effects. The most successful example of this design is the National Longitudinal Surveys of Labour Market Experience (NLS) project funded by the US Department of Labor and designed and organised by Ohio State University's Center for Human Resource Research (CHRR) and the US Bureau of the Census (Parnes, 1975; Bielby *et al.*, 1979; Sproat *et al.*, 1985; Center for Human Resource Research, 1995).

The NLS project was initiated in the mid-1960s with four nationally representative samples of people in wide age bands, thus combining the advantages of panels and age cohorts. Each panel was designed to focus on a key transitional phase in labour force participation, and associated problems, by means of surveys carried out at one- or two-year intervals over a period of 15 years.

The panel of 5,000 *older men* aged 45–59 years in 1966 was studied up to 1981, when survivors were aged 60–74 years. The surveys focused on the transition from work to retirement, early retirement, declining rates of labour force participation, skill obsolescence, deteriorating health, age discrimination, and related factors.

The panel of 5,000 *mature women* aged 30–44 years in 1967 was studied up to 1982, when they were aged 45–59 years. The surveys focused on the special problems of re-entry to the labour force after periods of absence, during which there may have been a deterioration in vocational and labour market skills, and related factors.

The panel of 5,000 *young men* aged 14–24 years in 1966 was studied up to 1981 when aged 29–39 years, and a panel of 5,000 *young women* aged 14–24 in 1968 was studied up to 1992 when aged 40–48 years. These surveys focused on the transition from school to work, the process of occupational choice and accommodation to the labour market during which job sampling, turnover and unemployment rates are high, and on the way in which women's work histories are affected by marriage and childrearing.

Owing to the success of the first round of panel studies, a second youth cohort study was started in 1979, covering a sample of 13,000 males and females aged 14–21 years in 1979 who were surveyed annually up to the 1990s. The second youth panel was designed to provide comparability with the two earlier youth panels, but gave greater emphasis to employment and vocational training, and data obtained from personal interviews was supplemented with data extracted from high school records, largely because people proved unreliable informants on this matter.

Between them, the first four panel studies covered most of the population of working age within a relatively short period of 15 years, and comparisons of period effects can also be made between the first and second youth cohorts. To ensure comparability across all the panels, certain 'core' topics are included in all the surveys (such as current employment status, employment experience since the previous survey, health, training, work orientations, family circumstances and sources of income and wealth). Another feature of the design is that members of two or even three panels were sometimes drawn from the same household, giving small sub-samples of mother–daughter, father–son, husband–wife and sister–brother pairs for more controlled intergenerational and sex differential analyses (Parnes, 1975; Mott, 1982).

The NLS is designed as a multi-disciplinary study of all aspects of labour force participation, with data from each survey released into the public domain as soon as edited, and usable tapes are prepared by the CHRR (and before any reports are produced by the Center). As a result, the NLS has become one of the most widely used longitudinal studies, with hundreds of reports produced by academic and other researchers, in addition to the main series of reports from the CHRR research team (Andrisani, 1978; Mott, 1978; Bielby *et al.*, 1979; Osterman, 1980; Parnes, 1981; Mott, 1982; Sproat *et al.*, 1985). Waldfogel (1998) presents a comparative analysis of the NCDS and NLS second youth cohort.

A study by Rexroat and Shehan (1984) provides a good example of the type of longitudinal analysis that becomes feasible only after a study has been running for a long stretch of time, and of the way in which longitudinal studies can conclusively answer questions about causal processes, frequently giving quite different answers to those drawn from cross-sectional surveys. Data from cross-sectional surveys, population censuses and even surveys collecting retrospective life histories have repeatedly shown that the number and ages of a woman's children, if any, determine female labour force participation – a finding that supported the common sense view (held by employers, for example) that women work as and when their family commitments permit them to do so. Rexroat and Shehan (1984) compared young women's career plans at age 22–24 years (in 1968) with the eventual outcome in their mid-30s (in 1980). They found that long-range work plans had a considerable impact on women's employment status in their mid-30s, largely reflecting the realisation of plans for those (the minority) who had expected to be working at age 35. Being married, and having young children to look after, affected the employment only of those (the majority) who had expected to be at home raising a family at age 35. Similarly, another analysis of NLS data by Waite and Stolzenberg (1976; see also Stolzenberg and Waite, 1977) showed that fertility expectations have only a small negative effect on young women's work plans, whereas work plans exert a powerful negative effect on young women's childbearing plans. Thus longitudinal research shows that women limit their fertility plans to accommodate their plans to participate in the labour force, so that those who work only if their family responsibilities permit them to do so are fulfilling a prior choice of emphasis on a 'marriage career'. In a similar vein, a longitudinal study carried out by Himmelweit *et al.* (1981) found that social and political attitudes proved to be far more important determinants of party choice during an election than was past voting behaviour, and that changes in attitudes produced changes in vote choice.

All the longitudinal studies have repeatedly demonstrated the importance of attitudes, values, aspirations and motivations as key determinants of subsequent labour market behaviour, occupational status and even earnings. This influence is independent of conventional human capital factors (Parnes, 1975: 246–7; Andrisani, 1978; Pilling, 1990; Szekelyi and Tardos, 1993; Dale and Egerton, 1997; Saunders, 1997; see also Hakim, 2000: Chapter 5) and has repeatedly surprised economists and sociologists alike, although established by social psychologists from other longitudinal studies (see, for example, Eichorn *et al.*, 1982).

A major assessment of attrition in longitudinal studies in the spring 1998 issue of the *Journal of Human Resources* reviewed experience with the PSID, the NLS second youth cohort and the USA Survey of Income and Program Participation (SIPP). Contributors concluded that the 50% attrition rate in the original PSID sample by 1989 had only a small or negligible impact on research findings. Cohort studies, in particular youth cohort studies, had the lowest attrition rates. In general, attrition is concentrated among people of lower socio-economic status and those who have frequent changes in residence and other circumstances.

## Studies focused on specific groups or issues

Multi-purpose longitudinal studies provide a good basis for studying special groups, owing to the advantage of built-in comparison groups, but some longitudinal studies are specially designed to focus on specific groups or issues (usually without any control or comparison sample). A typical example would be a longitudinal study of a cohort of persons entering a spell of unemployment, with repeated surveys to collect information on the initial spell and subsequent work histories (including any further spells of unemployment), as well as related factors such as health, the effects of unemployment benefits and pensions on work incentives, work orientations, standards of living and labour market withdrawal. Three such studies were carried out in Britain in the late 1970s to assess the causes and consequences of long-term unemployment, the effect of unemployment benefits on male breadwinners' work incentives, and the effectiveness of job placement services for the unemployed (White, 1983; Moylan, Millar and Davies, 1984; Daniel, 1986; see also Hakim, 1982b; Narendranathan, Nickell and Stern, 1985).

An unusual policy research example is the Cabinet Office's People's Panel, which is a nationally representative panel of about 5,000 people recruited to act as a barometer of public opinion on policy issues and public sector service delivery in Britain. The panel was set up in 1998, with surveys carried out twice a year by MORI. The panel has also provided information on women's priorities and needs, through the Listening to

Women programme of research and consultation. Results of this panel study are available at http://www.servicefirst.gov.uk/.

## Inter-generational studies

Many multi-purpose studies permit analysis of inter-generational continuity and change, as illustrated by the PSID and NCDS described above. Specially designed inter-generational longitudinal studies are rare, partly because of the practical difficulties of collecting data directly from parents and their children over any length of time. Studies of this nature address questions about the transmission of life chances, attitudes and values, life styles and patterns of behaviour from one generation to the next, the process of socialisation in the family, social mobility and social inequality issues.

A good example is a study of the political socialisation process, inter-generational continuity and change in social and political attitudes and behaviour conducted by Jennings and Niemi (1974, 1981) in the United States. In 1965, a nationally representative sample of high school seniors (in effect, a narrowly defined age cohort) was interviewed and their parents were also interviewed separately; eight years later, in 1973, both the young adult and parent samples were re-interviewed. The four surveys provided the basis for a study of continuity and change in political orientations both within each generation and between the two. Another example is the follow-up survey carried out in 1975–8 of the adult children of a sample of working-class families that had originally been surveyed in 1950 to study income mobility over two generations in Britain (Atkinson, Maynard and Trinder, 1983).

## Retrospective studies

Retrospective studies must be distinguished from prospective longitudinal studies because they are really quasi-longitudinal studies, which do not offer the same strengths for research on causal processes.

Retrospective studies typically interview a nationally representative sample once only, collecting information retrospectively on education, work, health and family histories, usually in a more abbreviated form than is feasible in prospective studies. Some surveys ask respondents to provide information, from memory, on their family situation in childhood and their parents' education, employment and attitudes, using the retrospective study as a short cut to an inter-generational study. Information on attitudes, values and motivations is collected with reference to the present, and retrospective information on reasons for earlier decisions is of uncertain value, given the distortions that can colour explanations recalled after the event. It is too much to expect people to remember quickly and in detail the reasons and processes that played a part in earlier decisions and events, and structured survey questionnaires do not encourage complex accounts, even if they are recalled. (Depth interviews can obtain complex accounts, as noted in Chapter 3, but they take far longer than survey interviews and require a very different sort of skilled interviewing.) Also, research addressed to individuals is sometimes seeking causal explanations that actually lie beyond their personal experience or understanding (as is cogently illustrated by Rutter, 1981: 329). Finally, explanations offered after the event may be distorted by a concern to maintain or restore 'face', by *post hoc* rationalisation, or by seeking to establish consistency between the past and the present, or between the present and the future (Semin and Manstead, 1983). Retrospective studies provide a much cheaper and quicker alternative to the prospective study in cases where broad descriptive information on life histories is required, but they do not have any advantage over the *ad hoc* or regular survey for explanatory research (see Andrisani, 1980: 109–10, 158–66).

A good example of this type is the 1980 Women and Employment Survey, which obtained detailed work histories from a nationally representative sample of women of working age in Britain (Martin and Roberts, 1984a, 1984b). The survey provided a clear picture of patterns of movement in and out of the labour force over the life cycle (at least for older women, the picture for younger women being incomplete), which was substantiated by comparisons with national statistics, but it was unable to explore the reasons for the different work profiles *post hoc*.

Another alternative to the true longitudinal study is the analysis of synthetic cohort data from existing sources (see Chapter 2), which offers some improvement on purely cross-sectional analyses of net change over time.

## Cross-national comparative studies

The success of the PSID in the USA prompted social scientists in Europe to develop equivalent panel studies of households.

The German Socio-Economic Panel has been running since 1984, with an initial sample of about 6,000 households and 12,250 respondents in West Germany. All persons in the household aged 16 and over are interviewed, and the first sweep collected retrospective work history data. In addition to being representative of the West German population, the study is designed to allow separate analyses of foreign nationals by oversampling heads of households with Turkish, Greek, Yugoslavian, Spanish or Italian nationality. Following unification, the study was extended to include the former East Germany: the first survey was carried out in 1990, covering an extra sample of 2,200 households and 4,450 persons. The Dutch Socio-Economic Panel Study has also been running since 1984, with two sweeps a year from 1984 to 1990, then a single annual survey from April 1991 onwards (Statistics Netherlands, 1992). All members of the household aged 15 and over are invited to participate. Unfortunately, the study suffers from high levels of non-participation: non-response in the first wave was 49%. Data for about 3,000 households and 6,000 persons is available. The British Household Panel Study is based on a sample of 5,000 households and about 13,000 individuals. The study began in 1991, but a lifetime employment history was only collected in 1992 (Taylor, 1998).

These three studies display the range of household panel studies now available in western European countries. Together with retrospective life history surveys and LFS panels, they are used for cross-national comparative research as well as for national studies, as illustrated by the contributions to Blossfeld (1995) and Blossfeld and Hakim (1997).

All the European household panel studies are modelled on the PSID, but each adopted variations to meet local information needs. Attempts to produce a harmonised EU dataset from existing surveys failed. The European Community Household Panel (ECHP) was thus designed and organised centrally to produce comparable data across all EU countries from 1994 onwards. Surveys focus on individual and household income, employment, housing, fertility and migration, with some limited questioning on welfare benefits, satisfaction levels and other attitudes. The first wave in 1994 had a sample of 60,000 households and 130,000 persons aged 16 and over in 12 member states. The second wave in 1995 maintained the sample at 60,000 households and 130,000 persons covering 13 member states. The study was gradually expanded to cover new EU member states joining in the 1990s. Basic documentation is available on the annual surveys (Eurostat, 1996), and results are occasionally reported in EC documents, but so far there have been no full reports on the study's results. However, ECHP data are sold to academics and others for secondary analysis, and cross-national comparative reports are gradually emerging.

Finally, there are similar panel studies of households and surveys collecting retrospective work/life history data in many other countries. For example, the Malaysia Family Life Survey collected retrospective histories and is used to study links between geographic mobility, work histories and family formation (Smith and Thomas, 1998). The potential for comparative research based on longitudinal data extends well beyond the OECD countries.

## Overlaps and combinations

The overlap between regular surveys and longitudinal studies was noted in Chapter 7. Examples of longitudinal studies based on administrative records were discussed in Chapter 4. For certain topics, longitudinal case studies offer an alternative to national longitudinal studies, but they may also be used in combination with them. One option is to carry out separate case studies in parallel with the main study, for example individual life histories might be used to complement a larger-scale study of criminal careers. Alternatively, case studies of special groups within a larger national study can be done, which are, in effect, selective follow-up sweeps. For example, Pilling (1990) did follow-up interviews at age 27 with two groups within the NCDS cohort who had been socially disadvantaged when children: one group that nevertheless became high achievers and a comparison group of low achievers. Her study tried to identify the factors that enabled some people to escape from disadvantage by their 20s: aspirations and motivation emerged as important factors, challenging the thesis that childhood poverty is the dominant factor in the transmission of deprivation (Gregg and Machin, 1999).

Unlike experimental studies, longitudinal studies do not intentionally set out to assess the effects of a particular change or policy innovation. But it may be possible to use an existing longitudinal study to assess the impact of a change or innovation that happens to occur within the life span of a study – for example, by drawing comparisons between those who were or were not affected by the change or had experience of the new measures.

## Practical considerations

Because they both involve repeated data collections over a long period of time, longitudinal studies have many features and practical problems in common with regular surveys (see Chapter 7). Other problems are specific to longitudinal studies, such as the need to keep in touch with study members.

One additional cost of a longitudinal study arises from the necessity of creating a more personalised relationship with study members and promoting their active interest in the study, in order to keep sample attrition and non-response as low as possible. For example, the NCDS research team has regularly sent birthday cards to all 17,000 cohort members (and thereby obtained the new addresses of movers). The PSID research team regularly sends summaries of the results of each survey to the 6,000 panel members. People who are being asked to participate in a study for any length of time cannot be treated as impersonally as respondents to an *ad hoc* survey. Maintaining the confidentiality of the identities of study participants also requires greater care, although this is less of a problem with national panel samples than with narrowly defined age cohorts.

The difficulties of tracing study participants after a lapse of time are greatly reduced in European countries (such as Sweden and Belgium) that have a population register. Self-regenerating sample designs offer one solution to the problem of wasting samples. Statistical methods have been developed for dealing with sample attrition and data-censoring (that is, the fact that event histories will be incomplete for certain members of a panel, or for young age cohorts) at the analysis stage (Tuma and Hannan, 1979; Abeles and Wise, 1980); these offer a more constructive alternative to the routine analyses of response bias, which simply state how the sample of respondents at each wave differs from the fuller sample at previous waves. Some studies have found that untraced study members are more deviant than non-respondents, so that the final sample at completion of a study may seriously under-represent marginal groups (Fogelman, 1976: 67). However, there is increasing awareness that some sources of sample attrition, such as deaths, can be used as substantive information in its own right (Parnes, 1981).

It is often difficult to get funding for longitudinal studies, especially those of long duration. Longitudinal studies are most vulnerable in their early stages, before the benefits of a long run of data are manifested in research reports, so a convincing research design document is crucial at the start. Continuity of research staff, particularly at senior levels, and a permanent institutional base are important if a longitudinal study is to maintain its sense of direction and purpose. It is indicative that the successful American longitudinal studies all had one or two guiding lights (Parnes on the NLS, Morgan and Duncan on the PSID), perhaps because such studies require large, multi-disciplinary research teams, with the practical problems these entail (see Chapters 11 and 12).

Difficult choices on data collection methods must be made at the design stage, with realistic appraisals of the implications for data quality and costs. Some studies rely almost entirely on personal interviews carried out by experienced survey agencies, sometimes with follow-up sweeps based on telephone or mail surveys in order to reduce costs. Some studies have used non-research staff for interviewing and data collection, for example social workers, community health staff, teachers and doctors, who do the task as part of their job and often without any briefing on the study's aims and procedures. While this reduces costs significantly, it can seriously damage the quality, consistency and value of the resulting data and cannot be recommended unless, at the minimum, research briefings are carried out with all those collaborating with the study. For one example of how this can be done see Todd and Dodd (1985). The extraction of data from administrative records and case files sometimes has to be done by non-research staff who are on the spot, again with implications for the quality, consistency and interpretation of the data (see Chapter 4). When a variety of data collection methods are used and/or they are changed over time, data documentation becomes a particularly crucial and resource-consuming task, more so than in any other kind of national study, because data analysts are unable to make assumptions about the nature and validity of any particular item of evidence from a multi-source dataset. Funding may also need to make allowance for user support staff to service and advise the large number of secondary analysts who wish to exploit rich longitudinal datasets.

The analysis of data from a longitudinal study will often be substantially more complex and time-consuming than equivalent analysis of regular surveys. True longitudinal analysis of linked data from a series of surveys frequently involves extremely large data files. While there have been significant developments in techniques for the longitudinal analysis of individual growth and change (Goldstein, 1979) and event histories (Tuma, Hannan and Groeneveld, 1979; Andrisani, 1980; Kessler and Greenberg, 1981; Dex, 1984b; Ni Bhrolchain and Timaeus, 1985; Blossfeld, Hamerle and Mayer, 1989; Blossfeld and Rohwer, 1995), special programming is often necessary to cope with the unique characteristics and problems of particular datasets. The Transitions Data Analysis (TDA) package developed by Rohwer, and enclosed with the Blossfeld and Rohwer (1995) book, is widely used for event history analysis. However, large quantities of exploratory analysis may be required to identify 'sleeper effects' and serendipitous discoveries, given that theory is generally better developed in relation to proximate than to distant causes.

In Britain, the Centre for Longitudinal Studies at the University of London Institute of Education is responsible for three cohort studies: the NCDS, a 1946 cohort study with an emphasis on epidemiological research, and a 1970 cohort study, which started with a study of a sample of 17,000 births in April 1970, with further data collections in 1975, 1980, 1986, 1996 and 2000. The Centre carried out new surveys of all three cohorts in 1999/2000. Another centre at the University of Essex is responsible for the British Household Panel Study. A guide to all sources of longitudinal data in Britain is available in ONS (1999).

# 9 Experimental social research

The sole purpose of experimental research is to study causal links: to assess whether a given factor X has an impact on another factor Y, or whether changes in one variable produce changes in another. The simplest studies seek only to ascertain whether or not there is a direct link between the two factors. More complex studies seek, in addition, to assess the magnitude or importance of the effect produced (the size of the effect) and even the *relative* importance of the effect, that is, relative to other factors that also produce a similar impact. Experimental social research is thus relatively narrow, or focused, in the type of information it produces, but it can provide more definitive answers to questions about causal links than do other types of study, and is hence essential for the development of soundly based explanations of social events, behaviour and attitudes.

As noted in Chapter 11, sample selection bias can be a problem in some studies. Experimental studies should completely eliminate this problem. The two essential elements of the experimental design are randomisation and controlled application of the factor X that is to be studied. *Experimental control* involves deciding which individuals, groups or organisations will be exposed to the information, experience or event whose impact is to be tested, rather than allowing them to choose (or even allowing someone else to make the choice for them) – on the grounds that those who voluntarily elect to participate are immediately identified as different from those choosing not to, so that the impact of the experimental factor will be confounded with the impact of selection effects (also termed self-selection effects). *Randomisation* involves allocating the people or other units being studied to the experimental group (which is exposed to the information, experience or event being tested) or to a control group (which is not exposed to the same experience, or is given a 'placebo' treatment instead) on an entirely random basis, taking no account of their characteristics or preferences. The logic of random allocation to the experimental and control groups is that the two groups thus formed will be exactly similar in all aspects relevant to the study, except for the single difference of being exposed, or not, to the experimental treatment. The two groups are studied before and after the experimental treatment and at the same points in time. Comparisons of the 'before' and 'after' information for the two groups then allows conclusions to be drawn about the impact of the treatment, if any. More complex versions of this design are also available, for example using four groups instead of two; using several levels of intensity in the treatment applied to the experimental group; or carrying out repeated follow-ups of the two groups in order to differentiate the immediate short-term impact from the longer-term impact, as these may differ in strength and in character (Stouffer, 1950; Campbell, 1957; Campbell and Stanley, 1963; Cook and Campbell, 1979).

It is immediately obvious that experimental designs are simply not feasible for many of the topics and questions addressed by social research. People cannot be randomly assigned to experience unemployment, imprisonment, marriage, war or migration. Professional and other ethical principles generally prevent exposing people to stressful or distressing treatments purely for experimental research purposes, although some scholars have defended the propriety of doing so in the interests of science (Milgram, 1963; Kelman, 1967). However, it is feasible to carry out experiments in relation to treatments of a beneficial nature (such as increased income or improved quality of education); the ethics of giving the treatment to the experimental group, while denying it to the control group, are justified where the treatment in question is in short supply (such as a new vaccine not yet produced on a large enough scale to treat everyone).

Apart from practical constraints on the type of treatments that can be tested, feasibility problems arise also in relation to people's willingness to be experimental guinea-pigs in research. Many adults are simply not 'available' for participation in experiments, and volunteers may not be representative. This tends to limit experimental research to captive populations, such as students in schools and other educational institutions, offenders in correctional institutions, workers in factories, members of the armed forces, social welfare recipients, and so on. A great deal of research in experimental psychology is carried out with students in higher education, who are readily available as subjects for academic research, but there is often good reason to believe that results obtained with such groups cannot be generalised to the population as a whole.

If the stringent requirements of experimental research designs are to be met, the design often becomes feasible only with small and untypical groups, in which case the conclusions cannot be generalised with any certainty. Conducting true experiments with large and representative samples is an enormously complex and costly design, but it is necessary if the results are to be reliably generalised from the groups studied to the populations they represent. It also follows that research reviews need to distinguish clearly between experiments in real-life settings and experiments using students purely for convenience, with the latter category often excluded altogether from research reviews on non-educational topics (Farrington, 1983).

Another problem is that experimental researchers' full control of the experiment can be self-defeating, in that they artificially produce the results they expect to obtain or, in some cases, directly contrary results (since some people react rebelliously rather than compliantly to these expectations). As noted in Chapter 2, the self-fulfilling prophecy operates in real-life settings as well as in laboratory experiments, and it can in practice entirely invalidate the superiority claimed for experimental research as the most rigorous test and proof of causal relationships. This finding led Rosenthal to list the research procedures that would avoid artificially creating the expected results, such as double-blind procedures (see Chapter 11), the use of larger numbers of data collectors, and subcontracting data collection (Rosenthal, 1976: 331–413; see also Campbell and Stanley, 1963: 20–2, 41).

Given these important constraints on the feasibility of social experiments, other types of study must often be used instead: longitudinal studies, case studies, regular or *ad hoc* surveys, research analyses of administrative records and even qualitative research (for example, where actors' motives, intentions and choices are important). Campbell and Stanley (1963), Campbell (1969) and Cook and Campbell (1979) have set out the analyses that can be applied to data from such non-experimental studies to test for causal relationships. They call them 'quasi-experimental' designs, to emphasise that they offer less rigorous tests than the true experimental design, list their respective weaknesses (such as the absence of a control group, or assignment to treatments on the basis of self-selection or by an administrator's decision) and show how the limitations of the non-experimental design can be overcome by additional tests (such as applying a rigorous logic to assessing the validity of the results and the elimination of plausible rival explanations for the results obtained). However, they also recognise that these other designs offer compensating strengths, improving upon true experiments in certain respects.

The non-experimental designs can more readily be used in real-world settings, but for some topics there is no real choice at all, and the only option is quasi-experimental analysis of a particular type of data – such as time series obtained from administrative records, regular surveys or longitudinal studies. Studies based on secondary analysis of existing data or involving large-scale data collections are characterised by double-blind conditions, and are hence immune from the artefactual results created by an experimenter's expectations, which can invisibly, unconsciously and unintentionally colour and bias conspicuous experimental procedures (Rosenthal, 1976: 367–400).

Experiments are designed to show the effects of a particular factor net of all the other factors that may produce the same effect, or moderate or exaggerate it, including (self-)selection effects. But there may be little practical value in seeking a precise separation of selection and treatment effects if, in the real world, they inevitably operate together. For example, if participation in certain programmes is voluntary, there is no point in seeking to know their effects on those groups choosing not to participate; similarly, there is no point in seeking to know the effects of certain experiences or benefits independently of the fact that they will be allocated to, or taken up by, particular groups with particular characteristics. So for some research topics there is no meaningful control group (whether precisely or only loosely matched) that might be included in the study. In fact, volunteer samples may actually be more appropriate for a study seeking to assess the impact of a programme with voluntary participation, although non-volunteer samples and, ideally, experimental research would be required for an equivalent study of a policy that is expected to be universal and compulsory in its application. Social science does not invariably seek to identify causal processes which exclude any reference to people's choices, intentions and active involvement in the real world (Sayer, 1984: 123–6; see also Byrne, 1999: 6, 41–2).

Experiments are appropriate for research on unidirectional causal processes (where the influence works one way only), but other types of study can be more effective for research on reciprocal causal processes (where a change in X produces a change in Y, and a change in Y also produces a change in X). Thornberry and Christenson (1984) illustrate how longitudinal studies provide a better design for such complex situations; they show that unemployment and crime mutually influence one another over the individual's life span.

The procedures recommended for quasi-experimental designs include using combinations of different research designs (such as cross-sectional and longitudinal designs, case studies and qualitative studies) as well as multiple replications of the same design (Campbell and

Stanley, 1963: 36, 42–4, 55–8, 60; see also Cook and Campbell, 1979), in effect arguing for multiple triangulation (see Chapter 11) and accepting that all research designs contribute to the study of causal processes by helping to eliminate plausible rival explanations.

All experimental research is longitudinal, in that observations are required for at least two points in time (before and after treatment), so that the two designs are readily confused. A review of school desegregation research by Crain and Mahard (1983) showed that experiments reveal stronger positive effects than other designs, such as quasi-experimental analysis of longitudinal studies and cross-sectional studies with weakly defined control groups. Meta-analysis of all the studies helped to identify the precise size of the effect of desegregation on educational attainment, and showed that policy experiments obtained the same results as natural experiments – because self-selection bias is sometimes non-existent.

For many decades, the randomised controlled experiment was presented in textbooks as the norm, or at least the ideal to strive for, in the design and conduct of social research. But the utility of experiments cannot be taken for granted as a self-evident assumption in social science research. One must set out the arguments showing that an experimental research design is more appropriate than other designs for the particular issue or question to be studied. Many causal processes are straightforward and fairly well understood in 'ordinary knowledge' (Lindblom and Cohen, 1979: 12); explanation and prediction are not synonymous or symmetric – they are different kinds of operation conducted for different purposes; and assessing the predictive adequacy of a model or an explanatory framework (which may take account of contingent conditions or ignore them as constants) can be a separate exercise from the analysis of causal mechanisms (Sayer, 1984: 94–106, 119–26, 193–203). Experiments are appropriate when there is disagreement as to the very existence of a causal relationship between X and Y (net of other contextual or related factors), or when a precise measure of the size and direction of the effect is needed. Other study designs may be more appropriate if one needs a measure of the effect size relative to other related factors, for example, or if one wants to look more closely at the beliefs and motivations that enter into the causal process. And experiments would be quite unnecessary for prediction and projections – until, of course, contextual conditions cease to be constant and the models used need to be re-formulated with reference to new or changing circumstances. Experimental research has never been, in practice, the dominant mode in empirical social research, except perhaps in social psychology, where the emphasis has been on experiments in artificial settings (or, as they are more commonly known, laboratory experiments).

## Experiments in real-life settings

Policy research provides the best examples of true experiments carried out in real-life settings and, in some cases, with samples sufficiently large and representative for the results to be extrapolated to the national level (Boruch *et al.*, 1978; Ferber and Hirsch, 1979; Hausman and Wise, 1985). Purely theoretical research is rarely accorded sufficient importance for all the practical barriers to the conduct of experiments in natural settings to be overcome.

In the 1970s, the governments of Canada and the United States both funded guaranteed annual income maintenance experiments based on Milton Friedman's proposal for a negative income tax (NIT) system to replace and consolidate various discrete welfare benefits. The NIT involved extending the conventional income tax system to low-income families, who would receive cash rebates in place of other types of transfer payments, providing a basic level of support to families without other sources of income, but reducing these benefits as income increased.

The largest of these experiments was the Seattle/Denver Income Maintenance Experiment (SIME and DIME), which cost about $70 million and involved 4,800 families. Funded mainly by the US Department of Health, Education and Welfare, plus the states of Washington and Colorado, the experiment was designed and evaluated by SRI International, which subcontracted the distribution of payments to families and regular household interviewing to another agency. Local community colleges in Seattle and Denver also participated in the experiment, which, at its peak, involved a team of over 200 persons all told.

The experiment was designed to assess the economic, social and psychological consequences of an NIT system, especially any unintended effects of such a reform to the welfare system. The primary concern was the impact of NIT on labour supply (work effort or work incentives), measured by the hours worked by individuals. (It reduced work hours by 10%–30%.) The second focus was the impact of NIT on marital stability, measured by separation or divorce (this being the relevant measure with reference to income maintenance policy). The experiment also assessed the impact of NIT on a wide spectrum of other behaviour and attitudes: fertility, migration and geographic mobility; the take-up of education and training options; demand for subsidised public housing; health and psychological well-being or stress; job satisfaction; job changes and wage rate changes; use of childcare services; family expenditure patterns; family assets and savings, and so on.

A complex experimental design was evolved to isolate the effects of NIT independently of related factors (such as previous family income, family composition and other family characteristics); to obtain precise measurement of NIT effects by varying the level of the guaranteed annual income and taxation rates; and to assess both short-term and long-term effects. Families were enrolled in the experiment for a period of three or five years, with a small sample enrolled for 20 years, and it was found that labour supply responses, for example, did vary significantly with the duration of the schemes tested (Robins *et al.*, 1980; Burtless and Greenberg, 1982). The design involved 84 experimental treatment categories and 60 stratified samples, with stratified random assignment of families to a treatment category or the control group. One effect of the complex design was that regression analysis had to be used to assess the effects of the NIT (rather than the simple comparison of mean scores for experimental and control groups typical of laboratory experiments). Although the experiment was limited to low-income families (excluding families with incomes too high to be affected by NIT), the design ensured that the results could be extrapolated to the national population by using Current Population Survey data (Robins *et al.*, 1980).

The SIME/DIME results were sufficiently detailed to provide the basis for national simulations of the costs and consequences not only of the NIT schemes tested but also of subsequent proposals for welfare reform. But some of the experiment's most valuable (and controversial) results concerned the unexpected consequences of NIT schemes. For example, it was believed that NIT would increase the stability of two-parent families, but the experiment showed an immediate 50% increase in divorce rates (Gauthier, 1996: 319; see also Nathan, 1988: 44–68). The experiment also prompted methodological developments (Tuma, Hannan and Groeneveld, 1979), and the control group (which did not receive the special payments but for whom equally detailed longitudinal data was obtained) provides the basis for more general studies of labour economics (Lundberg, 1985).

One advantage of experiments is that the results consist of a simple statement on whether or not the treatment made a difference and whether this effect was large or small, thus making reports readily accessible to policy-makers and social scientists alike. But experiments do not, of themselves, provide any explanation for the results, which is especially annoying when the results go contrary to expectation!

Because large-scale experiments in natural settings are such a major exercise, there is a tendency to maximise their utility by collecting extra data, which can be used to study causal processes as well. As a result, the distinction between the experimental results (which are narrow but definitive) and the additional analyses of causal mechanisms (which will be broader in scope but less conclusive) can become blurred in reports, causing confusion for some readers. One illustration of this is the debate over the results of the TARP experiment – a large-scale, randomised, controlled experiment in the USA designed to find out whether providing a modest income and job counselling to ex-convicts during their first months after their release from prison would improve their employability and reduce recidivism. The experiment produced no reduction in recidivism; however, the report went on to consider why, and argued that in this case (unlike a previous similar experiment) the effect of financial help in decreasing re-offending had been cancelled out by its effect in increasing unemployment (given that the amount of time spent working was inversely related to the re-arrest rate). Thus the report appeared to offer contradictory conclusions instead of the clear-cut results produced by experiments, leading to some debate as to the 'correct' results (Berk, Lenihan and Rossi, 1980; Rossi, Berk and Lenihan, 1980; Zeisel, 1982; see also Englander, 1983; Lattimore and Witte, 1985). Such debates in academic journals can be clouded by arguments over trivial details and veiled personal insults, which obscure matters still further.

The SIME/DIME and TARP experiments were concerned essentially with the effects of financial assistance, which is a fairly clear-cut type of experimental treatment. Other experiments are concerned with the effects of different ways of treating people and hence require the active participation of the people who have to administer different treatments. This poses more problems than simply giving people money. For example, the nature of the treatments becomes more variable (given that different individuals may be more successful giving one treatment rather than another), or one may need to exclude from the experiment those who are opposed to the idea of different treatments, even on an experimental basis. Although implementation of the research design may entail some slippage from the original plan, tests can sometimes be carried out to see whether this biased the data and results obtained, and if so how. An example of this kind is the Minneapolis Police Department experiment designed to assess the deterrent effects of arrest for domestic violence as compared with the more usual police responses of advice/mediation or separation (Sherman and Berk, 1984). This experiment was replicated with a quasi-experimental analysis of information on some 800 wife-battering incidents extracted from police records for a two-year period in California, with the same results: arrest had a strong deterrent effect on subsequent incidents of wife-battering (Berk and Newton, 1985). In other cases, practical problems with implementing an experiment in a natural setting may be so great as to vitiate the results (Clarke and Cornish, 1972; see also Farrington, 1983, for a broader review with reference to North American and British experimental research in the crime and justice field).

Experiments do not always require large scale-resources, or the active and knowing participation of many others. A particularly imaginative and discreet type of experiment has been developed for discrimination testing with reference to sex, race, criminal convictions, or other factors that might produce discriminatory behaviour. Brown and Gay (1985) report on a 1984 study with experimental comparisons of an employer's reactions to applicants of different ethnic origin but with equivalent qualifications for the job, and compare the results with earlier studies to assess trends in recent decades in Britain. The design involved sampling job advertisements and mailing two or three job applications to each employer, the applications being matched on everything except the applicants' ethnic group.

## Natural experiments

Although the examples described so far concern experiments in real-life, or 'natural' settings, they are all artificial experiments in that they occurred purely for research purposes. As noted earlier, practical and ethical considerations rule out true experiments on some topics, such as the effects of parental divorce on children, so that research (if done at all) must rely on naturally occurring events. The classic examples of naturally occurring experiments are identical twins reared apart, adopted children reared alongside natural children, and experimental or innovatory communities such as the kibbutz.

Some natural experiments are 'accidental' deviant or strategic cases, the outcome of rare conjunctures, as in the case of identical twins reared apart, or of adopted children reared alongside natural children, which form the basis for research on the relative impact of 'nature versus nurture' (Mednick and Baert, 1981: 215–30).

The discovery of oil near isolated, poor and rural communities, and the ensuing major and rapid changes that transform them into affluent and industrialised communities, provides just one example of the naturally occurring event around which an experimental study can be designed. The decision to locate an oil industrial complex in the

Shetland Islands offered particular advantages for such a study, owing to the natural boundaries preventing migration and creating a relatively homogeneous and stable population. A study by Voorhees-Rosen and Rosen (1981) focused on two communities, one in the area surrounding the oil port and industrial complex and most directly affected by the changes, and a control community in a designated conservation area in a remote part of Shetland that would be relatively little affected by the changes but that had a population and life style very similar to those in the target area. The study was concerned primarily with the effects of major social change and life stresses on mental health, but also collected data from administrative records for the island as a whole on other social consequences, such as crime, suicide and divorce.

Other natural experiments are distinguished by the fact that they are carried out autonomously by those directly involved for their own purposes rather than for research purposes (even though they may permit, or even invite, research to evaluate the effects). This usually means that they are implemented as a *permanent* innovation or change, with the active participation and positive commitment of at least some, if not all, of those involved – although some innovations are abandoned or fade away after a while (Blackler and Brown, 1980; Lavin *et al.*, 1981). This can be an important advantage in that the effects of the innovation might be telescoped in time, and thus be manifested within a shorter period than in artificial experiments, which are known to be of limited duration (so that many do not bother to adapt or respond to the purely temporary change). The disadvantage is that, precisely because the innovation is a permanent change rather than a short-term experiment, and because many individuals and groups may be involved in its implementation, the nature of the innovation (its aims, procedures, coverage, and so forth) may be defined less precisely and may be subject to modification as it proceeds. From the research design perspective, contraction or expansion of coverage is less of a problem than substantive modification of aims and procedures, because this may affect the choice of relevant outcome measures and of appropriate control groups or comparators.

Examples of natural experiments and social innovations that have formed the basis for quasi-experimental studies are the industrial democracy experiment in the Post Office Corporation (Batstone *et al.*, 1984), the participatory management experiment in the Shell Company in Britain (Blackler and Brown, 1980), the egalitarian communes and co-operatives of the kibbutz (Rosner 1982; Krausz, 1983), the short-lived open admissions programme of the City University of New York

(Lavin *et al.*, 1981) and many other experiments and innovations that have been the subject of evaluation research (for example, Herriott and Gross, 1979). The parallel development of the 'two Germanies' from World War Two up to 1989 is another natural experiment that attracted many comparative studies in the 1990s (Kuechler, 1998). Evaluation research is usually narrower in focus than studies of natural experiments, because it looks only at whether the policy achieved its aims and objectives, rather than at the whole spectrum of outcomes (Rossi and Freeman, 1999).

Studies of natural experiments and social innovations merge into studies of deviant and strategic cases (see Chapter 5), particularly when no appropriate control group or comparator can be incorporated in the study, or when the innovation is so subtle or complex in character and broad in potential impact that a multi-method case study approach is required to tap the full variety of qualitative effects. Like well-chosen case studies, natural experiments have to be found rather than artificially created. The most famous ones, like the Mondragón worker co-operatives in Spain, tend to be repetitively studied for that reason, and Whyte (1982) suggests that sociologists should devote more attention to other social innovations, in part because they cast light on the role of actors' intentions and motivations in social change – a factor that is completely eliminated from artificial experiments.

Countries with a federal government give rise to a special type of natural experiment. In the USA, for example, laws adopted at federal level have often been implemented previously in several states. Implementation of the federal law can be studied as a quasi-experimental situation, with before-and-after comparisons of states that had already implemented the policy with states introducing it for the first time, which were treated as 'control' and 'experimental' groups respectively. In practice, this may not work because of contradictory and unexplained results from the paired comparisons, as illustrated by Waldfogel's (1999) analysis of the impact of the 1993 Family and Medical Leave Act, which gave American women the right to short unpaid maternity leave, long after this became standard practice in Europe. Donovan (1995) reviews the methodological difficulties that arise in evaluations of this form of quasi-experimental study.

## Experiments in artificial settings

Artificial experiments in artificial settings, more commonly referred to as 'laboratory' experiments, are used extensively by psychologists. They allow complete control by the researcher, and hence achieve the 'model' random allocation to treatment and control groups and the well-defined treatment that are the aims of the true experiment. However, they are typically carried out with students and often focus on trivial questions, so that the typical laboratory experiment has been described as 'a temporary collection of late adolescent strangers given a puzzle to solve under bizarre conditions in a limited time during their first meeting while being peered at from behind a mirror' (Tajfel, 1984: 474). Not surprisingly, the results can rarely be generalised to any other social group, and the problem of the self-fulfilling prophecy arises precisely because malleable students allow the researcher unquestioned control over even the most meaningless experiments (Orne, 1962).

Nonetheless, laboratory experiments can sometimes be useful. An immediate example is Rosenthal's research on the self-fulfilling prophecy, which was based largely on laboratory experiments (Rosenthal, 1976) before being extended to experiments in natural settings (Rosenthal and Jacobson, 1968).

Students can offer an appropriate basis for some experimental research precisely because they do not have extensive work (or any other) experience and so provide a strong test of hypotheses. For example, Humphrey (1985) created an experimental corporate office staffed by students to test the process of self-fulfilling role expectations. He found that although everyone was told that participants in the experiment were students who were randomly assigned to the roles of manager and clerk (that is, with no relevant prior experience), both clerks and managers subsequently rated the managers highly on a range of role-related characteristics and tended to underevaluate the clerks. He concluded that those who are high in the organisational hierarchy and who do high-skill tasks are perceived more favourably than others of equal ability.

The potential for generalising from experiments is increased if normal adult groups are used instead of students and the experiment takes place in a real-world location rather than a university. This approach was used by Gamson *et al.* (1982) to study group response to the demands of an unjust authority and the factors that enabled weak or strong collective rebellion to develop. Initially, they analysed three critical incidents in the growth of social movements taken from real-life events in the USA: a 1936–7 plant strike and two conflictual encounters between the police and the public in the early 1960s. They then fabricated an unjust authority called the Manufacturers' Human Relations Consultants, which hired people and tried to get them to help it use unfair tactics to win a legal case of unfair dismissal, so as to test their model of the rebellion process in controlled experiments. The design involved running the experiment with 80 groups of people, but the project was curtailed after the thirty-third group because participants experienced so much stress in dealing with an unjust authority. The study was similar to Milgram's experiments on obedience to authority carried out in the 1960s, which provoked a good deal of debate over the ethical issues involved (Milgram, 1963; Kelman, 1967). This approach was also used by Rosen and Jerdee (1975) to study managers' reactions to employee grievances. They took advantage of a management training course to test reactions to threatening versus pleading styles of written complaint embedded in an in-basket exercise, so the experiment was carried out unobtrusively with bank employees on the course.

## Simulation and modelling

The advent of much more powerful computers and sophisticated data analysis software have prompted a rapid expansion in simulation and modelling work (Hoaglin *et al.*, 1982: 191–272; Gilbert and Doran, 1993; Gilbert and Conte, 1995; Gilbert and Troitzsch, 1999). This is frequently presented as a form of experimental research. For example, economists will often say that a study simulates 'experimentally' the impact of a policy innovation – for example, the impact of a change in tax rates or social security benefits on work effort or retirement decisions (Fields and Mitchell, 1984, 1985). However, a great deal depends on the nature of the data used for such work, and much of it bears no relation at all to experimental research: it assumes that causal processes are already known and unchanging, and addresses instead the question of the size of their possible effects. As noted earlier, the results of the SIME/DIME experiment have provided the basis for much simulation and modelling work that shows the consequences and costs, at the national level, of alternative proposals for reforms to the income maintenance system. Projections to the national level of the results of experimental research incorporate the unintended side effects of a policy change as well as the intended or expected effects.

Simulations and modelling work based on non-experimental data are a different matter. They are based on the assumption (rarely stated explicitly) that unexpected or unintended side effects can be ignored: the *ceteris paribus* assumption that everything remains constant except for the policy change that is being modelled. This simplifies the researcher's modelling work, but it is an oversimplification with reference to the real world. Models vary greatly in their sophistication (some take account of feedback effects, interactions, and so on), but so long as they rest on secondary analysis of descriptive non-experimental data from surveys and official statistics, they cannot incorporate side effects that might unforeseeably result from the proposed change in policy, rules and regulations. Surveys describe the present, or the recent past, but cannot describe possible futures. True experiments (such as SIME/ DIME) can show effects that are contrary to received wisdom and significantly affect the overall results. If experimental data are not available, it can help to refer to the results of case studies, qualitative research and similar micro-level research to gain some notion of the motivations, values and rationales that might in reality influence response to a particular change, but the results of qualitative research cannot readily be incorporated in quantitive models. Most models and simulations include a large element of guesswork and assumptions with varying degrees of credibility and validity (Gustman, 1984; Gilbert and Conte, 1995).

In the late 1970s, two major research programmes on the national minimum wage were undertaken in the USA, one of them a government-funded exercise spending $17 million over three years. Reviewing the results, Eccles and Freeman found that policy-makers had made little use of the reports, and they themselves felt that the research programme had been underdesigned and the money wasted. Virtually all the studies had been carried out by economists relying on secondary analysis of existing data (such as the CPS and NLS), many of them using modelling and simulation to assess the effects of changes in the minimum wage. They concluded that the money might have been better spent on a genuine experimental study to test the effects of a youth differential in the minimum wage (Eccles and Freeman, 1982: 231; see also Griliches, 1985: 196).

These problems arise only with simulations that purport to show 'experimentally' the impact of policy changes. They do not arise in purely descriptive work, which provides statistical estimates of the numbers of people who would be affected by proposed changes – such as increasing or decreasing the normal retirement age. This is a factual statement that says nothing at all about likely or actual behavioural responses to such a change and its overall effects. However, this distinction easily becomes blurred in reports, as illustrated by a study advocating one type of negative income tax system for Britain (Dilnot, Kay and Morris, 1984). In practice, modelling, simulation and forecasting are often conflated, especially in policy research (Hoaglin *et al.*, 1982: 191–272).

Some types of computer simulation have the characteristics of true experimental research. A classic example is Axelrod's research on the evolution of co-operation in a society of completely self-interested individuals. He carried out a series of computer simulations to assess the effectiveness of various strategies in the Prisoners' Dilemma or Commons Dilemma game – an issue that is more commonly studied with laboratory experiments (Maital, 1982: 12–37; Antonides, 1991). Contrary to expectation, one of the simplest strategies, named TIT FOR TAT, emerged repeatedly as the winner, owing to 'a combination of being nice, retaliatory, forgiving and clear' (Axelrod, 1984: 54). By using computer simulations of the strategies pitted against each other, the 'game' could be run for a much longer time and with a larger number of diverse players than if the study were carried out as a laboratory experiment. Strategies were submitted to the tournament by 62 players in six countries from the fields of psychology, economics, political science, mathematics and sociology. The results are relevant to situations where choices must be made between competition and co-operation, between pursuing self-interest versus collective interests, and hence rational choice theory, industrial relations, economic and sociological theory (Axelrod, 1984). Another simulation demonstrated how patterns of political domination can arise from a few rules followed by hypothetical nation states (Axelrod in Gilbert and Conte, 1995). Other examples of simulation and modelling are presented by contributors to Gilbert and Doran (1993) and Gilbert and Conte (1995).

## Cross-national comparative studies

Comparisons of experiments, in laboratory settings or natural settings, are used in theoretical research to identify patterns of behaviour that are culture-specific and those that are universal – as illustrated by comparative studies of bargaining behaviour, risk-taking and responses to innovations in work organisation in several modern societies (Bruins in Whitfield and Strauss, 1998).

In policy research and historical research, comparisons of natural experiments are more common. For example, Skocpol (1979) studied social revolutions in France, Russia and China, plus the contrary cases of Prussia, Japan and England, to test theories about the causes of revolutions. Ruhm (1998) compared the effects of policies providing maternity leave across 16 European countries, and concluded that short leaves had a positive effect on mothers' employment and no wage effect, whereas policies allowing long maternity leaves had negative effects on mothers' employment and wage levels.

Experimental studies that explicitly set out to be comparative are rare. One example is a study by Tallman *et al.* (1974, 1983) based on a game simulation method (called SIMCAR) falling between the sample survey (which can easily be replicated in several countries) and the laboratory experiment, which they developed and used in a comparative study of adolescent socialisation in the United States and Mexico. They found that Mexican peasant children were more flexible and open to change and had a greater career orientation than American adolescents – a result that went contrary to the American mobility ideology (Erikson and Goldthorpe, 1985).

## Overlaps and combinations

Overlaps between the experiment and other types of study have already been illustrated by some of the examples described above. Some projects combine experimental treatments with a longitudinal study in order to assess the long-term effects of the treatment (as in the case of SIME/DIME) and/or to study causal mechanisms more closely (as in the TARP experiment). Experiments must have at least one quantifiable outcome variable; if the results of a treatment are very diverse, or if they include qualitative changes, then the multi-method case study design may be an appropriate complement to, or even a substitute for, an experimental design. Studies of natural experiments verge into deviant and strategic case studies, as noted above.

Direct linkage between experiments and other types of study is rare. But it is feasible to combine experimental research and large-scale surveys within a research programme. The experimental study of discrimination in responses to job applications described above (Brown and Gay, 1985) was an adjunct to the 1982 national survey of ethnic minorities described in Chapter 5. The survey provided data on ethnic minority perceptions of racial discrimination as a factor limiting their employment opportunities (Brown, 1984: 170–3, 264–92), but the existence and significance of discrimination by employers was tested more rigorously, and independently, by the experiment.

## Practical considerations

The practical constraints on carrying out artificial experiments in real-life settings are the main disadvantage of this design. But the examples presented, both large scale and small scale, have demonstrated that this design is not necessarily limited to social psychological laboratory experiments with students, even though this is the example most commonly presented in textbooks (see, for example, Myers, 1966; Brown *et al.*, 1975).

The large-scale income maintenance experiments described here are not isolated examples. Other experiments have been conducted in the United States on health insurance plans, educational vouchers, educational performance contracts and housing allowances (Bradbury and Downs, 1981; Tanur, 1983; Hausman and Wise, 1985). The ethical issues involved in policy experiments go beyond the issues of deception and of whether the experiment has harmful effects for the participants, which are the focus of social psychological laboratory experiments (Boruch and Cecil, 1983). The issue of deception may not arise, because many real-world experiments (such as SIME/DIME and TARP) require that participants fully understand the experimental treatment, and the new options it opens up to them, for it to have an impact on their behaviour and attitudes. Informed consent becomes a necessary condition rather than a luxury or an impediment, so much so that assessments of participants' understanding of the treatment may be incorporated into analyses of their responses (Nicholson and Wright, 1977; Tanur, 1983: 47). Harmful effects are less readily defined when families or larger social units are involved. For example, the effects of the NIT treatments in increasing the divorce rate was seen as noxious by some of the husbands (who complained publicly) but as beneficial by the wives, who were enabled to quit unsatisfactory marriages. When ethical issues do arise, as in phasing out the small 20-year DIME scheme after the experiment had run for only six years, the associated political and financial constraints may be on a very large scale indeed (over $5 million in this case), with decision-making responsibility shared by many organisations (Thompson, 1981).

Textbooks by Campbell and Stanley (1963), Cook and Campbell (1979), Saxe and Fine (1981) and Cochran (1983) present general guidelines and statistical techniques for quasi-experimental analysis of data from non-experimental studies. Apart from Cochran, they also discuss designs for true experimental studies in real-life settings and the practical problems of their implementation. Briefer discussions of experimental and quasi-experimental designs can be found in Krausz and Miller (1974) and Denzin (1978a, 1978b). Hoaglin *et al.* (1982: 17–75) and Tanur (1983) provide concise non-technical reviews of the design issues arising in American social policy experiments. The contributors to Hausman and Wise's (1985) collection review the design, results and policy uses of experiments in social, health and housing policy in the USA, including self-selection bias; differences between short-term and long-term impacts; the need for multivariate modelling of results to measure treatment effects; the advantages and disadvantages of experiments focusing on individuals and those focused on communities or social groups; and issues in policy application. Unfortunately, the discussion is presented within an almost exclusively economic framework.

# Part II

# Putting together a research design

# 10 Choices and combinations

This chapter and the next discuss strategies for choosing between, or combining, different types of study and other general considerations in research design, such as the discrepancies between data collection units and the units of analysis, the use of focused sampling, and the need to cover conflicting interests in research on policy issues. The emphasis in this chapter is on decisions arising within single projects – such as choosing between alternative designs, and multiple replications of the same study. The emphasis in Chapter 11 is on the design of research programmes that combine different types of study into an integrated whole, and related topics – such as triangulation in research design, and the problems of multi-disciplinary research. The dividing line between the two chapters is somewhat arbitrary, because similar issues arise in the design of single projects and research programmes, so they should be read together. Chapter 12 considers some of the practical aspects of research design that can be crucial for translating the initial blueprint into a feasible and successful project.

The first rule for designing a project or research programme is to start at the beginning. Attempts to hurry things forward by skimping on the groundwork will always produce a mess. The first job of thinking the design through, sorting out options and their relative merits, deciding whether choices must be made or that two or more logically linked studies can be combined, doing preparatory work with available data-sets or statistics, and reviewing the literature cannot be hurried or completed later on. The beginning takes a long time, and necessarily so. Too often research proposals are rejected or referred back for further development because the initial design work is self-evidently incomplete, producing a confused proposal with ambiguous or incompatible objectives, or one that unknowingly duplicates existing studies.

We are concerned here with choices between *types of study*, not with choices between the data collection techniques and methods that go into any single study. For example, some type of interview survey may be used in its own right, or it may be an element of a case study or of an experimental social research project. Each of these three research designs will have differing objectives, and the specific proposals for the interview survey will differ accordingly, with reference to the type of sample (if any), the breadth or narrowness of the sampling frame or universe to be covered, and the nature and purpose of the data to be collected from the interviews. To say that an interview survey will be carried out does not, of itself, provide much information on the research design and the study's objectives.

A good research design is clear both about what can, and what cannot, be tackled by a project. Even research programmes have to omit some aspects of the issue, or some sub-groups, and such omissions will be even more significant in single projects. Perhaps the most common mistake in research design is the overambitious small study that lacks a clear focus and produces patchy output. It is better to have a first study that does one thing well and provides a good foundation on which to build further studies in a logical fashion if the initial project proves fruitful.

It is as well to be clear about whether the research design is exploratory, descriptive, or is intended to address causal processes. Because of the emphasis on tests and proof of causality in social science methodology textbooks, there is a tendency to regard non-experimental types of research as less prestigious, to overlook their particular merits and hence, perhaps, to oversell essentially descriptive studies as testing causal explanations. As Part I has shown, most studies can be used to elucidate causal processes as well as providing descriptive data, but the relative emphasis differs. Case studies, for example, might be designed as rigorous tests of a thesis or to provide descriptive accounts of representative examples.

These points apply equally to what can be termed *opportunistic research projects*, which seek to take advantage of some chance event or special opportunity that arises: access to an institution, group or event that is normally closed to outsiders; a naturally occurring social experiment; or a rare opportunity to study a deviant case; and so on. In such cases there can be pressures of time that tempt one to make the case for the project primarily with reference to the opportunity offered, instead of the use one proposes to make of it. But without the latter the opportunity will be wasted anyway, whether or not a study of some sort is done. Badly designed research can become a hostage to fortune, and this is rather more likely with opportunistic research, because the events, institutions or groups in question are more likely to have a high visibility. In the long term, it can damage public support for social research in terms of reducing access, co-operation and even funding.

## Student dissertations and theses

Most people confront research design issues for the first time for a student dissertation or thesis, and they are amazed at how long it can take. The only way to avoid the problem is to become a research worker within a research programme, where the programme directors can identify one or more specific blocks of work that are sufficiently self-contained to provide the basis for a dissertation or thesis. This arrangement has many advantages: good supervision is virtually guaranteed, because the programme directors have an interest in the successful completion of all elements of the research programme; practical problems will already have been sorted out by others, so that your energies can be concentrated on the research itself; there will be a ready-made group of colleagues with whom to discuss interesting or puzzling results as they emerge; and working in a well-organised research team can be more enjoyable than working entirely alone, unless one is already accustomed to solitude. There are also drawbacks, however: the thesis subject matter and research methods will already be fixed, and there will often be little or no scope for developing or pursuing new ideas as the work progresses. People differ greatly in how they react to this situation. Some people become interested in almost any subject after one or two weeks' work on it. Others can feel constrained by working within a research programme that has already been decided. Students who are doing their own independent study have more freedom but few resources.

The short timescales imposed on a dissertation or thesis mean that costs, time and feasibility are the overriding factors in the choice of design and subject. The requirement to complete the project successfully within the permitted time means that practical considerations always take precedence over theoretical issues or the search for innovation. The most important characteristic of the research design for a thesis is that it must be feasible, with no hidden or unknown problems that might prevent completion on time. All other considerations are secondary. In particular, there should be no major changes of direction, or methods, during the project. New ideas, new theories, new interests that are stimulated by the research process must be kept aside for future projects, *after* the thesis is finished and examined. This is not, in practice, an unusual situation. Researchers often find that by the time they are three-quarters of the way through a project they have lost interest in it or have changed their perspective so much that they are already looking ahead to the *next* study.

One of the best approaches to choosing a thesis topic is to build on any special knowledge or opportunities that one already has. Most people overlook their existing assets and advantages, but using them gives a project a quick start and increases the chances of eventual success. Contacts through family or friends can give access to research settings or social groups that are not readily accessible to most researchers. A student from one country who is attending university in another country can take advantage of trips home to do a study that would be prohibitively expensive for anyone else. Even cross-national comparative studies are a possibility, if the new data collected 'at home' are compared systematically with existing research results for another country. Someone who has an adequate knowledge of several languages can do a cross-national comparative study based on literature reviews or content analyses. Many of the best student theses consist of opportunistic research projects, exploiting an existing advantage. However, the most common problem encountered is the need to trade down from an initial research design that was too ambitious to something less costly in time and effort and/or less complex in its substantive focus.

## Trading down to a cheaper design

Sometimes the reaction to a research proposal is one of dismay at the costs and timetable involved. This cost-sensitive reaction can overwhelm any consideration of the substantive value of the research design, of whether it represents value for money, addresses the theoretical or policy issues in question, and represents a feasible design in terms of the staff resources, access problems and other factors that have to be taken into account. The cost-sensitive reaction inevitably becomes more common and carries more weight at times when there is strong competition for scarce research funds. The problem probably arises most often in relation to proposals involving surveys, partly because interview surveys are not cheap and partly because they are a popular choice owing to their many uses – in longitudinal studies and experimental social research as well as national studies. The usual reaction to this problem is to reduce costs by having smaller sample sizes, more clustered or narrowly defined samples, shorter questionnaires or minimal analysis of the results. Some local government surveys have recruited interviewers within a job creation scheme in order to get public funds to subsidise the fieldwork – with the result that young, untrained and inexperienced interviewers obtained poor-quality data. In the academic community, it is not uncommon to use inexperienced students as cheap fieldwork staff (Payne, 1979); this provides the students with valuable research training but can damage the quality of the research. Roth (1966) provides a salutary exposé of the commitment that can be expected from students and temporary research assistants hired by academics, who, as Osterman (1982: 354–5) points out, treat them as secondary workers. Attempts to trim costs can result in data not worth having.

It is often preferable to trade down to a different and cheaper type of study. The alternatives to surveys tend to be overlooked by those 'set' in the survey mould by the political attractions of sample surveys, the widespread availability of survey agencies and perhaps also the greater research design effort and thought required by alternatives that are cheaper in financial terms.

Trading down to a cheaper design – such as qualitative research, short case studies, research analysis of administrative records, or secondary analysis of existing data – needs to be done explicitly and with a clear statement of what is lost, and gained, in the process. In terms of the original objectives, there will be losses, so that one needs to state which objectives are curtailed or omitted entirely. But a good-quality cheaper alternative will have compensating strengths – whereas an inadequate interview survey may be useless. A typical example is the survey carried out by a cheap contractor that obtains a response rate of 50% or less (for example, Colledge and Bartholomew, 1980; King and Murray, 1996), so that there is little confidence in the results.

This is an area where research design skills are highlighted, for survey agencies cannot be expected to advise on the choice of *alternatives* to surveys, although some will readily do so (Harrop, 1980). The possible exception is qualitative research, which many survey agencies also offer, though usually only as exploratory work for a sample survey rather than as a substantive alternative offering different strengths. The approach in the second case is quite different, and survey agencies that have used qualitative research only to assist the development of a survey questionnaire will normally be unsuited for qualitative research used as a substantive alternative in its own right. This points up one of the main sources of resistance to the idea of trading down to a cheaper design: it frequently requires a change of research agency as well, or a research team with different interests and expertise.

On the other hand, the tasks of developing an alternative research design, completing preparatory work (for example, to identify suitable datasets for secondary analysis, or to locate appropriate case studies) and identifying an alternative research team take time and effort. In some cases, one has to balance the reduction in costs against the inevitable delays in the start-up date. If there is a premium on early results, the more expensive design may in practice be the more efficient option.

Trading down to case studies involves forcing oneself, or the client, to define more precisely the most important questions and issues to be addressed, because these determine the selection of appropriate cases or sites. If local case studies have to be used as a substitute for a national survey, at least two or three sites should be chosen in order to provide clear contrasts on the variables of interest (Sudman, 1976: 25–47).

Trading down to secondary analysis or to research analyses of administrative records means being constrained by the depth of information in existing data sources. The information may not be of very recent vintage, but the potential for generalising will usually be greater than with qualitative research and case studies.

What is gained in each case is the compensating strengths of each type of study outlined in Part I, which should be exploited to the full if they are to be treated as genuine alternatives rather than poor *substitutes* for a new interview survey, even if this means extending the study into somewhat different areas from those covered by the original proposal.

Sometimes the savings from trading down to a simpler design can be dramatic. One reason for the rarity of true longitudinal studies is their expense; *ad hoc* surveys that collect retrospective data can, if sufficient care is taken, provide good substitutes at far less cost (in time as well as money), at least for some topics.

## Trading up to a more complex design

Trading down may be the more common experience, but one should be equally prepared to take advantage of those fortunate occasions when the research topic strikes a chord with research sponsors and the option arises of trading up to a more complex design, or of combining two or more studies to achieve a more rounded design.

The option of trading up sometimes emerges in the form of wholly negative reactions to a research proposal, criticising it for failing to build on and extend existing studies. The previous research in question may be unknown to the research proposer because it was little publicised or, more often, because it was done within another disciplinary framework. But the key point here is the implicit invitation to upgrade the proposal to something more substantial, so long as it builds on the previous work and addresses new questions. This may involve a major change of focus after assimilating the literature that was overlooked.

In other cases it is the researcher who points out that a large body of evidence from surveys, case studies and qualitative research provides the basis for a more ambitious research design than was suggested in a research specification, and makes a convincing case for a more complex research design. For example, the Policy Studies Institute's design for a longitudinal study of the unemployed was accepted by the British Manpower Services Commission despite the fact that the original specification had been for a single-time cross-sectional survey. The case was made by showing how one could build on the numerous other surveys and case studies to move on to a more sophisticated cohort study design, in order to address the key issues and questions more sharply and reliably. By the time it was completed, the longitudinal study of a cohort of 4,000 unemployed people cost over £250,000 in its day, with PSI's original design for three interview sweeps extended to include fourth and fifth follow-up interviews of the cohort over a period of 30 months in 1980–2 (Daniel, 1986).

An even more dramatic example of trading up is the NLS project described in Chapter 8. The US Department of Labor originally approached Professor Parnes in the early 1960s with a request for a longitudinal study of declining rates of labour force participation among middle-aged men. Parnes convinced the Labor Department that the study should have a much broader scope while focusing on the transition to retirement. The eventual outcome was four separate panels that each ran for 15 years over the period 1966–83, with a second youth panel started in 1979. The NLS project cost over $25 million in its day, but proved one of the most ambitious and successful longitudinal designs, both for policy purposes and for theoretical research.

## Simultaneous replication

The replication of previous studies is essential for the cumulative development of social science knowledge – that is, empirically grounded knowledge as distinct from untested theoretical speculation. Replication of previous studies is relatively common in certain social sciences such as economics and psychology, but is relatively rare in sociology, where it carries low status (Denzin, 1978a: 40). In policy research, where the emphasis is on producing robust results and generalisations with broad application, the idea of replication, and even of simultaneous replication, is well accepted.

In its simplest form, *replication* involves doing the same study a second (or third, or fourth) time to re-test the same hypotheses, or to answer the same questions, in the same way. The setting, or sample, may be chosen to be exactly the same, or with one factor altered or changed in order to re-assess the relative importance of that particular factor in the overall results, or to test the generalisability of the conclusions across a variety of similar situations.

*Simultaneous replication* involves doing the same study two (or more) times simultaneously, either in the same contexts or in contexts carefully selected for their known variation on a relevant key factor or set of interrelated factors. Simultaneous replication is superior to simple replication because time, and all the time-related contextual and situational variables, are held constant.

One straightforward type of replication is to re-analyse research data held in archives in order to re-assess the conclusions presented in the original research reports – either because these were regarded as controversial, or because new techniques of analysis have subsequently been developed that permit more rigorous re-assessment or fuller analysis of significant early studies. Given the problems noted in Chapter 4 with data obtained from administrative records, studies based on official statistics are even more likely to be replicated in order to assess whether and how the results are affected by problems of definition and classification, as well as the particular techniques of analysis, the time periods and countries chosen, and the addition of relevant variables from other sources.

Since Durkeim's classic study of suicide carried out in the late nineteenth century, there have been continuing efforts to replicate and extend his analysis. Quasi-experimental research on the impact of the mass media on suicides and auto fatalities carried out by Phillips has been replicated to different locations in the United States, but has also been independently replicated using data for the Netherlands (see Phillips, 1983: 560). Another replication using USA suicide data was carried out more recently by Wasserman (1984). The replication used similar, updated, data on suicides, but applied a different method of analysis (multivariate time-series analysis instead of the quasi-experimental technique) and finer discrimination in the independent variable (differentiating between celebrity and non-celebrity suicides reported in the media), and also considered the effects of an alternative explanatory variable (swings in the business cycle as reflected in the average duration of unemployment spells, chosen in preference to the unemployment rate). The results confirmed the conclusions of the previous studies, but with further refinements in the explanations offered for imitative suicides.

Replications are of special value with case studies, particularly when the original study was based on unselected examples, or examples chosen to be illustrative or broadly representative (as far as was known), or with a very small number of cases – such as Blau's 1948–9 study of interpersonal relations in government agencies (Blau, 1963). The 'choice' of the two government agencies for this case study (an employment agency and a tax office) was determined primarily by them granting him access for research, since virtually all the other organisations he approached had refused access. In the second edition of his book, Blau is obliged to note that a replication case study carried out by Cohen some 10 years later proved some of his earlier conclusions in relation to the employment agency to be wrong: he had failed to take account of labour market conditions (both in general and, more specifically, conditions prevailing in the particular labour market served by the employment agency), and certain aspects of the placement officers' behaviour were determined by their responsiveness to the demands of employers rather than by their racial prejudice towards job-seekers (Blau, 1963: 95–9). Blau himself also did another replication study in a somewhat different setting (a public welfare agency) some 10 years later, the results of which also led to significant modifications to his earlier conclusions in order to recognise the conflicting roles and responsibilities of officers in public agencies (Blau, 1963: 113–17).

Simultaneous replication of studies based on sample surveys is perhaps best illustrated by research programmes consisting of a series of surveys carried out at the same time in different countries. One example comes from the political science field. For the Comparative Elites Project, the same two surveys – of politicians and senior government bureaucrats – were repeated in seven Western democracies (the United States, Britain, France, Germany, Italy, the Netherlands and Sweden) in the period 1970–74. Designed and implemented by a core research team of half-a-dozen academics in three different American universities, there was a single central focus for all seven country studies: to identify the consistent features characteristic of administrators and parliamentary politicians and hence to develop generalisations about these roles in Western democracies. The research project was thus concerned primarily with the functions of these two key roles, the division of labour and the interaction between them, and only secondarily with comparisons of national differences. Simultaneous replication on this scale is both costly and time-consuming: the project started in 1968 and ran for well over a decade. The research was based on sample surveys, in preference to the main alternative of systematic case studies across comparable policy areas and nations (as illustrated, for example, by Heclo, 1974), on the grounds that this design provided a better basis for generalisations valid across policy domains and across nations (Rockman, 1976; Aberbach, Putnam and Rockman, 1981).

Other projects involving replication of the same study in a number of countries have focused instead on cross-national comparisons – for example, comparative research on the civic culture (Almond and Verba, 1965, 1980). But this is an altogether more ambitious design requiring a multi-level explanatory structure as well as more extensive data collections (Przeworski and Teune, 1970).

Replication also plays an important function in experimental social research, given that new policy schemes cannot be tested on a national scale. The SIME/DIME experiment described in Chapter 9 incorporated simultaneous replication of the same design in two sites, Seattle and Denver, chosen for their similarities and differences on key criteria. The TARP experiment was also carried out simultaneously with persons released in 1976 from the state prisons of Georgia and Texas, with small variations in the experimental treatment between the two sites. Furthermore, the SIME/DIME and TARP experiments had each been preceded by a series of smaller experimental studies in other sites, with progressive development and refinement of the policy schemes tested and the research methods used. Reports on the two final large-scale and comprehensive experiments refer back to the earlier experiments to consider how the results compared between treatments (Berk, Lenihan and Rossi, 1980; Robins *et al.*, 1980; Rossi, Berk and Lenihan, 1980).

For the cumulative development of a grounded body of social science theory and knowledge, replication and extension of previous studies is essential. The robust research results and generalisations required in a policy context make replication a necessity in some research designs, such as case studies, and desirable also for studies using national data. Since replication of a study frequently involves some modification to the design (be it in the methods of data collection or analysis, the location or cases selected), there is only a thin boundary line between replications and extensions of previous research. But research designs that demonstrably build on previous work are more likely to be useful not only for the development of theory but also in a policy context, where isolated studies carry relatively little weight.

## Units of analysis: time, space and social units

The choice of the units of analysis for a study can have significant implications both for the substantive content and costs. The proposed units of analysis should be stated in research proposals because they determine the appropriate data to be collected, or extracted from existing sources, and in due course the nature of the results. The choice can also affect costs and inform any discussions of trading up or down to a different type of study. The three key units of analysis for any study are the principal social unit, space and time. The last two tend to be overlooked, partly because they appear unproblematic, and partly because many disputes between theories and disciplines concern the choice of social unit and hence the relative emphasis on micro-level or macro-level analysis (Sayer, 1984: 87–9, 108–11, 132–5). In policy research, time and space are always of interest, whether they are held constant or treated as variables, and policy considerations may influence the choice of social unit.

Given the importance of fluctuations in the business cycle, economists invariably state the dates or periods to which their research relates. Academic sociologists who spend 10 years or longer analysing data from one study sometimes conceal the fact by omitting to state when the study was done (Prandy, Stewart and Blackburn, 1982). In politics, even a week can seem a long time, so any research report that claims to present policy-relevant findings must address the question of whether the results are dated or time-specific, particularly when some years have elapsed since data collection. A good example is Townsend's report, published in 1979, on a poverty survey carried out in 1968. Part of the introductory chapter was devoted to assessing evidence from national surveys and other sources in order to show that there was no reason to believe that the situation depicted by the study had changed significantly in the intervening years. In other cases changes may have occurred, but it is nevertheless possible to consider which, if any, of the findings might be affected by subsequent developments (White, 1983: 166–9; Hakim, 1985: 73–6). However, changes in legislation are likely to affect the continuing relevance of earlier studies.

Time is explicitly recognised as a variable in longitudinal studies, and is often incorporated as a variable in projects based on secondary analysis (Hyman, 1972: 209–90; Hyman, Wright and Reed, 1975). Replications of previous studies sometimes involve changing the temporal unit of analysis so as to improve the theoretical or policy relevance of the results. For example, Wasserman's replication of Phillips's study of imitative suicides discussed above used months, instead of years, as the unit of analysis. It was argued that months provided the better unit of analysis because yearly data made it impossible to examine the effects of economic business cycles, while daily data were subject to higher measurement errors; in addition, the causal processes being studied were thought to take place over a period of days, weeks or months rather than over periods as long as a year (Wasserman, 1984: 430).

Ideally, nationally representative information is needed in order for a study to draw conclusions with general application. In practice, it is often necessary to use data for selected locations, or types of area, sometimes with relatively small loss in the value of the results.

Secondary analysis may use data for selected areas as a substitute for analysis at the national level. For example, early studies of ethnic minorities in Britain tended to focus on areas with relatively high concentrations of ethnic minority groups; special tabulations from the 1961 and 1966 Population Censuses could be obtained at reasonable cost for the selected areas and supplemented by local surveys (Rose *et al.*, 1969; see also Hakim, 1982a: 69). It is only from the 1980s onwards that nationally representative surveys of ethnic minorities have been carried out (Brown, 1984), and in some cases 'national' surveys of ethnic minority groups still rely on samples taken in areas of high concentration only (Smith, 1981). This offers substantial savings in research costs, while a survey that covers all areas with significant concentrations of minority groups will give a good approximation to a fully national picture for these groups. However, this is unlikely to be the case for non-minority groups.

Case study research is often used as a traded-down substitute for a more costly national survey – for example, by carrying out case studies in a small number of selected areas or organisations. A great deal of academic research is based on small local studies as a *de facto* traded-down substitute for larger-scale research; but the obvious advantages of the case study design are not always balanced by a clear statement of the limitations of the results, in terms of representativeness and generalisability or, alternatively, a statement of the selection factors that make for a deviant, strategic, or other selective type of case study. Sometimes virtually no information is provided on the place where the study was carried out.

This weakness is most marked in studies carried out, purely for the researcher's convenience, in a single location; extending a project to cover even two or three sites dramatically increases the value of the results (Sudman, 1976: 26). Either way, there should be a statement locating the site, or sites, chosen for the study within the broader picture and identifying any distinctive characteristics (as illustrated by Goldthorpe *et al.*, 1969: 30–47). If the case study concerns a business or other organisation, national statistics will help to identify whether it was unusually large or small and other relevant characteristics that help to situate it within the broader spectrum. If the case study covers a small number of towns or communities, they can be placed in context by using small area statistics and social area classifications from recent population censuses (Hakim, 1982a: 52, 58, 75–81, 183; Dale and Marsh, 1993), supplemented by a description of the areas in question and the rationale for choosing them.

However, in social research the key decision in the design of a study is whether the main social unit of analysis is the individual, or some social group or larger collectivity such as the family, occupational group or organisation, or even some larger and more abstract entity such as a religious group, social class or industry. The choice of the social unit of analysis is easily overlooked at the design stage, when the focus tends to be on data collection rather than data analysis.

The individual is an easy choice because it is clear what a person is, and the characteristics of people included or excluded from a study (or from part of an analysis) can be described in terms of age, sex, principal activity or occupation and other standard classification variables, as well as other characteristics pertinent to the study (such as duration of unemployment, criminal record or religion). Also, the individual is clearly a significant actor, whose motivations and behaviour can be ascertained. But even if data is collected from, or about, individual persons, the main unit of analysis in social research is normally some larger social group or social unit, and the choice here needs some thought, given the wide range of options, each with substantive impli-cations. For example, one may need to choose between the family or the household as the unit of analysis, and the choice will vary according to the nature and purpose of the study. Despite its title, the Family Expenditure Survey is based on households as the main unit of data collection and analysis, because the household unit is more pertinent to the uses of the data within government. Studies of the labour market and industrial relations need to choose between the plant (or establish-ment), the organisation (or company) or the industry group as the key unit of analysis. In some cases, occupational groups (Walsh, 1982; Spenner, 1983), social classes (Goldthorpe, 1983, 1984), roles (Cole-man, 1961; Strong and Davis, 1977), events or social encounters (Bailey, 1983; Sykes and Brent, 1983; Torode, 1984; Kollock, Blumstein and Schwartz, 1985) are used as the unit of analysis. In both small-scale and large-scale studies, the choice will have implications for the type of data needed for the analysis.

For example, a study that takes roles as the unit of analysis will require information on the nature and boundaries of roles and their functions, as perceived by role-holders, and information on role-related beliefs, values and experiences, rather than extensive information on the social background, careers, religious beliefs or private interests of the incumbents (Aberbach, Putnam and Rockman, 1981: 30–3).

A study that takes organisations (or parts of them) as the unit of analysis may still collect information through interviews with individuals, but they would be asked to provide information on the organisation (rather than on themselves), on its characteristics and activities, and on processes and events taking place within it. As Namenwirth *et al.* (1981) have shown, organisational representatives are able to distinguish between their own views and those of the organisation, which may well differ in significant ways. So, for example, studies of management policy and practices towards women workers, or of industrial relations at workplace level, would require data about organisations as the main unit of analysis, and the best surveys interview multiple informants at each establishment, rather than relying on the knowledge of a single respondent (Hunt, 1975; Cully *et al.*, 1999). Similarly, Coleman (1961) collated data from many students to describe the internal social structure of the school.

It is often thought that the relevant social unit of analysis is determined by the substantive issues addressed by a study, but it is rather more likely that the choice will be determined by the researcher's disciplinary framework and theoretical perspective. Each of the social sciences is strongly oriented towards particular levels (or units) of analysis, and this readily becomes a source of disagreement or conflict within multi-disciplinary research terms. Psychologists tend to take it for granted that the focus of any research will be on individuals, their attitudes, motivations and values. Sociologists often take it as self-evident that research should focus on social structural factors (although, in practice, a great deal of sociological research consists of describing the attitudes and behaviour of individuals). Economists focus variously on trends in the economy or the labour market as a whole (in macro-economics) or on individual-level or firm-level choices and preferences (in micro-economics). In theoretical research, the choice of unit of analysis is determined largely by the disciplinary perspective brought to bear, rather than the subject-matter itself. As a result, economists and sociologists can be whole-heartedly at variance with each other on the 'appropriate' questions to address in a study, and psychologists and sociologists can regard each other's perspective as 'irrelevant' at best, if not positively misguided. These differences of perspective are highlighted when multi-disciplinary research reviews attempt to synthesise and consolidate knowledge on particular policy issues such as poverty (Covello, 1980; see also Townsend, 1979, versus Sen, 1981).

To add to the confusion (as it will appear to those, such as policy-makers, not attached to a particular disciplinary tribe) there are also disputes *within* disciplines about what is theoretically relevant or methodologically appropriate, especially in sociology, and debates sometimes become acrimonious. For example, there is a long-running debate within the field of social stratification research as to whether the individual or the family should be taken as the main unit of analysis, and whether the employment and occupations of wives should be taken into account in classifying the social class (or socio-economic status) of the family (see, for example, Rossi *et al.*, 1974; Erikson, 1984; Goldthorpe, 1984; Marshall *et al.*, 1991; Wright, 1997). Similarly, there are debates as to the value and implications of using the establishment, the organisation (or company) or the industry as the main unit of analysis in research concerned with economic or labour market segmentation theory (see, for example, Granovetter, 1984; Hodson, 1984). This list could be extended almost indefinitely in other research areas (see, for example, Blaug, 1980).

In policy research, the relevant unit of analysis is more likely to be determined by practical policy-related considerations, such as the level at which legislation becomes operative, than by the theoretical concerns of a particular discipline; and policy research often requires *multi-level analysis* rather than the choice of one main unit of analysis. Legislation and regulations concerned with income maintenance, for example, may operate at the level of the family, or the individual, or both. A good deal of equal opportunities legislation takes effect at the level of the company or organisation, or at plant or establishment level – again determining the relevant level of analysis for research. Multi-level analysis is usually necessary when research is intended to inform debate on the need for changes to existing legislation and possible options for new legislation. But this generally entails a research programme, with separate projects to assess, say, the macro-economic effects of existing policies, and the likely reactions of businesses, or of workers, to new proposals; it is rarely feasible to cover all the issues within a single multi-level project.

It should be obvious that no guidelines can be given on the choice of the social unit of analysis, and indeed that the issue provides fertile ground for arguments between social science disciplines, and between researchers and those commissioning and/or using policy research. The key point is that the issue needs to be addressed, and resolved, at the research design stage, because so much will follow from it. And the issue is likely to loom largest in multi-disciplinary research (which is discussed further in Chapter 11) and in policy research. Apart from these conclusions, two further points can be made.

Studies that establish correlations (or associations) between factors in area-based studies or time-series analysis cannot provide a basis (in the absence of other information) for drawing conclusions about any associations or causal processes at the individual level.

Studies based on *areas* as the unit of analysis can readily run into the *ecological fallacy* if one attempts to draw conclusions about the behaviour of individuals from them. The classic exposition of the ecological fallacy is given in Robinson (1950). For example, particular areas can have simultaneously high (or low) levels of crime and unemployment without there necessarily being any causal link between unemployment and crime at the individual level, because people with high rates of unemployment and people who engage in crime may happen both to be concentrated in the same residential areas. So if one is really interested in establishing causal links at the level of the individual, then area-based studies are the wrong way to go about it, although they are perfectly valid if the objective is rather to establish the simultaneous occurrence of particular social problems within cities or other areas (such as police districts).

The longitudinal research and time-series analysis counterparts to the ecological fallacy are rather less well recognised. Establishing an association between two factors (such as crime and unemployment) in a time-series analysis does not provide a basis, in the absence of other information, for drawing conclusions about the existence of a direct association at the individual level. Again, information on trends at the macro-level may be of interest in its own right, for example to predict that an increase in unemployment will normally entail an increase in crime, even if the underlying causal mechanisms are not precisely known.

The fact that individuals move (over time) between statuses, families, jobs, cities, and so forth does not mean that one can conclude that these statuses and social units are themselves unstable or ambiguous, and hence useless, analytical concepts. For example, marriage, unemployment and occupations do not lose their credibility or interest as categories for social research just because people move in and out of them. Similarly, social classes and other abstract analytical concepts do not cease to have utility purely because individual families move in and out of them in the course of upward or downward social mobility.

One reason for the sample survey being a particularly popular choice of study is that it provides the basis for a wide choice of units of analysis, and even for multi-level analysis. Surveys necessarily obtain data from individuals, but the data can be about the individual respondents themselves, their families, the companies or organisations they work in, the political groups they belong to, and so on. Contextual data on these broader social units can also be obtained from other sources and merged with the data from interview surveys to provide a broader database for research on schools (Rutter *et al.*, 1979), companies (Leggatt, 1974), political parties (Husbands, 1983) or any other larger social unit of interest. Ecological data (from population census and other statistics for local areas) can be added in for area-based analyses of survey microdata (Parcel and Mueller, 1983b; Smith, 1983a: 26–8, 34–54; White, 1983: 74–7; Joshi, 1984; Hakim, 1985: 304, 84; Hough and Mayhew, 1985: 35–9, 95–7). Time-series data can be merged with survey data providing work history information for individuals in order to study the effects of economic cycles on the labour market behaviour of age cohorts over time (Dex, 1984a). The variations seem almost endless, and sample surveys certainly offer a wider range of options for analysis than do many other types of study. It is one of the key characteristics of the survey, making it the most multi-purpose type of research design.

# 11 Research programmes

The key feature of a research programme is that it attempts to provide conclusive answers to a significant issue, or a set of closely interconnected questions, rather than one small piece of the jigsaw puzzle fitted into place. When completed, it should provide a significant addition to knowledge and understanding of the topic – a watershed or milestone. A successful research programme constitutes a major step forward at the very least, and may potentially completely re-shape the definition of the issue and public understanding of it. A research programme involves great expectations and hence a great deal more thought and care in its design (but not necessarily more money) than a single project, however large.

A research programme consists of four or more interrelated research projects that address the central topic from different angles: using different types of study, various data sources and methods and, usually, looking at it at both the 'macro' and 'micro' levels. Research programmes typically involve a number of researchers (either working together as a team or working separately with some form of central co-ordinating unit) and a variety of theoretical perspectives, so that they are more likely to be multi-disciplinary than stand-alone projects.

A properly designed research programme consists of more than a large portfolio of research projects on one topic. The defining characteristic of a research programme is an overarching strategy that integrates all the individual projects, rather than the size of the funds used, the length of the timetable or the combination of different types of study. Research programmes tend to cost more than the average single project, but there are cases of single national surveys that cost as much as several research programmes put together – such as the fourth sweep of the NCDS cohort study (see Chapter 8), which was based on an interview survey carried out in 1981 and cost £1.8 million in its day, spread over five years. Research programmes tend to run for a longer period than the average single project, but of course longitudinal and cohort studies can run for 30 years or longer, easily dwarfing the timescale required for a research programme. Research programmes typically use a variety of different studies, but then again research programmes in economics rely almost exclusively on secondary analysis of data collected by other people. Research programmes generally involve a number of research workers and may even develop into permanent research units, but then again individual scholars develop research programmes by their single-minded attention to a particular topic over their career.

Research programmes feature prominently in the research portfolios of central government departments – in some cases by funding research units (a particularly common approach within the British Departments of Health and Social Security, as illustrated by the Social Policy Research Unit at York University) and in other cases by carrying out their own programme of research on particular policy issues over a period of time. For example, Clarke and Cornish (1983) have described the British Home Office's research programme on the prevention and control of crime as it developed through two stages, each dominated by a particular theoretical framework, over a period of 25 years. Some academic social scientists have their own personal research programme in that they pursue one theme systematically over many years – for example, Brown's work on the social origins of depression (Brown and Harris, 1978; Brown, 1993; Nazroo, Edwards and Brown, 1997) or Himmelweit's work on the development of political orientations (Himmelweit *et al.*, 1981). Government-appointed commissions and committees of inquiry are more likely to rely on existing research evidence than to initiate new work (Komarovsky, 1975; Bulmer, 1980), but some have carried out substantial research programmes, such as the British Royal Commission on the Distribution of Income and Wealth, which produced a large number of research reports between 1974 and 1979, or the Committee of Inquiry on contract labour in the construction industry (Phelps Brown, 1968a, 1968b). Research institutes are well placed to design and co-ordinate research programmes – as illustrated by the substantial programme of research on the youth labour market carried out by the National Bureau of Economic Research in the USA (Freeman and Wise, 1982) and by the Policy Studies Institute's research programme on relations between the police and the public in Britain (Small, 1983; Smith, 1983a, 1983b; Smith and Gray, 1983).

Occasionally, all research projects in a programme are carried out by a single team – as illustrated by Drake's research programme on the single homeless carried out in the late 1970s for the Department of the Environment, which included an interview survey, qualitative research (both depth interviews and group discussions), case studies (based on non-participant observation) of centres for the homeless, and analysis of the administrative records of centres dealing with the homeless (Drake, O'Brien and Biebuyck, 1981). In other cases there is a central unit (a person or team) that designs and manages the research programme but contracts out all or some of the projects to researchers with special expertise and/or different disciplinary perspectives, as illustrated by a research programme on homeworking conducted by the Department of Employment (Hakim, 1985, 1987).

Some research programmes address long-standing issues, being prompted by the availability of new datasets – such as the ESRC-funded research programme on social exclusion initiated in 1998 at the London School of Economics. In other cases the impetus comes from the political arena, pressure groups and parliamentary debates producing a level of public concern sufficient for the necessary information to be created from new research – as illustrated by the Department of Employment's research programme on homeworking (Hakim, 1987), or the inquiry on contract labour that was stimulated by major stoppages of work on important public building sites in the 1960s (Phelps Brown, 1968a, 1968b).

In short, research programmes come in all shapes and sizes, costing trivial amounts or hugely expensive sums, lasting the working life of an academic or completed in a few years, involving major new data collections or systematic secondary analysis of existing data; and they may be carried out by virtually any organisation.

## Strategies for research programmes

Research programmes require an extra, higher order, layer of design work to ensure that the individual projects in a programme mesh together into an integrated whole. In contrast with the multi-method case study – in which data is obtained by a variety of means (surveys, observation, analysis of documents and records) but always relating to the same *specific* community, groups, activities or events – the links between projects in a programme will be at the *logical* and *conceptual* level. The design of programmes is thus substantively different from the design of individual studies. But the extra work is essential if the research programme is to be more than a suite of projects running in parallel.

As noted in Chapter 10, simultaneous replication provides one strategy for a research programme. Numerous replications of broadly the same type of study are carried out in different settings or locations, each study done by a separate research team. The settings for each project are chosen to offer both similarities and differences, so that the results as a whole allow controlled comparisons and contrasts in cross-site analysis.

One example is the International Social Survey Programme (see Chapter 7), which carries out social attitude surveys in several OECD countries (later extended to over 30 countries globally) using the same questionnaire, addressing a different topic each year of the survey.

Another variation, more common in economic research, is for a series of secondary analysis studies to be carried out by different teams, using different data sources and techniques of analysis, but all addressing the same topic. One example is the NBER research programme on youth unemployment noted above. The studies used NLS data, CPS gross flows data, the 1970 Census 1% Public Use Sample and other sources to assess the relationship between youth unemployment and minimum wages, labour turnover, family circumstances, geographical and temporal variations in the labour market (Freeman and Wise, 1982). Another example is the large programme of research on the minimum wage carried out in the late 1970s (see Chapter 9), which Eccles and Freeman (1982) criticise for being under-designed.

Multiple replication offers the simplest, and probably the weakest, strategy for a research programme. One weakness is that the design does not incorporate both intensive studies (at the micro-level) and extensive research (at the macro-level). But it is readily adopted for research programmes within a single discipline, or where time is short.

Other more complex strategies are possible. The two key factors of the logical relationship between the component parts, and hence the way the component studies are combined into a particular time sequence, suggest at least four other strategies for a research programme.

One approach is to carry out several small studies that provide the foundation for the design and analysis of a final, large study. The foundation studies are carried out before the main study, and may be characterised as exploratory studies. But they also provide substantive information at the micro-level that extends the main study results. The main study is the largest or most important element of the research programme, such as a national survey. This strategy is most useful for 'green field' topics where there is little or no previous research on which to build.

One example of this strategy is the research programme on modern and traditional homeworking carried out in Britain in the early 1980s:

five initial projects used a variety of research designs (qualitative research, case studies, analysis of data from administrative records, secondary analysis of survey data) to explore particular issues and aspects of homeworking in some detail, as well as providing the methodological groundwork for a more comprehensive national survey. In this case the main study consisted of not one but two national surveys – a survey of employers and a survey of homeworkers – so as to obtain a rounded perspective from both sides of the employment relationship. In the jargon of economists, the two surveys addressed the demand-side issues and the supply-side issues respectively. From the perspective of sociology, the two surveys address the structural factors and perspectives that each of the parties brings to the employment relationship. By combining small in-depth studies with nationally representative surveys, the research programme integrated micro-level and macro-level perspectives. All the component projects were interconnected, in that all key questions were addressed by at least two projects within the programme – a foundation study and a national survey (Hakim, 1985, 1987; see also Hakim, 1998: 178–220).

Another strategy consists of a centrepiece study, usually a national survey, which is linked to a variety of other studies carried out at roughly the same time. This strategy is suitable for topics where there is already a good deal of research information and well-developed theoretical perspectives. Each of the linked projects is a substantive study in its own right, which gains from the connection to the central survey.

One example of this strategy is the research programme on women's labour force participation carried out by the British Department of Employment in the 1980s. The centrepiece was a national survey of women of working age and a sub-sample of their husbands (Martin and Roberts, 1984a, 1984b), as described in Chapter 6. Several other studies were linked with it, either logically (in terms of the questions addressed) or more directly (by re-interviewing selected sub-groups of the main survey). The linked studies included case studies (Martin and Wallace, 1985; Craig *et al.*, 1985), secondary analysis projects extending the main survey report by more detailed analysis of selected issues (Dex, 1984a; Joshi, 1984), and qualitative research extending the survey results on female unemployment by depth interviews with selected sub-groups eight months later (Cragg and Dawson, 1984).

Some research programmes do not have a main study: all the projects contribute in roughly equal weight to the overall picture. This is one of the most elegant designs, with counterbalancing studies at the micro-level and the macro-level, and from both 'sides' of an issue. This strategy is appropriate for topics where there are well-defined contested issues, and when all the projects can be carried out together in a short period of time.

One example is the Policy Studies Institute's research programme on relations between the police and the public, initiated at a time when serious riots, increasing racialist attacks and other outbreaks of public disorder were bringing the police into confrontation with ethnic minority groups in London, and police–community relations were the subject of general debate. The research programme consisted of a survey of police officers and a case study of the police force, a survey of the general public (with over-sampling of ethnic minorities) and a case study of young black people, and was completed within four years 1980–3 (see Chapter 6). Although each study was reported in a separate volume, the four volumes were published simultaneously on completion of the research programme, with a single introduction to the set and a single concluding chapter. Throughout the report it is emphasised that each study constitutes only one part of the picture and that conclusions can properly be drawn only from the research programme as a whole (Small, 1983; Smith, 1983a, 1983b; Smith and Gray, 1983).

All the above strategies concern research programmes completed within about six years with a specific block of funding. The alternative is a series of studies carried out over an extended period of time, sometimes without any main project, even without funding, but with a central theme connecting all the projects. The central thread is clear when the research programme is centred on a longitudinal or cohort study, as illustrated by the National Children's Bureau research programme on child development, which used the NCDS cohort study as the central element (Fogelman, 1983). The central thread is less visible when it is a theory or model that is being developed and refined through a succession of studies.

This strategy underlies the personal research programmes of individual academics who pursue a selected theoretical area, or substantive topic, for many years. Inevitably the research design is revised, developed and progressively re-formulated over time – but at any point in time there is a coherent strategy for future work (Berger and Zelditch, 1993). Without such a plan the research work is in danger of shooting off on all sorts of tangents with opportunistic studies that go nowhere in particular.

One example is a research programme on the relationship between work conditions (especially occupational self-direction and job complexity), social stratification and psychological functioning pursued by Kohn and Schooler (1983) for over 25 years with studies in the USA, Poland and Japan (Slomczynski, Miller and Kohn, 1981; Naoi and

Schooler, 1985). At various stages of his research on the self-fulfilling prophecy, pursued for over 25 years, Rosenthal used literature reviews, meta-analysis, a series of laboratory experiments and experiments in real-life settings (Rosenthal, 1976; Rosenthal and Jacobson, 1968). Townsend's research on poverty was pursued through literature reviews, secondary analysis of data from regular surveys, case studies and a major survey (Abel-Smith and Townsend, 1965; Norris, 1978; Townsend, 1979).

Policy research examples are less easily identifiable. Until Clarke and Cornish revealed the research strategy underlying a series of studies spanning 25 years, the Home Office Research Unit had been criticised for carrying out research on a piecemeal basis with no reference to theoretical developments in criminology (Clarke and Cornish, 1983: 3–54).

## Focused sampling

The underlying logic (or strategy) of a research programme may remain hidden when extensive use is made of what Glaser and Strauss (1967) termed *theoretical sampling*, but is more appropriately termed *focused sampling*, in order to avoid the implicit assumption that research invariably addresses theoretical issues alone.

Focused sampling is the *selective* study of particular persons, groups or institutions, or of particular relationships, processes or interactions that are expected to offer especially illuminating examples, or to provide especially good tests for propositions of a broad nature. Strategic, deviant and critical test case studies offer the best examples of focused sampling for the study of processes and interactions. But focused sampling can also be applied to other types of study. Qualitative research can be focused selectively on particular persons or social groups of special interest for the research topic in question. Analyses of administrative records and secondary analysis of existing research datasets can also focus selectively on particular sub-groups or processes within the broader datasource. It is worth noting that focused sampling is the direct opposite of the usual procedure in designing survey samples and/or of creating data subsets for secondary analysis, in which certain 'outlier' cases or categories, and those with large amounts of missing data, are *excluded* from the sample and/or analysis; in the case of focused sampling the emphasis switches instead to giving specific reasons why particular cases are *selected for inclusion* in the study or analysis, and they may well be outlier or deviant cases.

Formulating projects that are logically interlinked within a research programme often leads to the use of focused sampling for studies that may be of little interest as stand-alone projects outside the context of the research programme as a whole. When the focus of a special project is a particular sub-group within the larger group being studied, the logical links between the two studies are visible and easy to explain – for example to research funders. The logical links between projects are less visible when a subsidiary project based on focused sampling deals with relationships, processes or interactions between selected factors, and generally require more care and effort to explain.

One illustration of focused sampling is to extend and complement a national survey with in-depth interviewing of selected sub-groups within the national sample, or to carry out case study research with selected types of cases covered by a broader study. Cases may be selected for more intensive study with reference to their characteristics (for example, people who have, against the odds, been successful in terms of educational attainment and occupational achievement, or people exhibiting status inconsistency), or with reference to some process or relationship exhibited (for example, institutions that exhibit high degrees of conflict, or cases with a close association between two factors that are usually unrelated). This type of focused sampling offers the benefits of both worlds – generalisability from the national survey which identifies the incidence of such cases and the more detailed information from the intensive study.

One example is a study that used depth interviews to obtain fuller information on non-working women who might be classified as unemployed on three different criteria: they were formally registered as unemployed with a local government office, were actively seeking employment, or intended to return to work within six months. The depth interviews were carried out eight months after the structured interview for the national survey, thus allowing the women's behaviour and experiences in the intervening period to be explored, and any effects on their self-classification as unemployed or economically inactive to be examined (Cragg and Dawson, 1984). Another example is a small project consisting of case studies of 22 families with an unemployed breadwinner husband, a dependent wife and children, which was used to provide fuller information on the social and health consequences of unemployment than could be obtained in the main, national, survey of families of this type (Fagin and Little, 1984). A third example is Pilling's (1990) study of young people who became successful despite growing up in homes that were socially and economically deprived. High achievers were contrasted with low achievers from poor families, both groups being identified within the 1958 NCDS cohort study.

The particular conjunction of factors needed to test some

proposition, or to gain access to some especially relevant social group for a study based on focused sampling, does not necessarily come to hand 'on demand', so research projects of this nature are often opportunistic.

## Selection effects

Focused sampling involves *knowing and intentional* selectivity. Unfortunately, some studies that intend to cover representative samples actually cover restricted samples, or overlook selection effects within the sample, and thus produce biased results. Sample selection bias and selection effects occur when research is based on a non-random subset of a wider population, typically because information is only available for cases that exceed a certain threshold. The systematic exclusion of cases with particular characteristics means that the validity of findings is in doubt. One example is studies of women's wages. One can observe wages only for women who are employed, and working women tend to be better-educated and to have stronger work commitment than women who choose not to work (Hakim, 1996: 129). Although techniques have been developed for the diagnosis of and correction for sample selection bias in quantitive studies, it cannot in practice be eliminated from research results (Berk, 1983; Lieberson, 1985; Stolzenberg and Relles, 1997).

One illustration is a study that concluded that the key determinant of good health was the power to control your own work and other aspects of your life. This conclusion was drawn from the Whitehall Study, which collected health and lifestyle information from a sample of 17,000 government employees over 30 years. People in the highest occupational grades had consistently lower morbidity and mortality rates (Marmot and Wilkinson, 1999: 17, 105–31, 166–9). Unfortunately, the study overlooked the fact that meritocratic bureaucracies select for promotion those people with the highest mental and physical health as well as the highest intellectual, social and organisational skills, who are thus able to deliver the best performance on the job. In a meritocracy, good health, like ability, is a contributory cause of promotion to high-grade posts rather than a consequence of occupying such jobs. Despite its large and representative sample, the results of the Whitehall Study were biased by selection effects.

## Multiple triangulation

Since research programmes involve multiple studies, they provide a ready context for combining different types of study in order to obtain the particular strengths each offers. Given the assessments in Part I of the respective strengths and weaknesses of each type of study, and the potential for linking them, the idea of combining different studies within a research programme would seem no more than common sense. It is already widespread practice in policy research and market research, which are both areas with pressures for valid, reliable and robust conclusions to provide a firm basis for decisions, on legislation or the marketing strategy to be adopted. The idea remains sufficiently novel in academic social science circles to stimulate entire books arguing the case for this approach, which has been given the unhappy term of *methodological triangulation* (Campbell and Fiske, 1959; Webb *et al.*, 1966; Smith, 1975; Denzin, 1978a, 1978b; McGrath, Martin and Kulka, 1982).

Denzin's two books provide the most comprehensive, indeed laborious, argument for the use of multiple studies. But he is concerned solely with sociological research, and identifies only five distinct types of research method or strategy: the experiment, the social survey, participant observation (the field method), the comparative life history method, and unobtrusive measures. So his presentation does not correspond to the perspective offered here – which encompasses all social science research and identifies eight distinct types of research *design* (rather than methods) – and it is also muddled in places. After reviewing the strengths and limitations of his five methods, Denzin goes on to consider very briefly five types of triangulation: methodological triangulation, data triangulation, investigator triangulation, theoretical triangulation and multiple triangulation (Denzin, 1978a: 291–307; Denzin, 1978b: 339–80).

Denzin's concept of *data triangulation* is perhaps the most muddled in that it encompasses focused sampling (described above), the use of case studies and replications of the same study in different settings, and – most importantly – introduces the idea that research should be carried out at both the micro-level (to cover interpersonal interactions in small group settings) and the macro-level (to cover social structural explanations). As noted in Part I, different types of study function best at different levels, so Denzin's point about data triangulation is perhaps no more than a reiteration of the case for combining different studies. But it also underlines the point that the design of a research programme is that much more solid if one can ensure that individual projects are selected with a view to ensuring that both micro-level and macro-level perspectives are covered – which means in practice that both large-scale or national data will be required as well as more focused and intensive studies.

Denzin is quite clear about the superiority of *investigator triangulation* over studies by one person (or one person and a research assistant). The use of multiple researchers is recommended as the only way of getting round the potential bias that comes from relying on a single researcher. The use of multiple researchers or research teams is virtually inevitable in research programmes, and should be regarded as one of their strengths, despite the problems of research organisation and management that are thereby created.

Relying heavily on Westie (1957), Denzin also recommends the use of *theoretical triangulation* on the grounds that it facilitates the development of integrated sociological theory, but he admits its relative rarity – perhaps because it entails research programmes rather than isolated projects. However, he refuses to go so far as commending the even greater benefits for the development of social science theory of multi-disciplinary research.

Finally, Denzin recommends *multiple triangulation*: multiple researchers, multiple studies, multiple sources of data and multiple theoretical perspectives all simultaneously combined. The idea is not developed, but logically must entail a research programme. Denzin commends it as 'the most refined goal any investigation can achieve' (Denzin, 1978a: 304). It is well illustrated by the three policy research programmes on women's labour force participation, homeworking and police–community relations described above.

## Conflicting interests

Research programmes or projects can be designed to cover the substantively different, and sometimes conflicting, interests of groups with a direct involvement in the subject-matter of the research. A good example is a project evaluating the effects of maternity rights legislation, which was first introduced in the mid-1970s in order to reduce the disadvantage that women experienced in the labour market as a result of leaving a job to have a baby. The design consisted of not one but two surveys: information on *women's* experience of maternity rights was obtained through a nationally representative survey of mothers of new babies, half of whom had been in work before pregnancy (Daniel, 1980); and information on *employers'* experience of maternity rights legislation was obtained from a national survey of employers who had recently employed at least one woman who had a baby soon afterwards (Daniel, 1981). Even in a single project, using only one type of study, care was taken to ensure that the interests and concerns of employers and workers were both represented in the research results. This approach has been maintained in subsequent replications (Callender *et al.*, 1997; Forth *et al.*, 1997).

The need to cover the conflicting interests of all parties typically arises in the design of policy research, especially when the issues in question are the subject of some debate. This approach is accepted practice in policy research, and is applied in single projects (as illustrated by the above example) and in research programmes (as illustrated by the police–community relations research programme described earlier).

The term *stakeholders* is used to refer to the various parties who are affected by policy decisions, whose interests are at stake when changes are proposed. Some extend the definition to include anyone who has some input to the decision-making process, and recommend that interviews be conducted with all potentially influential individuals and group representatives (Majchrzak, 1984: 28–9, 36–8). The identification of stakeholder groups depends on the research topic. For example, a study of child welfare or child-battering might need to treat parents (jointly) and children as two separate interest groups, whereas studies of wife-battering or of divorce procedures and legislation might need to deal with wives and husbands as two separate interest groups. Although the general role of government is to arbitrate between and reconcile conflicting interests within society at large, particular government agencies may, in some contexts, constitute a stakeholder group – for example, the tax service has an interest in maximising the revenue it collects. Similarly, the academic community generally carries out social and other research from a disinterested position, but in the particular context of debates about changes in higher education, for example, it becomes a stakeholder group with interests to defend.

Research carried out with reference to a single stakeholder group can be regarded as partial, and in that sense biased, whether it relies on a single project or on the more rounded perspective offered by a complex research programme. (It may even extend into advocacy research, as noted in Chapter 1.) The use of multiple studies is sometimes confused and conflated with the idea of research designed to cover conflicting interests, especially in critiques of research based on a single study. The single study sometimes combines two logically distinct weaknesses: it may cover a single stakeholder group and it exhibits the limitations of the particular study design (as noted in Part I). However, case studies are distinctive in offering the potential for providing information not only on the differing, even conflicting, accounts of the various parties to an event or debate (such as a strike) but also on the complex structure of *interests* that lie beyond these perspectives. The point is illustrated by the contrast between the Workplace Industrial/Employment Relations Surveys, which provide information on both managers' and worker representatives' accounts of the employment relations climate and industrial conflict in each establishment, and Lloyd's case study of the year-long miners' strike of 1984–5 in Britain, which goes beyond the parties' accounts to give the author's analysis of the underlying conflicting interests (Daniel and Millward, 1983: 12–13, 60–4, 151–4, 214–17; Lloyd, 1985; Cully *et al.*, 1999: 245, 277).

## Multi-disciplinary research

There must be few topics suitable for research programme treatment that do not automatically entail a multi-disciplinary approach to the subject. The arguments *against* a multi-disciplinary treatment would need to be justified to avoid the obvious criticism that the research proposal was blinkered by the research designer's prejudice in favour of their own discipline, or the types of study with which they were personally most comfortable, and their ignorance of the useful contributions of other social sciences. The case for a multi-disciplinary approach in a research programme is so strong that it is almost a defining characteristic.

One might expect that multi-disciplinary research programmes would be most common in universities, where a range of social sciences is normally represented. In practice, however, multi-disciplinary research programmes are more common and more successful in non-academic organisations – in the research units of central government departments, independent research institutes and research organisations that are clearly separated from their host university institution.

In effect, multi-disciplinary research programmes are more common in policy research and the operational types of applied research, where the focus is on elucidating the substantive issue or topic rather than on the development and testing of selected theories. In addition, multi-disciplinary research seems to proceed best when it is located in organisations divorced from the competitive rivalry between disciplines and faculties that seems to characterise the university environment. Academic rivalries present serious impediments to the development of the mutual trust and respect between disciplines that is essential for multi-disciplinary research. However, Luszki suggests that some social scientists also lack the personal qualities or intellectual abilities that are essential for the team research that is typical of multi-disciplinary programmes: emotional maturity, open mindedness, humility, tolerance, flexibility, curiosity, a recognition of one's own strengths and limitations, personal and professional security, the ability to integrate relationships among many different factors and to work at both a high level of abstraction and the detailed and concrete level (Luszki, 1957:

22; Luszki, 1958). This suggests that multi-disciplinary research is not for the novice or for the researcher without a proven record, both of whom are likely to be more concerned with establishing their disciplinary (or tribal) identity and defending their 'territories' against any pressure from other disciplines or indeed from factions within their own discipline (Luszki, 1957; see also Rose, 1976: 101). But the problem is also of a more general nature in that, *in practice*, disciplines represent vested interests and scientists often give precedence to their personal ambitions and career interests over their stated goal of the development of scientific knowledge. As Gieryn (1983) points out, scientists (like Orwell's pigs in *Animal Farm*) sometimes claim that they are 'more equal', or re-define scientific work so as to serve their self-interests and to maximise their material resources, independence, autonomy and other professional benefits. Birnbaum (1981) argued that closely integrated multi-disciplinary research teams simply do not work well, as measured by their output; however, his findings in fact show almost no impact at all on output as measured by published reports and papers.

The impetus towards more integrated multi-disciplinary research comes from funding bodies and the policy research field more often than from the academic community (Cunningham, 1969; Rose, 1976: 115; Clarke and Cornish, 1983: 50–2). Policy research also contributes to the development of multi-disciplinary research within the social sciences by insisting that specialists adopt the 'plain English' that is accessible to civil servants, politicians, journalists and pressure groups alike, and hence is accessible also to other social science disciplines. The use of technical terms and disciplinary jargon is not as necessary as academics claim, especially in reports on empirical research. As Einstein pointed out, the whole of science is nothing more than a refinement of everyday thinking (Einstein, 1936: 349). The use of jargon and specialist terminology is often a technique for defending one's territory and closing out 'outsiders' from other disciplines, and it can also be used to conceal the paucity of non-trivial findings from a study. Policy research appears, in practice, to emphasise the search for explanation and full knowledge of causal processes to no lesser extent than the academic community – because the results will be used in a decision-making context where the price of mistakes can be very high.

The benefits of multi-disciplinary research are highlighted in policy research fields such as education, crime, health, the labour market, housing, leisure, fertility and family studies. In these fields, the emphasis is more readily focused on the issues and questions addressed than on the development of a particular discipline, and no single discipline has a complete monopoly of the topic to the exclusion of all others.

Arguments in favour of multi-disciplinary research are more commonly found in relation to such 'real-world' topics and issues. For example, Maital (1982) and Antonides (1991) argue that economics and social psychology should be combined in the study of taxation, tax evasion behaviour, the relationship between taxation and labour supply, fiscal policy and related matters. Earl (1983) goes further in building an alternative behavioural theory of choice that incorporates elements of psychological and sociological theory into an economic framework for analysing how people think as they make choices, giving examples of how this might be applied to price determination by firms and consumer choice. Located more directly in the policy research field, the research programme on homeworking described earlier drew on the perspectives of economics, sociology, psychology and law. Reviewing a research programme spanning 25 years, Clarke and Cornish (1983) show how theoretical frameworks from psychology and sociology were applied in research on the prevention and control of crime.

Some disciplinary combinations are already well established – such as historical sociology, political economy, social psychology, socio-legal studies, social geography, epidemiology, and social economics. The foundations for a fuller multi-disciplinary approach to research are not lacking, and some social scientists are seeking to develop a broader theoretical base for multi-disciplinary research through some combination of rational choice theory and structural theory that might span the micro/macro divide (Schelling, 1978; Himmelweit *et al.*, 1981; Banton, 1983; Hechter, 1983; Hammersley, 1984; Hakim, 1999a, 2000) or complexity theory (Byrne, 1999).

At present, however, organising multi-disciplinary research poses additional problems. One approach is to subject the same database to secondary analysis by researchers with different disciplinary or theoretical perspectives. This is easily organised as a series of separate projects by different teams, although the final task of integrating the various study results may prove difficult.

The second approach is to develop a multi-disciplinary research programme wherein each project is based within one discipline (either single disciplines or established combinations of two disciplines, such as socio-legal research or social psychology). Integrating the results in a final report is easier here, especially if each disciplinary team is allocated the type of study in which it specialises (psychologists for depth interviews, economists for secondary analysis, sociologists for survey work, and so forth).

The third approach is to create a single multi-disciplinary research team working together on a project or research programme. In this case there is the danger that the usual problems of team research will be exacerbated by the team's multi-disciplinary character. Since teams must have a lead researcher, the success or otherwise of this approach depends largely on his or her ability to incorporate all the disciplines represented, instead of favouring his or her own, whether from habit and familiarity or from bias. Basing the research on a multi-disciplinary perspective would aid this process.

## Programme organisation and management

Although we are concerned here with the *design* of research programmes, the organisation and management of a large number of studies is a more integral feature of research design than it is for individual projects. The point is made by considering a negative example. The ESRC's strategy of developing Research Initiatives on selected topics has produced substantial concentrations of new research on particular themes, but not well-designed research programmes, because the ESRC, like most national research-funding bodies, has been unable to move away from the traditional 'responsive' mode of grant-funding research projects designed by academics towards a pro-active role in the design and implementation of a research programme, even when invited by ministers to address specific issues (Berthoud, 1983). The results of such Research Initiatives have been very variable taken as a whole (see, for example, Brown and Madge, 1982; Storey, 1994), and sometimes so fragmented that no summary report was feasible, as in the case of the Social Change and Economic Life Initiative (see for example Gallie *et al.*, 1994). Another example of an underdesigned research programme is that carried out by the United States government's Minimum Wage Study Commission at a cost of $17 million, as noted in Chapter 9.

The SIME/DIME experiment (see Chapter 9) illustrates that mistakes can happen even in studies that are carefully planned and well funded, sometimes with serious consequences. Researchers, like other people, are fallible. The decision to phase out the small 20-year DIME scheme after the experiment had run for only six years was due largely to errors in the procedures for random allocation of families to experimental and control groups that were of sufficient importance to render the results useless for research purposes (Thompson, 1981). But an *unintentional* technical error in one part of a project is rather different from the failure of an entire research programme to deliver substantive results because of inadequate design and poor management. The latter is more likely to be used as concrete evidence of the intellectual poverty and organisational incompetence of the social sciences by those who wish to cut funds.

One of the key practical issues in the design of a research programme is the question of whether a single research team does all the work (as illustrated by Drake, O'Brien and Biebuyck, 1981) or whether the programme is designed in detail and centrally co-ordinated by a lead researcher who contracts out some of the projects to other researchers or research teams (as illustrated by Hakim, 1985, 1987). The second approach makes it easier to engage experienced specialists for particular projects, but it also entails more careful design and management of the subcontracted projects so as to ensure that they produce the information required, as distinct from a successful study that has little relevance to the programme as a whole.

The combination of subcontracting and focused sampling can present special problems. For example, it raises the question of whether a subcontractor should be fully informed of the underlying logic, the particular hypotheses and the questions addressed in the focused sample project (such as a case study or deviant case analysis) for which they are responsible. Much will depend on the circumstances of the case, but the question needs to be addressed; there is no automatic reason for doing so, any more than one tells the interviewing field force about the specific questions and hypotheses underlying a sample survey. There are advantages in carrying out projects with a *double-blind* test, that is, with *neither* the respondents or other participants nor the researcher working on the project being aware of the hypotheses being tested. The results carry even more weight because one has eliminated the possibility of the researcher introducing a bias in favour of or against the hypotheses in question, purely as a result of selective perception or selective interest. Double-blind procedures are a long-standing practice in medical research and well established in psychological research as well (Rosenthal, 1976: 367–400). But, apart from the *de facto* double-blind procedures in large-scale interview surveys that employ professional interviewers, they have not yet been taken up in social research generally.

Independent research institutes and other permanent non-academic research units are best placed to handle the special organisation and management requirements of large-scale research programmes. Such centres can accumulate experience in developing and implementing major programmes of research work; acquire the right mix of specialist expertise, including the range of social science disciplines needed for multi-disciplinary research and general support staff; and develop sufficient team spirit or programme loyalty to overcome many of the problems arising in *ad hoc* team research. In the United States there is a large number of such institutes, some of them specialising in policy research, such as the National Opinion Research Center in Chicago, the Institute of Social Research at the University of Michigan, the Brookings Institution in Washington, Abt Associates in Cambridge, Mathematica at Princeton, the Stanford Research Institute in California, and many others. Even excluding the commercial institutes, their histories, funding arrangements, research programmes and links with universities have varied greatly (Orlans, 1972). Equivalent institutes in Britain include the Policy Studies Institute, previously known as Political and Economic Planning (Pinder, 1981), the National Institute of Economic and Social Research, the National Centre for Social Research (formerly Social and Community Planning Research), the Tavistock Institute and the National Children's Bureau (Bulmer, Sykes and Moorhouse, 1998).

In the academic community, where teaching responsibilities and large-scale research work are not compatible, it has been necessary to create separate centres with full-time research staff to conduct research programmes, such as the Centre for Research on Ethnic Relations at the University of Warwick and the Centre for the History of Population and Social Structure at Cambridge University. The research programmes of centres such as these consist of more loosely interlinked projects than with *ad hoc* and highly focused research programmes.

## Presentation of reports

The presentation of results in published reports requires special care in the case of a research programme to ensure that the interlocking and logically interrelated individual projects are brought together at the end of the exercise. In the case of research programmes spanning a number of years, it will almost never be advantageous to postpone publication of all the reports till the end of the programme, so some thought has to be given to how results are presented and published while the programme is still in progress. These two questions need to be considered at the design stage because they can substantively affect the research work (especially report-writing). Similar issues can arise in longitudinal studies that span a number of years, and the appropriateness or otherwise of publishing early reports on the first round of interviews or equivalent data collection needs to be considered. For example, in a project that involved follow-up interviews with a sample of long-term unemployed people about 18 months after they were first interviewed, it was decided not to allow any publications reporting on the first, and most detailed, interview survey in case it affected response rates to the follow-up survey. Instead there was a single overall report published after the follow-up survey was completed (White, 1983). It is in cases like these that the benefits of using experienced and established researchers are seen: they are less likely to attempt to rush through early publications purely to serve their career at the expense of the interests of the research.

Reports on each project within a programme should offer not only an account of the individual study and its results, but also some indication of how it fits into the overall design of the research programme. The progressive publication of a series of free-standing reports on individual projects is rarely sufficient, because the purpose, value and meaning of the results, their interpretation and the conclusions to be drawn will depend on the project's specific position within the programme as a whole. This is particularly true of selective case studies and projects based on focused sampling, but it will be more generally true of any project within the programme.

One option is to publish the results of each project as a free-standing report, but with a preface, introduction or some other section that sets the study within the context of the research programme. This approach was adopted in the research programme on homeworking, with separate 'prefaces' by the lead researcher within each of the reports written by the contractors for individual projects.

Another option is for the lead researcher to be a co-author of reports on individual projects, with the function of threading in information on the design strategy, and enhancing the presentation of results, conclusions and interpretations with reference to results from other elements in the research programme. The report would thus be set firmly in the context of the research programme as a whole, and the full value of the contribution it makes would be clear. Interestingly, there are no examples of this approach, even from research programmes carried out by a single research team with no contractors (Drake, O'Brien and Biebuyck, 1981).

The publication of reports on individual projects as they are completed is usually beneficial, because it allows for feedback from a range of interested parties. This feedback can be valuable, providing comment, advice and reactions from the audience for the research results (pressure groups, politicians, government departments, or international bodies like the EU, ILO and United Nations) as well as comment from other researchers and academics. One may also get reactions from people who belong to the social groups or types of organisation covered by the research. Although these reactions may be perceived as distracting or inconvenient at the time, they will ultimately be beneficial to the research, helping to ensure that the presentation of results in a final report avoids any of the misunderstandings revealed at an earlier stage.

Research programmes were defined as providing a significant addition to knowledge or substantive re-definition of issues. It follows that they should attract a much greater volume of interest and attention than single projects – be it praise or criticism. Reactions usually commence while the research programme is still in progress, as soon as first reports are published. This should not only be foreseen by careful attention to the manner of presentation of reports, but should also be used constructively as a substantive input to the design and conduct of the research programme.

In many cases, the full value of a complex research design will become clear only when the results of the component projects are being pulled together within a single 'umbrella' final report. In a well-designed programme, this stage should yield additional findings, over and beyond those that were consciously planned; thus the whole will be more than the sum of its parts.

# 12  Organisation and funding of research

Until recently, the practical aspects of research design were under-valued. When funds for social research were relatively plentiful, the business of obtaining funding for a project (or even a programme) could be seen as a tedious chore that had to be gone through before one got down to the serious business of doing research. If poor organisation and management meant that a project failed or was never properly completed, one would simply move on to a new project with little fretting over what went wrong or why. Textbooks on research design would focus almost exclusively on the niceties of designing research to test causal hypotheses, with scarcely a glance at the practical aspects of mounting a study (Ackoff, 1953; Krausz and Miller, 1974; Bynner and Stribley, 1978; Miller, 1992). As universities came under pressure to demonstrate their outputs and productivity, the organisation, management and funding of research attracted greater attention (O'Toole, 1971; Orlans, 1973; Bernstein and Freeman, 1975; Useem, 1976; Gibbons and Gummett, 1976; Platt, 1976; Crawford and Perry, 1976; Abramson, 1978; Rossi, 1980; Kogan and Henkel, 1983; St Pierre, 1983).

The organisation and funding of social research had changed fundamentally by the start of the 21st century. The centre of gravity for the conduct of social research shifted away from universities and other teaching institutions towards institutes and centres specifically dedicated to the conduct, dissemination and (sometimes) utilisation of research, and staffed accordingly, as illustrated in Bulmer, Sykes and Moorhouse, (1998). Think tanks also became important (Kandiah and Seldon, 1996). Funding for social research now comes predominantly from government, pressure groups, service organisations and other non-academic bodies, with the foundations and other grant-funding bodies like the SSRC (USA) and ESRC (Britain) providing a diminishing proportion of the increasing total. The change is further advanced and better accepted in North America than in Britain and other European countries (see, for example, Lazarsfeld, Sewell and Wilensky, 1967; O'Toole, 1971; Lazarsfeld and Reitz, 1975; Crawford and Perry, 1976; Weiss, 1977; Rossi, 1980; Rossi and Freeman, 1999). Initially, this stimulated a defensive reaction among some academics, who sought to discredit the output from non-academic research centres, demean the value of policy research, and reiterate the academic community's monopoly rights over the conduct and control of social research (Bernstein and Freeman, 1975; see also Rossi, 1980: 889; Bulmer, 1983: 108; Clarke and Cornish, 1983: 3, 18, 50–3; Rossi and Freeman, 1999). By the 1990s, some scientists argued that the expansion of policy research had significantly changed the nature of knowledge production (Gibbons *et al.*, 1994). In addition, the shift towards dedicated research institutes, contract research, large research programmes and research initiatives has dictated greater emphasis on the organisation, costing and management of research.

Part and parcel of these trends is a more pragmatic approach to research and a recognition that the practical reality of carrying out a study is a more complex process than is admitted by the models offered in textbooks (Smelser, 1980).

Space does not permit a full review of the numerous (and frequently tedious) matters that arise under the heading of research-funding and research management. The focus here is on those practical aspects of research design that make a proposal feasible and successful rather than a piously theoretical but unworkable proposal that never gets beyond the blueprint stage. The special needs of cross-national comparative research are discussed in Chapter 14.

## Practical aspects of research design

The first, and obvious, step is to think through the practical details of carrying out the study: the timetable; the level of staffing needed; special costs (travel costs are rarely overlooked, but postage is more easily forgotten); and any specialist tasks that may need to be subcontracted such as sampling, interviewing or data-processing. This will enable one to decide whether research-funding will be needed, and its relative scale. If survey or other work will be subcontracted, outline costs must be sought.

The second task is to think through any problems that might arise on access to key informants, organisations or information. If funding needs to be sought, questions of access must be resolved before a proposal is presented to a funding body, particularly because social scientists cannot take their welcome for granted nowadays.

Perhaps the most common practical mistake in research proposals is to underestimate the budget, in time and money, required for a project. Underestimates are often attributable to inexperience, but when the funding climate for research veers towards the wintry, there is a strong temptation to err on the low side and present a shoestring budget. If the funding body is experienced enough to detect this and demand more realistic estimates, all is well; but a project that goes ahead on a shoestring budget is likely to fail unless it is treated as a 'loss leader' or unless there are other, hidden subsidies available.

Research is a messy and chaotic business even for the experienced researcher, and will be even more chaotic for the researcher with little practical experience. Research budgets that allow no room for manoeuvre, or for any mistakes, can create significant problems. In this respect, contract research has the edge on research grants. Because the funding body has a direct interest in seeing the study completed, unforeseen additional costs can be discussed, and the extra funds usually agreed, at the time when decisions need to be made. Indeed it is common for contracts for very large research projects to include a contingency fund to be used for additional work and unforeseen problems, as agreed jointly by the research contractor and the organisation commissioning the study. In contrast, it is rarely possible to go back to a grant-funding body for more money before the initial grant has been exhausted; this is often too late (research decisions will already have been taken and cannot usually be amended retrospectively) and there is rather less certainty that the case for an extension of funding might be accepted (the researcher is likely to be seen as having failed to deliver on his/her own costings for the study).

If the available funding restricts a study to a shoestring budget, one should consider trading down to a different and cheaper design that can be completed with greater assurance of success and quality within the available funds or even on a self-funding basis (see Chapter 10).

As a rule, estimates of budgets (both time and money) are better in relation to data collection and other fieldwork than in relation to data analysis and report-writing, which always take longer than expected, partly because analysis is an infinitely extendable feast. One solution is to allow for the possibility of separate and additional contracts or grants for further work on specific topics or aspects of the study, which might include methodological assessments as well as substantive analyses. However, there should be no guarantee that the original researchers will automatically get preference for any secondary analysis extension studies; indeed it is often advantageous for highly focused additional analyses to be carried out by researchers with different disciplinary approaches or specialist knowledge.

When a project of any size or significance is being undertaken, the budget should include an allowance for the final dataset to be tidied up and the necessary documentation to be produced for archive deposit. This has become a standard requirement for large and important studies, in the interests of both the researcher and the funding body. Many funders now include archive deposit as a standard requirement – in some cases at the point when an edited datafile is ready, rather than at the very end of a project, on the grounds that any data collected at public expense are in the public domain and must be available to others.

It is sometimes argued that research timetables and budgets should include an allowance for the preparation of reports for publication. The argument is more likely to succeed in projects where there is a particular need to disseminate findings to an audience beyond the social science community (for example, studies of 'best practice' and many types of policy research, which can be expected to attract wide public interest), or where it is necessary to produce a variety of non-technical summaries of findings for particular audiences. The argument is unlikely to succeed when researchers simply want to maximise their record of publications in academic journals with a view to furthering their career. Here again contract research can score over grant research, because the funding body may be willing to take on or subsidise publication costs.

Some research designs depend crucially on having access to key informants, organisations, sources of information, sampling frames, official statistics and the like, while others require the consent or active support of interested parties (such as trade unions or the senior management of an organisation). It is almost pointless developing a detailed research design of this nature, or preparing a research proposal for funding, before checking its feasibility in relation to such access issues. Obtaining access often depends on the presentation of a study design that is meaningful and interesting to those concerned. It is usually necessary to provide a separate, shorter, outline of the study for this purpose, quite different from the main proposal, focusing on the issues and questions addressed rather than on the methods and data collection techniques to be used, with a view to stimulating the interest of any gatekeepers. Once their interest is aroused, they may be able to make suggestions on the study design or its conduct that could not have been foreseen – for example, by pointing to other sources of information or to better cases, alerting the researcher to significant practical difficulties, as well as smoothing out special access difficulties. Although the focus in such contacts will inevitably be on the access issues, one should also be keeping an eye out for any factors that might substantively affect the study design.

## Funding

There are essentially four types of funding for a research project, which can have implications for the study design:

- self-funding;
- research carried out in the context of consultancy work;
- obtaining specific funds under grant research and/or contract research terms; and
- linking into existing major projects.

*Self-funding* involves carrying out a study using the existing resources provided by the researcher's institution, which will usually include data-processing services, library services and other support services as well as time and money budgets for research and development work. Institutions of higher education make provision for their staff to do research – for example, teaching loads in old British universities are lower than in new universities due to the tradition that academics devote one-third of their time to research. Government departments and many business and other organisations have research units to carry out 'internal' or 'in-house' studies. Independent research institutes (commercial and non-profit) often build an element into their overheads to provide for some quantity of internal research and development work. The relatively small scale of resources that are typically available within institutions implies that self-funded projects have to rely primarily on the cheaper type of study designs, such as literature reviews, secondary analysis of existing data, qualitative research and small-scale case study research, which are less expensive in money if not in time as well. One way of funding case studies is to take a job in an organisation or community that provides the subject-matter for the project (Dalton, 1964; see also Chapter 5).

*Research combined with consultancy work* is concentrated in institutions that have organised themselves on this basis (such as the Tavistock Institute in London, and the Institute of Employment Studies in the University of Sussex), but is also undertaken, with varying degree of frankness, by academics and other organisations that engage in the multifarious activities coming under the rubric of consultancy work. This approach to funding research affords the opportunity for studies that might otherwise be ruled out (owing to access problems), but it can present significant problems for research ethics and/or research design. Research carried out on this basis will rarely be formulated very explicitly and clearly, since it is essentially opportunistic and has to be accommodated within options that are opened or closed by the consultancy work, but it tends to consist of case study research. It can offer opportunities for multi-disciplinary research and even, over an extended period of time, for an informal research programme. Blackler and Brown's (1980) critique of the research and consultancy work of the Tavistock Institute indicates the controversies that this approach can give rise to, while Brown (1967) provides a more sympathetic assessment of the benefits and value of the type of research that can be carried out in this way. Klein (1976) offers another account of the Tavistock Institute's approach to combining consultancy and research work, in her case as an 'internal consultant' with Esso in the 1960s.

The opportunities and difficulties of research combined with consultancy work depend to some extent on the particular social science discipline. Sociologists, for example, are less likely to be sought for consultancy work than psychologists, who are often able to utilise training and consultancy work as the basis for social experiments in field settings (Rosen and Jerdee, 1975) or for case studies (Moore, 1984), which offer significant advantages over the alternative of laboratory studies conducted with students as subjects. Some consultancy work provides privileged access to data for secondary analysis (Webber and Craig, 1978).

*Explicit research-funding* consists of *research grants, research contracts*, or some combination of the two. The key distinction between research contracts and grants is not the source of the funds but the question of who has the overall, or ultimate, responsibility for and control of the project and project funds. In the case of research grants, the researcher has sole responsibility for the design of the study, any modification to it, and implementation of the project. In research contracts there is joint responsibility for the conduct of the project, and the funding body may have ultimate control in that the contract can be curtailed, or broken, if the contractor fails or refuses to proceed with the research design as originally agreed, or as jointly amended. The key distinction, then, is whether the researcher is left to their own devices once the grant has been obtained – with the funding body having little or no interest in the specific results, and no interest also in dealing with any unforeseen problems or costs that may arise, as noted above – or whether the organisation providing the money also has an active interest and role in the study, and will thus be averse to the study being deflected, diverted or even changed wholesale to address different questions. All other distinctions between grant research and contract research are contingent rather than necessary. The particular terms and conditions attached to each will vary over time between organisations and between countries, with the distinctions between them (and even the labels adopted for each type) often blurred in practice. For example, some organisations require that contracts be let only after a tendering process (either an open competition or invited tenders) but others will develop a research contract out of intensive discussion and negotiation with a single researcher or research institute. If there is any doubt about terms and conditions, obtain a copy of the standard research contract – most organisations that commission research with any regularity will have one. The distinction between research grants and contracts has important implications for research design. Most of the academic literature on this matter has focused on the contingent distinctions and refers to particular examples, which may be outdated or unrepresentative. For example, although decades have elapsed since Project Camelot, it is still referred to as a relevant example of contract research (Denzin, 1978a: 169, 322–4; Denzin, 1978b: 385, 406–21; see also Bulmer and Warwick, 1983), and similar warnings are offered with reference to equally idiosyncratic, if more obscure, examples (Fevre, 1983). Only rarely do researchers admit to their selective focus on bad examples of contract research, because good news is uninteresting (Cox *et al.* in Bell and Encel, 1978: 138). Even more rarely do successful research contractors set out the advantages of working on research contracts (Rossi, 1980), or provide guidelines for dealing with the contingencies (Majchrzak, 1984; Rossi and Freeman, 1999). The advice commonly proffered by academics, especially by sociologists, and particulary by those with no experience of such work, is that the researcher should have complete control of a study and that 'the researcher, and only the researcher, should decide what is to be studied' (Denzin, 1978a: 331; Denzin, 1978b: 385; see also Platt, 1976: 179). Such advice is vacuous, since the organisation that lets a research contract is a co-researcher with the contractor. The immorality of this advice is revealed by transposing it to another field, where it becomes 'The military, and only the military, should decide when and how to wage war'. However, it is reasonable to expect that the commissioning body's representative should be a trained researcher or social scientist in order to ensure fruitful collaboration with the contractor.

When the researcher is seeking a grant, the research design needs to be sufficiently detailed to meet the funding body's requirements and to justify the particular level of funding sought; but there is the option of making significant changes, or even re-designing the whole study, after the grant is obtained. (Whyte [1955] and Blau [1963] offer unusually frank accounts of how their changing interests and other contingencies led to modifications of their research designs after they had begun their case studies.) In the case of research contracts, the research design may be supplied by the funder, to be developed jointly into a final, more detailed, outline; alternatively, the funder may specify the issues and questions to be addressed and invite tenders for research designs that tackle them, sometimes with two stages of tendering: initial broad outlines of the proposed approach followed, at a more selective second round of tendering, by research designs worked out in detail with timetables and budgets specified. Any subsequent amendments and alterations to the design that forms the basis of the agreement will need to be discussed and agreed. This takes time and may cause delays in the progress of the study, so there is a far greater need to work out a detailed research design before the work starts. To researchers who are not accustomed to it, this process looks like 'endless delays' in getting the study under way. But it avoids the need for detailed negotiations at subsequent stages, and once the study has begun it should proceed fairly smoothly along the lines already hammered out. Unlike grant research, design issues are worked out intensively at the *front end* of a project or programme, before an agreement is drawn up. This does not mean that research contracts are inflexible, only that key decisions that must be taken at later stages of the project will be identified at the start as options on which discussion is postponed. One advantage is that a researcher who is considering working on such a project will be able to read documents setting out very clearly what the study is, and where it is going, before deciding to join the team (instead of trusting to luck that the project will develop along lines of interest to him or her), making it easier to recruit a team with appropriate interests. Contract research is in many ways equivalent to team research (see below) and rarely is suitable for lone riders.

Combining both grant and contract funding for a project or research programme can offer the best of both worlds. For example, one might fund a major survey under a research contract and then use a series of grants for additional studies: secondary analyses on topics or questions that were of little or no interest to the original funder, or selective case studies of respondents who were of special theoretical or policy interest. Combining research contracts and grants for a single study can allow one to cover a wider range of issues or aspects of a topic (for example, both politically sensitive questions and the more mundane range of factual information might be included in a survey). However, it is important to draw clear distinctions between the work funded by each source, partly because research contracts normally have much tighter timetables than grants, and partly because the design of the grant-funded elements need not necessarily be defined in as much detail at the start. Also, both funding bodies must be informed of the arrangements.

Finally, some studies can be funded by *linking into existing major projects*. This approach imposes most restrictions on the research design, since much will depend on the nature of the existing project and on the arrangements offered for linking into it. Post-graduate student research is often carried out in this way, with schemes ranging from those where the student is effectively a 'hired hand' assistant on part, or parts, of the study, to those where the student is responsible for the design and implementation of a specific element within the whole study. Another arrangement is for researchers to link into major surveys by taking on specific blocks of analysis, usually topics on which they offer specialist knowledge. For example, the British Home Office has a scheme for 'consultants' to join its internal research unit on a temporary basis to work on analyses of specific topics covered by its regular series of British Crime Surveys; the scheme attracts criminologists from North American as well as British universities. With the increasing scale of social research projects and programmes, this type of arrangement may become more common.

Major studies and research programmes are frequently funded by a combination of two or more of the four options outlined above, and may also involve the combined resources of two or more research organisations. In fields where there is already a large body of knowledge based on smaller-scale studies, the natural progression is towards larger and more complex studies, which can require multi-agency funding and resources. For example, a university-based project may combine internal resources (self-funding) for the first stages of literature review and exploratory case study work, then move to a research grant or contract for the larger-scale main study involving fieldwork, then revert back to internal funding for more extensive further analyses of the data collected.

A research programme conducted by a government department can utilise all four funding options for the various component studies: commissioning external studies on a research contract basis; carrying out some projects internally; providing for academic specialists in particular topics to link into the programme by carrying out special analyses of certain themes in the data collected; and using existing liaison networks with 'client' groups to collect information in the course of advisory work.

Multi-agency funding of research may involve different sources of funding being used for separate stages of a project, or for particular studies in a programme, as in the above examples. But it is used also for the funding of very large single projects, and is leading to the development of new styles of collaborative research.

Major national studies (especially multi-purpose national surveys with large samples) may be funded by a consortium of several organisations. One example of university-based research is the Comparative Elites Project carried out by a team of academics in three American universities using a combination of grants from different sources (see Chapter 10). Another example of multi-funding is the British Workplace Employment Relations Survey series, which is jointly funded and staffed by a consortium of four organisations: the Department of Trade and Industry, the ESRC, the Policy Studies Institute (an independent research institute relying on research grants from foundations for its share of the funding) and the Advisory, Conciliation and Arbitration Service (ACAS) – an independent public agency (Cully *et al.*, 1998, 1999; Millward, Bryson and Forth, 2000). In this case, the project has a two-tier management structure: a management committee, which includes representatives of all funders and makes decisions about the timetable for surveys, expenditure, staffing, the content of the survey questionnaire and outputs, publications, publicity and release of the edited datatape for secondary analysis; and a research team, which develops specifications for each stage of the project and does all the work once their ideas are accepted. Only the head of the research team is a member of the management committee, but other researchers may sit in on their meetings to understand how and why decisions are reached. Collaborative arrangements such as these combine theoretical research with policy research, grant-funding with research contracts, and make distinctions between them increasingly tenuous.

One implication of these developments is that research of any size or complexity becomes a team effort, and will almost invariably require additional resources for the collective management of the project or programme – a point considered further in the following section.

## Organisation and management of research work

The organisation and management of research is not wholly determined by the funding used, although larger projects will invariably have more formal arrangements than smaller studies. There are three main options for the organisation of a research project or research programme.

The *hierarchically organised research team* will have the status of lead researcher(s) clearly stated and will usually have well-defined roles for other members of the team. Notwithstanding the egalitarian ideology given lip-service in some social science disciplines (but much rarer in the natural sciences), this format is typical of university-based research, where it can give rise to 'hired hand' rebellions (Roth, 1966). It is also widespread in large research organisations and in research units located within bureaucratic organisations, where it causes fewer problems, being in line with the organisational culture and ethos, and because there is a well-defined career ladder for everyone. Research design decisions are ultimately the prerogative of the lead researcher(s), which obviates the need for protracted negotiations with other members of the team. (Group problem-solving and decision-making is a more time-consuming, and therefore costly, process than individual decision-making.) The success of this format depends ultimately on the research experience and management skills of the lead researcher(s); management skills are scarcer than admitted in the social sciences, where the status of lead researcher is determined more by prestige as a specialist than by management skills (which are not of themselves publishable material).

One alternative is the *research team of formal equals*, which is often used for multi-disciplinary studies, where there is a need to draw on the different and complementary expertise of a number of people. Perhaps because of the special difficulties of multi-disciplinary research (see Chapter 11), this format seems particularly prone to organisation and management problems, which may affect the success, in practice, of a good research design.

The third option is the *collaborative research team*, which draws together members from different institutions who will often have somewhat different interests in the project and differing contributions to make. This arrangement is common in studies with multiple funding (such as the WERS surveys mentioned earlier) and research teams spanning a number of academic institutions (such as the Comparative Elites Project). In this case it is helpful, if not essential, to have some body (a person or a committee) to fulfil a central co-ordinating role, to arbitrate between incompatible interests, mediate on issues where differences can be reconciled, or at least rendered understandably acceptable to dissenting parties, and generally pull the team together on decisions required at various stages of the project. This role may be independent of the research design function, because it comes into play only during the implementation of the study, after a mutually acceptable research design has been agreed by all the parties concerned. Indeed, the role is sometimes best filled by someone who does not have a personal stake in the study, although it frequently is (if only because of the difficulties of obtaining the services of a sufficiently interested but independent chairman).

On large, complex and costly projects, and on those with large research teams, project management is likely to be formalised in a separate group (variously termed Steering Committee, Working Party, Management Group, and so forth), which meets at periodic intervals to review progress, sort out problems and take any decisions required on the implementation of the research design. This style of research management and review is particularly common with research programmes, multi-funded projects, contract research and projects carried out by government departments (where there is a requirement of public accountability for the funds used and work done). The disadvantage is that it takes up time and other resources, for example, to produce progress reports, for which allowance must be made in cost estimates. The advantage is that the management group provides a ready forum for negotiating and agreeing additional projects in a programme, modifications to the design of a project, and support for extension projects. Management groups can also incorporate independent 'advisers' or 'consultants' who are not members of the research team, and can facilitate the work in various ways (such as resolving problems of access to institutions or sources of information, providing specialist advice on specific difficulties, or offering alternative solutions to unforeseen problems). The benefits of good research management need to be underlined because management tends to be undervalued (and done badly) in the academic community where social scientists get their basic research training. Indeed, the individualistic ethos of the university, which contributes to an organisational culture described by some as organised anarchy (Baldridge and Deal, 1983), is largely antipathetic to the kind of well-organised management required on projects of any scale.

## Issues in research management

One general question arising in research implementation is whether to do the entire project oneself, by specially recruiting or pulling together a research team, or whether part of the work will be subcontracted. The question arises most often in relation to the use of fieldwork agencies for interview surveys, but it needs also to be addressed for other elements of a project such as particular parts of the data-processing, specialised bits of the analysis and writing up, depth interviews, and so on. Research programmes offer even greater potential for subcontracting discrete projects to separate research teams. Multi-disciplinary research projects and programmes may also raise the choice between specially recruiting a single research team with representation of the relevant disciplines, or splitting up the research into discrete blocks that can be covered separately by researchers from the separate disciplines. Sometimes there may be two levels of subcontracting; for example, a government organisation may commission a large study from a research institute, which subcontracts part of the work to other agencies – as illustrated by the SIME/DIME experiment.

The issue of subcontracting elements of a project, or entire projects within a programme, can stimulate as much heated debate as the issue of contract research. Some academics take the view that subcontractors should never be used, especially not commercial research agencies, even though they admit that the alternative is the use of inexperienced but easily exploited student labour and junior research assistants (Payne, 1979), with the data quality problems outlined by Roth (1966) and research management and supervision problems described by Platt (1976). Others argue that the use of students is indefensible, and point to the advantages of sub-contracting fieldwork in particular (O'Toole, 1971: 165, 200, 232). In practice, the choice will depend very much on the circumstances of each research project, the organisational location and the resources of the main research team. However, the desire of researchers to 'have a go' at a type of work or study that is new to them must be weighed against the interests of the study and its successful completion. The interests of the individual researcher are not synonymous with the interests of the study, and may even be entirely at odds with it.

The main advantages of university-based research are that a greater depth of theoretical work will usually be brought into a project, often from a single discipline. But because academics have competing teaching responsibilities, being in effect part-time researchers, the work may be subject to long delays, and the individualistic ethos of the academic community impedes team research (Douglas, 1976: 222; Useem, 1976: 614–15). The main advantages of the research institute and of specialist agencies are that their full-time research staff can complete studies more quickly, and they are able to retain a variety of specialists and general support staff who are needed only on an occasional basis for particular aspects of a study – such as sampling experts, statisticians, data-processors or clerical support staff. They have more experience in the organisation, management and costing of research studies, so reports will normally be delivered on time and to budget; however, these will often be reports on the study itself with little explicit attempt to set the results in the context of the social research literature. The main advantages of research that is carried out in-house (for example, by research units within government departments and other large organisations) are fewer problems of access to confidential information (such as internal records and case files), research designs and reports that more closely match organisational information needs, and professionally staffed research units that can offer many, if not all, the advantages of the independent research institute as well. On the other hand, the research may be vulnerable to disruptions from the wider organisational environment.

These differing strengths and weaknesses suggest that subcontracting parts of a project to an appropriate organisation offers significant gains. The arguments for multiple triangulation (see Chapter 11) might be extrapolated to encompass the complementary usage of different types of research organisation as well as different types of study and multiple researchers. For example, the respective strengths of university-based research and of research institutes can be maximised by subcontracting national survey fieldwork to a survey agency up to the production of an edited and documented dataset, possibly with a general descriptive summary report on the results, with the detailed and more considerative analyses of the data allocated to academics and other topic experts. This is, in effect, the underlying principle for the organisation of the General Social Survey in the USA and the International Social Survey Programme. In both cases academics contribute to the design of the survey content, and the early release of the datasets into the public domain leaves the field free to anyone wishing to do more substantive analyses. These examples of collaborative research arrangements contrast markedly with the academic practice of 'hoarding' datasets as personal property until the last ounce of value has been extracted by the original researcher. Another format is for academics to do case study and qualitative research based on samples or selected cases drawn from, or simply highlighted by, national surveys – with various examples discussed in Chapter 11.

The possibility remains that some researchers will prefer to carry out an entire project themselves by recruiting their own research team, irrespective of the costs, as illustrated by Townsend's poverty survey, which took some 15 years from its original conception and design to the final report.

Another general issue arising in research organisation and management is the problem of the 'Us versus Them' mentality. This often forms an undercurrent to discussions of subcontracting, publication and authorship rights, relations with those who are the subjects of the research (especially the communities and organisations that are the subjects of case study research), contacts with 'clients', 'sponsors' or other funding agencies, and it creates many of the so-called personality clashes that can arise in single-discipline or multi-disciplinary research teams. The key element of the 'Us versus Them' game is that 'We' have a pure and selfless interest in the pursuit of knowledge and truth, while 'They' are venal, biased, self-seeking, and much else besides. The game rests on bad faith, seeking to equate the vested interests of researchers (in their careers, publications record and freedom to do as they please) with the interests of the project, while denying that other parties such as sponsors, subjects and contractors are capable of disinterested concerns. The popularity of the game is not limited to the social sciences (Gieryn, 1983; Gilbert and Mulkay, 1984). Research managers will differ in their views as to whether the interests of the study always take priority, but one needs to be clear that the moralistic and ideological smoke-screen thrown up by the 'Us versus Them' mentality often obfuscates choices that may need to be made between the interests of the study, the researchers' professional interests, and the rights and interests of the subjects of the study and of other parties.

Conventionally, research reports provide a *post hoc* account of the research process that clears away the undergrowth of false starts, serendipitous discoveries, disputes within the research team, and so forth, to focus on the central lines of the study in its final form. But there is now a growing literature on the practical aspects of developing and implementing research. This includes personal accounts and broader discussions of the contrasting styles of management and organisation of policy research and theoretical research; interpersonal relationships within research teams; the reiterative process of developing theoretical perspectives as data are generated by the research process; changing patterns of research funding; the procedures adopted by foundations, social science research councils and government agencies for commissioning and funding research; the implications of institutional location for the research process; relationships between research contractors and funding bodies; relationships with organisations and communities that are the subjects of case study research; and related issues (Hammond, 1964; O'Toole, 1971; Nagi and Corwin, 1972; Orlans, 1972, 1973; Bernstein and Freeman, 1975; Abt, 1976; Crawford and Perry, 1976; Klein, 1976; Platt, 1976; Bell and Newby, 1977; Bell and Encel, 1978; Blalock, 1980; Pinder, 1981; Bulmer, 1983, Clarke and Cornish, 1983; Kogan and Henkel, 1983; St Pierre, 1983; Bell and Roberts, 1984; Thomas, 1985). Of these, the contributions to the books edited by Hammond (1964) and O'Toole (1971) are of continuing wide interest.

There is also a growing literature devoted to policy research more specifically. This includes personal accounts of careers in policy research; discussions of whether policy research makes a difference to policies; practical questions of designing, carrying through and reporting on research in this field; and how policy research is changing the nature of knowledge production as well as policy analysis (Abt, 1976, 1980; Olsen and Micklin, 1981; Merton, 1982; Freeman *et al.*, 1983; Booth, 1988; Nathan, 1988; Gibbons *et al.*, 1994; McRae and Whittington, 1997; Steele *et al.*, 1999). A particularly good text, which is concise, well written, and draws on extensive personal experience of policy research, is provided by Majchrzak (1984). She shows how the contingent features of policy research affect each stage of the research process, and offers guidance on how to deal with them. Also drawing on personal experience, Weiss (1983) presents an incisive analysis of the role and contribution of research results to the policy process that remains valid today, in all political and cultural contexts.

The successful implementation of a research design depends on the location, organisation and management of the study. This is an area where opinions are frequently clouded by particular experiences. But the general consensus appears to be that what is variously termed charisma, flair, experience or nous plays an important part over and beyond specialist and research management skills. Research is, ultimately, a creative activity, and dull people produce dull research reports.

# 13 Cross-national comparative studies

Cross-national comparative research must be the most challenging of all types of study because it aims to produce a genuinely universal social science (Galtung, 1990). In terms of research design and methods, these studies are no different from national or local projects. Examples of comparative studies can be identified for every research design in Chapters 2 to 9. In large and culturally diverse countries, such as India, Indonesia or Nigeria, a national study can be just as challenging as a cross-national comparative study. In most cases, however, the comparative element adds another layer of work – both theoretical and organisational. Studying the country where one lives and works never demands explanation. It seems obvious. But research on other countries always requires explanation. Why these particular countries? How are the extra effort and cost justified? And how will such a study be carried out?

## The logic of comparative analysis

Theory-driven academic research is only one type of comparative study. Equally important, in sheer volume, is the policy-driven research carried out by or for international organisations.

Policy-driven comparative research is carried out by all international organisations, such as the European Commission, the OECD, the United Nations and its agencies, the International Labour Office (ILO), World Health Organisation and UNESCO (the education and culture body). This research is often presented as basic descriptive work, published in collections of statistical and other information harmonised to present reasonably comparable data. But all these statistical and other compendia present selective indicators, chosen to reflect the particular concerns and policy objectives of the organisation. More substantial research studies shade into advocacy research (see Chapter 1), because they invariably serve to inform, support and promote the policy objectives of the organisation, broadly defined, even if this is never stated explicitly.

One example is the ILO's comparative study of the sex segregation of occupations described in Chapter 2. This report was explicit about the ILO's policy on occupational segregation as noxious, something to be reduced to the minimum possible, even if its complete elimination was recognised as impossible and inappropriate (Anker, 1998: 8). Unfortunately for the ILO, countries with the strongest gender equality policies – the Nordic countries of Finland, Sweden and Norway – were also found to have the highest levels of occupational segregation in modern societies, and even in the world (Anker, 1998; Melkas and Anker, 1998), as well as the largest gender gap in workplace authority (Wright, 1997: 318–70). In a theoretical study, this would have led the authors to reconsider their thesis that gender equality policies reduce occupational segregation. Writing within an advocacy research framework, the authors were forced to ignore this element of their results and reiterate the need to reduce occupational segregation, as a matter of social justice.

Most comparative studies and statistical compendia of the European Commission are focused on the issue of convergence between member states, although independent studies underline the lack of convergence in attitudes and behaviour across Europe (Hakim, 1999a, 1999b; Boh *et al.*, 1989). Other international bodies focus on minimum standards, for example in health or standards of living, or in styles of living. Either way, all have a bias of some sort, even if this remains implicit.

Nonetheless, the publications of the international bodies provide valuable background information for comparative studies, and sometimes the main source of data, as noted in Chapter 2. These publications include reference volumes setting out agreed international definitions and classifications; glossaries of terms in several languages (such as the *Glossaries* on labour market topics produced for every EU member country by the European Foundation); and statistical compendia that present data in the most comparable formats that can be achieved.

There is an extensive literature on theory-driven comparative research, informed by research in comparative sociology, comparative politics and (social) policy analysis (Rokkan, 1968; Przeworski and Teune, 1970; Warwick and Osherson, 1973; Smelser, 1976; Jones, 1985; Ragin, 1987, 1991; Johnson and Tuttle, 1989; Kohn, 1989; Heidenheimer, Heclo and Adams, 1990; Oyen, 1990; Castles, 1993). Inevitably, attempts to formulate general principles for the design and conduct of comparative studies are influenced by the disciplinary perspective that authors bring to the task and by the diverse issues and questions on which each social science focuses. Kohn's classification of the main approaches is perhaps the most general, and is informed by his review of several earlier classifications (Kohn, 1989: 20–23). Policy-driven studies simply cover *all* countries within a given administrative area, such as the European Union, or even all countries in the world, or as many as possible. In contrast, the principal feature of theory-driven comparative research is that the countries studied are always carefully *selected* on some criterion, which must be stated. The criteria for selection are similar to those for case studies (see Chapter 5), but with greater emphasis on theoretical issues. Comparative research can be seen as a special type of case study research.

Countries can be chosen as substantively interesting in their own right: the society itself, or some aspect of it, such as the political system or policies, is the main object of study. This is especially common in policy research, where the aim is to describe and analyse the main features of the countries chosen as case studies, as illustrated by Jones' (1985) comparative analysis of social policy in the USA, Britain, France, West Germany and Sweden. Such studies are often richly descriptive.

Sometimes the research focus is a theory, and countries are selected to illustrate or test particular aspects of that theory. Typical cases and exceptions (deviant cases) are both studied (Köbben in Rokkan, 1968: 17–53; Ragin, 1987). The aim is to test the generality of a thesis on how institutions operate, or the process of change, or how the social environment impacts on individuals, groups or social movements. One example is the research programme of Kohn and his colleagues on the relationship between social stratification and social–psychological functioning. The initial study was carried out in the USA (Kohn, 1969; Kohn and Schooler, 1983), followed by comparative replications in Poland and Japan (Slomczynski, Miller and Kohn, 1981; Naoi and Schooler, 1985). These showed the reciprocal impact of job status and job conditions on desire for self-direction, intellectual functioning and social orientations in all modern societies, irrespective of historical, cultural, economic and political circumstances (Kohn, 1989: 77–102). Another example is Skocpol's (1979) comparative analysis of the causes and consequences of social revolutions in France, Russia and China. A classic example is Barrington Moore's study of *The Origins of Dictatorship and Democracy*, which compared England, France, the USA, Germany, Russia, China, Japan and India. In this type of study, countries must be selected for characteristics relevant to the theory being tested, wherever they are in the world. Another type of comparative study collects data for a variety of countries in order to test a theory through variable-centred analysis. Because the special characteristics of each country are not examined closely, a greater number of countries can be included. Research on the causes and correlates of economic growth and development fall into this category. Classic examples are the studies of social change and modernisation in developing countries by McClelland (1961), Almond and Verba (1965) and Smith and Inkeles (1966). These studies sometimes rely on secondary analysis and select all countries with reasonably similar characteristics for which the right data is available (see the contributions to Rokkan, 1968, and Oyen, 1990).

There is a growing category of *global studies*, which study nations and multi-national organisations as part of the global economic, political, social and cultural system. As globalisation proceeds, these studies become more common. They demand new indicators and new theoretical perspectives, such as world-systems theory, and the focus shifts away from the nation state to other transnational organisations and global processes. Classic examples are the thesis of the development of underdevelopment, and Cardoso and Faletto's (1969) analysis of dependency and development in Latin America (see Calderon and Piscitelli in Oyen, 1990: 81–95). More recently, Sklair has studied the policies and activities of the largest transnational corporations to identify the emerging characteristics of a new transnational capitalist class that is gradually supplanting national political elites in importance (Sklair, 1999a, 1999b, 2000).

Finally, there are always opportunistic studies, where people take advantage of some special situation, existing cross-national datasets, or even of their linguistic abilities, to do comparative studies. Many secondary analysis studies are of this type, and the ISSP has stimulated many data-driven comparative studies.

## Organisation of research work

There is a tendency to assume that comparative research entails teamwork and requires substantial research funding. In reality, it is still possible for the solo researcher to mastermind, and even carry out, comparative studies. Some of the most successful studies are designed and led by a single academic, with a well-defined thesis and a clear research strategy, who is able to persuade others to join in the endeavour.

The first option for the solo researcher is the *safari style*. This involves a series of visits to the countries selected for study, to collect information and carry out any interviews or surveys required. This can be done by visits to colleagues or research centres in other universities, and by judicious use of sabbaticals and summer vacations (which are dedicated to research anyway). The safari style of research is sometimes criticised for being too ambitious: it is argued that no single scholar can fully understand several cultures on the basis of brief country visits. But the scope of most studies is much narrower than this, and the country visits may contribute only one element of intensive studies of each country in the research programme, carried out over a period of years, or even decades. Very exceptionally, well-funded studies allow the solo researcher to carry out national surveys in a series of countries, using local survey firms. One example is Almond and Verba's (1965) study of the civic culture in five nations: the USA, Mexico, Britain, West Germany and Italy. Omnibus surveys make this option even more accessible, and quicker than in the past.

The second option for the solo researcher is to act as the *lead researcher* for a dispersed team effort, with each country carrying out its own independent replication within the theoretical and methodological framework specified by the lead researcher. The globalisation of scholarly research makes this an increasingly common arrangement. One example is the Comparative Project on Class Structure and Class Consciousness co-ordinated by Wright with national surveys in the USA, Sweden, Norway, Britain, Germany, Portugal, Canada, Australia, Japan and six other countries eventually over two decades (Marshall *et al.*, 1991; Wright, 1985, 1997). This looked at class formation and class ideology in modern societies, identifying variations across societies, with the final synthesis report produced by Wright (1997). Another example is the series of World Values Surveys designed and organised by Inglehart in 1970, 1981, 1990 and 1996 (Inglehart, 1977, 1990, 1997; Abramson and Inglehart, 1995; Inglehart *et al.*, 1998). In this case, the lead researcher developed the theory to be tested, produced a bank of social and political attitude items to be used in national surveys, carried out analyses that identified a shortlist of diagnostic indicators of materialist and post-materialist attitudes, produced a *Sourcebook* guide to all 43 national surveys, and wrote reports on the comparative analyses, drawing on numerous national reports. In contrast, the ISSP (see Chapter 7) is run by a loose association of 31 participating countries, covers a diversity of topics with no single theoretical focus, and produces no major reports synthesising the results of each comparative survey. The lead researcher option may be open to few people, because it requires an established position within the academic community. But the point here is that it remains possible for a solo researcher to mastermind a global research programme, and these are among the most successful comparative studies, certainly more successful than some research programmes run by teamwork or by committee.

The *duo* is a popular arrangement among academics and one that normally works well. Two academics in different countries agree to collaborate on a comparative study. Each person remains responsible for their own national report, and comparative analyses are jointly produced. This arrangement assumes that the two parties know each other well enough to work constructively together. Interpretation of research results benefits from the country expertise of each partner, and the limited size of the research team reduces communication problems to the minimum. This arrangement can sometimes be made to work with three partners, as illustrated by a series of ISSP analyses by Alwin, Braun and Scott (1992; see also Scott, Braun and Alwin, 1998).

Finally, some comparative studies are produced by *teamwork*. Two approaches can be identified. The first option is a comparative study led, or carried out, by a dedicated, full-time central research team, which designs and co-ordinates the entire study, produces the comparative analysis and writes the final overview report.

A good example of this approach is the World Fertility Survey described in Chapter 6. The WFS was designed and organised by a small dedicated team of demographers and statisticians in London working for the International Statistical Institute. This team designed the essential features of the survey, the common module of core questions applied in all countries, and the optional additional modules. This approach was used to accommodate the varying interests and concerns of the 61 participating countries, and to ensure that comparability was retained across all topics covered by the national surveys. The lead team also provided model instruments and manuals, technical advice on sampling and data analysis software, and assistance on practical matters such as funding. As the project extended over 12 years, with some countries participating early and others joining late, the leading team also ensured co-ordination and consistency across the entire project, organised the final synthesis and evaluation reports (Cleland and Hobcraft, 1985; Cleland and Scott, 1987), produced a standardised dataset for all countries, and undertook dissemination and archival work. The WFS was a good example of collaborative research, combining the efforts of the team of experts in London, the efforts of national research teams and the resources of several funding agencies. Because of this tripartite involvement, the WFS had to be broadly descriptive; there was no attempt to structure the survey around any theory about fertility. Even so, the results did change thinking, prompting a change of emphasis from the economic determinants of fertility to situational and attitudinal factors.

The dedicated team is also used by some international organisations. For example, most of the OECD's comparative studies are produced by its own full-time research staff. Additional studies on specific topics are commissioned as necessary, feeding into the OECD's final synthesis reports. This approach is used to produce regular reports, such as the annual *OECD Employment Outlook*, and one-off studies, such as the *OECD Jobs Study* (1994).

A completely different approach to organising cross-national comparative research is illustrated by the European Commission's Observatories and Networks of Experts covering a range of social policy topics, including employment, family policy, social exclusion, older people, minimum income, and the development and convergence of social protection policies. (Some of these issues have been pursued despite the limitations of Commission competence in the social field.) In this case, experts are appointed in all EU member countries, with an independent coordinator hired to liaise with the Commission and lead the work of the Network of Experts for a period of five years. Almost all the experts are academics, who retain their university commitments, in full or in part. The Commission retains control over the Networks' research activities, which are often directed towards immediate policy issues and short-term horizons. In practice, much of the work done by the Networks consists of advocacy research designed to support policy positions that the Commission has already chosen privately. These arrangements have led to some worthwhile comparative studies (for example, Rubery and Fagan, 1993), but they also lead to patchy and superficial analyses based mainly on secondary analysis of available data. Reviews reveal frequent dissatisfaction with the operation of such Networks, with their unrealistic objectives, and with the conflict between theoretical research and advocacy research, as illustrated by Rubery and other contributors to Hantrais and Mangen's (1996) collection. One problem is the Commission's desire to identify policy initiatives that can be applied uniformly across the EU, whereas research confirms that country differences in Europe are significant enough for this to be frequently inappropriate or even counterproductive.

## Funding and practical problems

Obtaining funds can be more difficult because large comparative studies are more expensive than single-nation studies. One solution is for each country in a research programme to seek its own funding. Being part of a wider, cross-national comparative project can increase the chances of obtaining funding substantially, because most countries want to be seen to participate. Within the EU, there is a tendency for comparative projects to be favoured over single-nation studies, all else equal. Thus funding can sometimes be easier for comparative studies.

The practical problems of carrying out cross-national or cross-cultural research are emphasised in most textbooks, but can easily be exaggerated. True, there are cultural differences in styles of work, and in relations between members of a team, or between strangers, that must be taken into account. But there are similar differences between organisational cultures *within* countries – for example, differences between organisational styles in the public and private sectors, or between government research departments, commercial firms and academics. In the case of cross-cultural research, such differences are at least half anticipated, making it easier to respond and adapt, or to excuse eccentric behaviour. Cultural differences never seem to matter much in a research team that is motivated and has a good research design that everyone understands and can follow.

Cultural differences can be more important for the content of the research, affecting the substantive meaning of concepts, ideas, scales, themes or the wording of questions (Scheuch and Mitchell in Rokkan, 1968). For example, there is no appropriate word or phrase in Japanese that approximates the idea of god that is so well established in countries with a Judeo–Christian–Moslem culture. This obviously affects the design of surveys on religious beliefs and behaviour (Jowell, 1998: 172), but it also indicates more diffuse differences in conceptions of morality and cultural differences. It is common for English to be adopted, formally or informally, as the language for discussion in international research teams and, where surveys are carried out, for English to be used as the language for questionnaire drafting. One procedure used to check the translations of the final questionnaire is back translation into English from the other languages. If a back translation is too different from the original questionnaire, adjustments are needed to achieve a good match across all versions of the questionnaire. However, most researchers agree that the aim is never a literal translation but functional equivalence of meaning. There are different ways of achieving this, but ultimately it remains a matter of judgement (Scheuch in Rokkan, 1968: 176–209). In general, questions about behaviour seem to cause fewer translation problems than questions about attitudes, values and preferences. This is perhaps one reason why the efforts of the ILO and other international bodies to standardise survey procedures have been more successful in relation to studies of behaviour than of attitudes.

Problems of cross-cultural research are not specific to cross-national studies; they arise also in research on different ethnic groups within a single nation (Johnson and Tuttle, 1989). This is illustrated by Marín and Marín's (1991) guide to research with Hispanic populations within the USA. Some of the difficulties, and solutions, apply equally to research on Hispanic populations in Latin America, poor communities in any country, and to Asian cultures that also exhibit the courtesy bias (Mitchell in Rokkan, 1968: 229; Jones, 1983) that leads people to acquiesce and offer socially desirable responses to questions (Ross and Mirowsky, 1984). For example, Marín and Marín (1991: 101–3) point out that in certain cultures, younger and less educated people all tend to offer more extreme responses to attitude questions. One study had to include the item 'I wish somebody would kill all these people' to represent adequately the full range of attitudes to social groups (Scheuch in Rokkan, 1968: 185). One solution is to group all degrees of approval and disapproval, agreement and disagreement, into single bands. Another approach accepts extreme responses as valid and locally meaningful. Cultural dissimilarities *within* a nation are sometimes ignored, especially if ethnic groups constitute minorities. In cross-national comparative research, these issues have to be addressed.

Social and political attitude research probably poses the greatest difficulties for comparative studies, partly because so much depends on the precise wording and meaning of attitude questions and partly because there are few or no other datasources to use as checks on validity. Surveys that enquire about purchasing behaviour, employment patterns or religious practices, for example, can check that results are roughly in line with what is already known from other sources. Such validity checks are rarely possible with attitude data, and some surveys deliver results that are puzzling or even baffling. For example, surveys carried out in East Germany in spring 1990, shortly after the Berlin wall came down, suggested that 40 years of socialism had left no discernible trace: there was hardly any difference between East and West Germans in the acceptance of democratic norms and values. As Kuechler (1998: 192–3) points out, several interpretations were possible: access to West German television from the 1970s onwards had neutralised the effects of political socialisation in school and workplace; East Germans had internalised Western political values in just four months; or East Germans were smart enough to give the socially desirable answers, as they may have done for decades under socialism.

Many of the practical difficulties of comparative research can be overcome if data collection and interpretation in each country is carried out by a local research team or survey agency. However, this introduces another problem, of multi-disciplinary collaboration. The social sciences are organised differently even across European countries, and even more so across all regions of the world. For example, employment topics that would be studied by sociologists in one country will be studied by labour lawyers in another country, by labour economists in a third country, and by industrial relations specialists in a fourth country. Even if they are all working on the same project, scholars from different countries may be thinking within different disciplinary perspectives. Cross-national and cross-cultural research often becomes multi-disciplinary research as well, even if this was not intended. This is most likely to happen with studies based on secondary analysis and case studies. This, and other hidden problems of teamwork, may explain the disproportional success of studies designed and carried out by a solo researcher.

Theoretically driven comparative studies tend to be located firmly within a specific disciplinary framework, and so are the texts discussing comparative research. Most assume a graduate audience and some familiarity with social science methods and disciplines – mainly sociology and political science. Rokkan (1968), Warwick and Osherson (1973), Smelser (1976), Kohn (1989) and Oyen (1990) all provide practical and theoretical guidance on comparative research, with a wide range of illustrative examples. Whitfield and Strauss (1998) discuss comparative research in industrial relations. Przeworski and Teune (1970) present a systematic review of the theoretical and measurement issues involved in variable-centred statistical analysis of data for several countries, again with many examples. Ragin (1987) presents the advantages of a holistic case study approach instead of a variable-centred approach to comparative research, illustrated by examples.

The practical difficulties of cross-national research are increased if a project includes late developing countries as well as industrialised societies. Cultural differences will be extended by differences in standards of living and, possibly, in educational standards. In some cultures, it is considered appropriate for interviewers and researchers to recompense interviewees and informants for their time and help, sometimes in the form of a gift offered when introducing oneself, sometimes in the form of a gift, small service or monetary reward offered at the end of an interview. Failure to offer a reward for the time-consuming assistance of someone who is markedly less affluent than the researcher/interviewer is considered exploitative. In some countries, interviews typically take place in the presence of other people, sometimes in a group context. Mitchell in Rokkan (1968: 210–38), Peil (1982), Bulmer and Warwick (1983), O'Barr, Spain and Tessler, (1973) and Warwick and Osherson (1973) offer guides to doing research in developing countries.

The publications of international bodies are the best source of information on the international classifications and definitions that underlie their comparative statistical reports and also the statistical reports of many nation states, which use these classifications, suitably abbreviated, or expanded as necessary. OECD reports are a particularly good source of information on the datasources, definitions and classifications used in advanced economies, as well as in OECD's comparative analyses. There are several academic international classifications of social/occupational status, occupational prestige and social class created by Goldthorpe (Erikson and Goldthorpe, 1993), Ganzeboom and Treiman (1996) and Treiman (1977). These are all described in Hakim (1998: 254–8) along with British social status scales. Hakim (1991) describes the potential of the European Labour Force Surveys for comparative research.

Finally, the development of e-mail and the internet are transforming cross-national communication and collaboration in ways that will have huge implications for research in future decades, because they offer access to colleagues, data archives and libraries from anywhere in the world.

# 14  Conclusions

Research is in the nature of sailing off to chart unexplored seas or, more concretely, trudging off to map unexplored territories. Research design is about aiming in the right direction, getting your bearings right (from previous studies) and making sure you are adequately equipped to get there and back. Methods texts explain how to build a ship, but it is navigators who take ships to sea and sail them. Columbus set sail to find the western route to the East Indies and came across the West Indies and America instead. Research designs that fail in their original intentions are not always so lucky, but it helps if one is clear that the original plan made sense, can offer some reasons on why it went awry and describes what was discovered instead. However, research projects are more likely to fail from being over ambitious or poorly designed in the first place.

The usual focus in the presentation of a research report is on the questions to be addressed in relation to theoretical issues within the discipline and relevant literature. Methods textbooks focus on the detailed practical procedures of carrying out research, the methods and techniques to be used. This leaves an enormous gap in between. This book has been about the research design process, the crucial intervening task that links together theory and methods, the questions to be addressed and the types of answer that can be obtained from particular research efforts. It has been noted throughout that there is often more than one way of tackling a question, and that research design issues are not reducible to a choice of research methods and techniques. Each of the eight types of study offers particular strengths and weaknesses, which can be maximised by combining or linking two or more studies within a project or research programme. The task of research design is intellectually demanding and time-consuming, but it needs to be done well if empirical research is to produce information worth having. From this review of the research design process, and the examples chosen to reflect the full range of social science disciplines, a number of themes emerge that merit further consideration.

The discussion has been illustrated throughout with examples from theoretical research and policy research in equal numbers. The fact that this has been possible disposes of the idea that there is any major or necessary dividing line between the two, or that there is a significant or substantive gap that dictates different research designs for theoretical research and for policy research. For example, experiments have long been presented as the ideal design for theoretical research, but the best examples of experimental research in real-life settings are found in policy research. However, *all* research has one major limitation for policy relevance: research can describe or explain the present or the recent past, but it provides only tentative information on possible futures and how to achieve them (Hoaglin *et al.*, 1982). To underline the importance and value of information from empirical research is not to deny the importance of ideology and conflicting interests within the policy process (Weiss, 1983).

If one ignores the contingent factors that differentiate policy research – such as the funding source and the intended audience – its two most distinguishing features are, first, an emphasis on the substantive or practical importance of research results rather than on merely 'statistically significant' findings, and second, a multi-disciplinary approach that in turn leads to the eclectic and catholic use of any and all research designs that might prove helpful in answering the questions posed. This raises the question of whether the current division of the social sciences into separate disciplines, with continuous proliferation of sub-disciplines, is beneficial for empirical social research, or even for the development of social science theory. This book has shown that research design can be discussed outside a disciplinary framework. The theoretical framework brought to bear on a study is a logically separate matter, and one may choose a multi-disciplinary framework instead. The development of a research design framework that cuts across disciplinary boundaries should facilitate communication across social science disciplines (as well as improving communication between researchers, research funders and research users) and smooth the path of multi-disciplinary research. The eventual outcome should be more comprehensive multi-disciplinary theory and understanding of social processes in place of the partial accounts currently offered by intellectually segregated disciplines. The expansion of policy research is fundamentally changing knowledge production (Gibbons *et al.*, 1994), but this seems to be ultimately beneficial for the development of social science theory.

It is readily accepted that *intensive* and *extensive* research differ, as illustrated by the contrasts between case studies and sample surveys: they address different questions at different levels. The differences between them are sometimes reduced to a superficial distinction between 'depth versus breadth'; or between studies that address causal processes on the ground versus studies providing broad-brush but representative data, but their complementarity is generally emphasised (Sayer, 1984: 219–28). The distinction between intensive and extensive research, which are ultimately compatible, has led to the idea that micro-level studies provide results that are in some sense more 'real' or valid than studies at the macro-level. However, emphasis on the different perspectives of intensive and extensive research has produced a tendency to overlook another, equally important, distinction: between micro-level and macro-level analyses that produce different and incompatible answers to the *same* question, even from the *same* data. Robinson (1950) has shown that correlations at higher levels of aggregation will, all other things being equal, be larger than at the less aggregated, or individual, level, and also that it is quite possible for correlations at the two levels of aggregation to be substantively different, even contradictory. Although this is routinely referred to as 'the well-known ecological fallacy', it is nonetheless frequently overlooked in disputes over discrepant research findings. Failure to take account of it is particularly likely when disputes are between a discipline that almost always does macro-level research (as in macro-economics) and a discipline that almost always does micro-level research (as in social psychology). And it does mean that research carried out at different levels can produce discontinuous and contradictory results rather than complementary findings.

Similar problems regularly arise from the failure to distinguish between gross and net measures of change, at the micro-level and macro-level respectively. It is not unknown for scholars to ridicule regular surveys for showing *no* change (no net change, that is) when their own, more detailed, studies reveal quite dramatic amounts of change (that is, gross change at the micro-level) in attitudes, voting preferences or behaviour.

In general, there will be smaller differences between social units or areas, less change across time, and stronger correlations between factors, the larger the unit of analysis; and there will be larger differences between social units or areas, more change across time, and weaker associations between factors, the smaller the unit of analysis. Taken together, these can add up to substantial differences between research results at the macro-level and the micro-level, which may be magnified further by contradictory associations being found at the two levels. One consequence is that macro-level studies usually appear to produce more notable and worthwhile findings, while micro-level studies reveal a more chaotic and changing reality – and the two kinds of results may even be generated from the same source (such as a longitudinal dataset that permits cross-sectional analysis as well as longitudinal analysis). These points go beyond the traditional, even routinised, arguments over the relative merits of intensive versus extensive, qualitative versus quanti-tive, research designs, but they provide an additional reason for multi-level, as well as multi-method, research.

Another theme emerging from the review of research designs is that all eight types of study contribute in different ways to the tasks of description and explanation of social realities and social processes. Some of the arguments about the relative merits of each are not disputes about the value of particular research designs as such, but arguments about the types of explanation that are most 'important' or 'useful'. For example, qualitative research is most likely to be rejected as irrelevant by scholars who disregard the impact of psychological and motivational factors. Yet all longitudinal studies demonstrate the importance of these factors in the long term as well as the short term.

Some social scientists, especially economists, insist that the central aim is to predict and 'not merely to explain' (Blaug, 1980: 262), and prediction is important in policy research (Hoaglin *et al.*, 1982). Putting aside the fact that the two activities can be discrete – since projections of current patterns into the near future do not invariably require under-standing of the underlying causal processes – prediction immediately runs into the problems of the macro/micro divide and the distinction between diagnostic, actionable and causative factors, as well as all the unknowns of future contingencies. All other things do *not* conveniently remain the same, and analyses of national trends in crime and recidiv-ism will be of little use in predicting whether a particular individual, John Smith, will return to crime on release from prison. Prediction remains the long-term objective, but at present social research mainly offers description and explanation, in varying proportions. This is quite an achievement in itself and is reflected in substantively worthwhile additions to knowledge, as illustrated by many of the examples quoted in previous chapters.

The final theme emerging from this review of the research design process is the declining importance of small-scale craft work in university-based social research as the emphasis shifts towards large-scale projects, cross-national comparative studies and co-ordinated research programmes, with a concomitant increase in large research teams, research institutes outside the sphere of higher education, contract research, and large-scale exercises that are costly in time and money. This change is the consequence of policy research becoming the dominant form of social research today (Gibbons *et al.*, 1994). It also suggests that research design and research management are becoming separate specialist functions, as they did somewhat earlier in another field with the division of labour between architect and builder.

# Bibliography

Abeles, R.P. and Wise, L.L. (1980) 'Coping with attrition in a longitudinal study: the case of Project TALENT', *Journal of Economics and Business*, 32: 170–81.

Abel-Smith, B. and Townsend, P. (1965) *The Poor and the Poorest*, London: Bell.

Aberbach, J.D., Putnam, R.D. and Rockman, B.A. (1981) *Bureaucrats and Politicians in Western Democracies*, Cambridge MA: Harvard University Press.

Abramson, M.A. (1978) *The Funding of Social Knowledge Production and Application: A Survey of Federal Agencies*, Washington DC: National Academy of Sciences.

Abramson, P.R. and Inglehart, R. (1995) *Value Change in Global Perspective*, Ann Arbor: University of Michigan Press.

Abt, C.C. (ed.) (1976) *The Evaluation of Social Programs*, Beverly Hills: Sage.

Abt, C.C. (ed.) (1980) *Problems in American Social Policy Research*, Cambridge MA: Abt Books.

Ackoff, R.L. (1953) *The Design of Social Research*, Chicago: University of Chicago Press.

Ahlstrand, B.W. (1990) *The Quest for Productivity: A Case Study of Fawley after Flanders*, Cambridge: Cambridge University Press.

Almond, G.A. and Verba, S. (1965) *The Civic Culture: Political Attitudes and Democracy in Five Nations*, Boston: Little Brown.

Almond, G.A. and Verba, S. (eds) (1980) *The Civic Culture Revisited*, Boston: Little Brown.

Alwin, D.F., Braun, M. and Scott, J. (1992) 'The separation of work and the family: attitudes towards women's labour-force participation in Germany, Great Britain and the United States', *European Sociological Review*, 8: 13–37.

Andrisani, P.J. (1978) *Work Attitudes and Labor Market Experience: Evidence from the National Longitudinal Surveys*, New York: Praeger.

Andrisani, P.J. (ed.) (1980) 'Longitudinal research and labor force behaviour: a symposium', *Journal of Economics and Business*, 32: 89–181.

Anker, R. (1998) *Gender and Jobs: Sex Segregation of Occupations in the World*, Geneva: ILO.

Antonides, G. (1991) *Psychology in Economics and Business*, Dordrecht: Kluwer Academic.

Apostle, R.A. *et al.*. (1983) *The Anatomy of Racial Attitudes*, Berkeley: University of California Press.

Archer, D. and Gartner, R. (1984) *Violence and Crime in Cross-National Perspective*, New Haven: Yale University Press.

Argyle, M. (1967) *The Psychology of Interpersonal Behaviour*, London: Penguin.

Atkinson, A.B., Maynard, A.K. and Trinder, C.G. (1983) *Parents and Children: Incomes in Two Generations*, London: Heinemann.

Aubel, J. (1994) *Guidelines for Studies Using the Group Interview Technique*, Geneva: International Labour Office.

Axelrod, R. (1984) *The Evolution of Cooperation*, New York: Basic Books.

Bailey, G. (1983) *The Tactical Uses of Passion: An Essay on Power, Reason, and Reality*, Ithaca: Cornell University Press.

Baldridge, J.V. and Deal, T. (eds) (1983) *The Dynamics of Organisational Change in Education*, Berkeley CA: McCutchan Publishing.

Banaka, W.H. (1971) *Training in Depth Interviewing*, New York: Harper & Row.

Banton, M. (1983) *Racial and Ethnic Competition*, Cambridge: Cambridge University Press.

Barbour, R.S. and Kitzinger, J. (eds) (1998) *Developing Focus Group Research*, London: Sage.

Barker, E. (1984) *The Making of a Moonie: Brainwashing or Choice?*, Oxford: Blackwell.

Barker, E. (2001) *Religious and Moral Pluralism in Britain*, forthcoming.

Barnes, S.H. *et al.* (1979) *Political Action: Mass Participation in Five Western Democracies*, Beverly Hills: Sage.

Bateman, F. and Weiss, T. (1981) *A Deplorable Scarcity: The Failure of Industrialisation in the Slave Economy*, Chapel Hill: University of North Carolina Press.

Bateson, N. (1984) *Data Construction in Social Surveys*, London: Allen & Unwin.

Batstone, E. (1985) 'International variations in strike activity', *European Sociological Review*, 1: 46–64.

Batstone, E. *et al.* (1984) *Consent and Efficiency: Labour Relations and Management Strategy in the State Enterprise*, Oxford: Blackwell.

Baxter, J. and Kane, E.W. (1995) 'Dependence and independence: a cross-national analysis of gender inequality and gender attitudes', *Gender and Society*, 9: 193–215.

BBC (1984) *Daily Life in the 1980s*, London: BBC.

Bechhofer, F. *et al.* (1984) 'Safety in numbers: on the use of multiple interviewers', *Sociology*, 18: 97–100.

Becker, H.S. (1998) *Tricks of the Trade: How to Think about Your Research While You're Doing It*, Chicago: University of Chicago Press.

Behrman, J.R. *et al.* (1983) 'The impact of minimum wages on the distribution of earnings for major race-sex groups; a dynamic analysis', *American Economic Review*, 73: 766–78.

Bell, C. and Encel, S. (eds) (1978) *Inside the Whale: Ten Personal Accounts of Social Research*, London: Pergamon.

Bell, C. and Newby, H. (1977) *Doing Sociological Research*, London: Allen & Unwin.

Bell, C. and Roberts, H. (eds) (1984) *Social Researching: Politics, Problems and Practice*, London: Routledge.

Berelson, B. (1952) *Content Analysis in Communication Research*, Glencoe IL: Free Press.

Berger, J. and Zelditch, M. (1993) *Theoretical Research Programs: Studies in the Growth of Theory*, Stanford CA: Stanford University Press.

Berk, R. (1983) 'An introduction to sample selection bias in sociological data', *American Sociological Review*, 48: 386–98.

Berk, R.A., Lenihan, K.J. and Rossi, P.H. (1980) 'Crime and poverty: some experimental evidence from ex-offenders', *American Sociological Review*, 45: 766–86.

Berk, R.A. and Newton, P.J. (1985) 'Does arrest really deter wife battery? An effort to replicate the findings of the Minneapolis spouse abuse experiment', *American Sociological Review*, 50: 253–62.

Berkman, L.F. and Breslow, L. (1983) *Health and Ways of Living: The Alameda County Study*, New York: Oxford University Press.

Bernstein, I.N. and Freeman, H.E. (1975) *Academic and Entrepreneurial Research*, New York: Russell Sage Foundation.

Berthoud, R. (1983) 'Transmitted deprivation: the kite that failed', *Policy Studies*, 3: 151–69.

Bielby, W.T. *et al.* (1979) *Research Uses of the National Longitudinal Surveys*, R&D Monograph No. 62, Washington DC: United States Department of Labor.

Birnbaum, P.H. (1981) 'Integration and specialisation in academic research', *Academy of Management Journal*, 24: 487–503.

Black, J. *et al.* (1983) *Social Work in Context: A Comparative Study of Three Social Services Teams*, London: Tavistock.

Blackler, F.H.M. and Brown, C.A. (1980) *Whatever Happened to Shell's New Philosophy of Management? Lessons for the 1980s from a Major Socio-Technical Intervention of the 1960s*, Farnborough, Hants: Saxon House.

Blake, J. and Donovan, J.J. (1971) *Western European Censuses 1960: An English Language Guide*, Berkeley: University of California, Institute of International Studies. Reprinted Westport: Greenwood Press, 1976.

Blalock, H.M. (ed.) (1980) *Sociological Theory and Research: A Critical Appraisal*, New York: Free Press and London: Collier Macmillan.

Blau, P.M. (1963) *The Dynamics of Bureaucracy: A Study of Interpersonal Relations in Two Government Agencies*, 2nd ed., Chicago: University of Chicago Press.

Blau, P.M. and Duncan, O.D. (1967) *The American Occupational Structure*, New York: Wiley.

Blaug, M. (1980) *The Methodology of Economics: Or How Economists Explain*, Cambridge: Cambridge University Press.

Blaxter, M. (ed.) (1979) 'The analysis of qualitative data: a symposium', *Sociological Review*, 27: 649–827.

Block, R. (1983) *Victimisation and Fear of Crime around the World*, Washington DC: US Department of Justice.

Blossfeld, H-P. (1995) *The New Role of Women: Family Formation in Modern Societies*, Boulder CO: Westview.

Blossfeld, H-P. and Hakim, C. (1997) *Between Equalization and Marginalization: Women Working Part-Time in Europe and the USA*, Oxford: Oxford University Press.

Blossfeld, H-P. and Rohwer, G. (1995) *Techniques of Event History Modelling: New Approaches to Causal Analysis*, Mahwah NJ: Lawrence Erlbaum.

Blossfeld, H-P., Hamerle, A. and Mayer, K.U. (1989) *Event History Analysis*, Hillsdale NJ: Lawrence Erlbaum.

Blumstein, A. and Cohen, J. (1979) 'Estimation of individual crime rates from arrest records', *Journal of Criminal Law and Criminology*, 70: 561–85.

Bogdan, R. and Taylor, S.J. (1975) *Introduction to Qualitative Research Methods: A Phenomenological Approach to the Social Sciences*, New York: Wiley.

Boh, K. *et al.* (eds) (1989) *Changing Patterns of European Family Life: A Comparative Analysis of 14 European Countries*, London: Routledge.

Booth, T. (1988) *Developing Policy Research*, Aldershot: Avebury.

Boruch, R.F. and Cecil, J.S. (eds) (1983) *Solutions to Ethical and Legal Problems in Social Research*, New York: Academic Press.

Boruch, R.F. *et al.* (1978) 'Randomized field experiments for program planning, development and evaluation: an illustrative bibliography', *Evaluation Quarterly*, 2: 655–95.

Boserup, E. (1970) *Women's Role in Economic Development*, New York: St Martin's Press.

Boudon, R. (1981) *The Logic of Social Action: An Introduction to Sociological Analysis*, London: Routledge.

Bradbury, K.L. and Downs, A. (eds) (1981) *Do Housing Allowances Work?*, Washington DC: Brookings Institution.

Bradbury, K.L. *et al.* (1982) *Urban Decline and the Future of American Cities*, Washington DC: Brookings Institution.

Braithwaite, J. (1981) 'The myth of social class and criminality reconsidered', *American Sociological Review*, 46: 36–57.

Brook, L. *et al.* (1992) *British Social Attitudes: Cumulative Sourcebook for the First Six Surveys*, Aldershot, Hants: Gower.

Brown, C. (1984) *Black and White Britain: The Third PSI Survey*, London: Heinemann.

Brown, C. and Gay, P. (1985) *Racial Discrimination: 17 Years After the Act*, London: Policy Studies Institute.

Brown, C. and Ritchie, J. (1981) *Focused Enumeration: The Development of a Method of Sampling Ethnic Minority Groups*, London: Policy Studies Institute.

Brown, G. *et al.* (1975) *Experiments in the Social Sciences*, London: Harper & Row.

Brown, G.W. (1993) 'The role of life events in the aetiology of depressive and anxiety disorders', pp. 23–50 in S.C. Stanford and P. Salmon (eds) *Stress: From Synapse to Syndrome*, New York: Academic Press.

Brown, G.W. and Harris, T. (1978) *The Social Origins of Depression: A Study of Psychiatric Disorder in Women*, London: Tavistock.

Brown, M. and Madge, N. (1982) *Despite the Welfare State:* A report on the SSRC/DHSS programme of research into transmitted deprivation, London: Heinemann.

Brown, R.K. (1967) 'Research and consultancy in industrial enterprises: a review of the contribution of the Tavistock Institute of Human Relations to the development of industrial sociology', *Sociology*, 1: 33–60.

Bryman, A. and Burgess, R.G. (eds) (1999) *Qualitative Research*, 4 vols, London: Sage.

Bulmer, M. (ed.) (1980) *Social Research and Royal Commissions*, London: Allen & Unwin.

Bulmer, M. (1983) 'The social sciences', pp. 102–17 in J.W. Chapman (ed.) *The Western University on Trial*, Berkeley: University of California Press.

Bulmer, M. and Warwick, P.D. (eds) (1983) *Social Research in Developing Countries: Surveys and Censuses in the Third World*, Chichester, Sussex: Wiley.

Bulmer, M., Sykes, W. and Moorhouse, J. (eds) (1998) *Directory of Social Research Organisations in the United Kingdom*, 2nd ed., London: Mansell.

Burgess, R.G. (ed.) (1982) *Field Research: A Sourcebook and Field Manual*, London: Allen & Unwin.

Burgess, R.G. (1984) *In the Field: An Introduction to Field Research*, London: Allen & Unwin.

Bursik, R.J. and Webb, J. (1982) 'Community change and patterns of delinquency', *American Journal of Sociology*, 88: 24–42.

Burtless, G. and Greenberg, D. (1982) 'Inferences concerning labour supply behaviour based on limited-duration experiments', *American Economic Review*, 72: 488–97.

Buxton, N.K. and Mackay, D.I. (1977) *British Employment Statistics: A Guide to Sources and Methods*, Oxford: Blackwell.

Bynner, J. and Stribley, K.M. (1978) *Social Research: Principles and Procedures*, London and New York: Longman/Open University Press.

Byrne, D. (1999) *Complexity Theory and the Social Sciences*, London: Routledge.

Cain, G.G. and Watts, H.W. (1970) 'Problems in making policy inferences from the Coleman report', *American Sociological Review*, 35: 228–42.

Cain, M.T. (1993) 'Patriarchal structure and demographic change', in N. Federici, K.O. Mason and S. Sogner (eds) *Women's Position and Demographic Change*, Oxford: Clarendon Press.

Cain, P.S. and Treiman, D.J. (1981) 'The *Dictionary of Occupational Titles* as a source of occupational data', *American Sociological Review*, 46: 253–78.

Calder, A. and Sheridan, D. (eds) (1984) *Speak for Yourself: A Mass Observation Anthology 1937–49*, London: Cape.

Callender, C. *et al.* (1997) *Maternity Rights and Benefits in Britain*, DSS Research Series No. 67, London: Department of Social Security.

Campbell, D.T. (1957) 'Factors relevant to the validity of experiments in social settings', *Psychological Bulletin*, 54: 297–311. Reprinted pp. 243–63 in N.K. Denzin (ed.) *Sociological Methods: A Sourcebook*, 1978, Chicago: Aldine.

Campbell, D.T. (1969) 'Reforms as experiments', *American Psychologist*, 24: 409–29. Reprinted pp. 79–112 in J. Bynner and K.M. Stribley (eds) *Social Research: Principles and Procedures*, London: Longman/Open University Press, 1979.

Campbell, D.T. and Fiske, D.W. (1959) 'Convergent and discriminant validation by the multitrait-multimethod matrix', *Psychological Bulletin*, 56: 81–105.

Campbell, D.T. and Stanley, J.C. (1963) *Experimental and Quasi-Experimental Designs for Research*, Chicago: Rand McNally.

Capen, M.M. *et al.* (1985) 'Labour supply effects of unemployment insurance benefits', *Applied Economics*, 17: 73–85.

Caplow, T. *et al.* (1982) *Middletown Families: Fifty Years of Change and Continuity*, Minneapolis: University of Minnesota Press.

Cardoso, F.H. and Faletto, E. (1969) *Dependencia y Desarollo en America Latina*, Mexico: Siglo XXI.

Carter, P.G. (1976) *US Census Data for Political and Social Research: A Resource Guide*, Washington DC: American Political Science Association.

Cartwright, A. and Anderson, R. (1981) *General Practice Revisited: A Second Study of Patients and their Doctors*, London: Tavistock.

Castles, F.G. (ed.) (1993) *Families of Nations: Patterns of Public Policy in Western Democracies*, Aldershot: Dartmouth.

Center for Human Resource Research (1995) *NLS Handbook 1995*, Columbus: Ohio State University.

Chambers, G. and Tombs, J. (eds) (1984) *The British Crime Survey: Scotland*, Scottish Office Social Research Study, Edinburgh: HMSO.

Champagne, D. (1983) 'Social structure, revitalisation movements and state building: social change in four native American societies', *American Sociological Review*, 48: 754–63.

Chelimsky, E. and Shadish, W.R. (eds) (1997) *Evaluation for the 21st Century*, London: Sage.

Cherlin, A. (1979) 'Worklife and marital dissolution', pp. 151–66 in G. Levinger and O. Moles (eds) *Divorce and Separation: Context, Causes and Consequences*, New York: Basic Books.

Chiplin, B. (1981) 'An alternative approach to the measurement of sex discrimination: an illustration from university entrance', *The Economic Journal*, 91: 988–97.

Chowdhury, G. and Nickell, S. (1985) 'Hourly earnings in the United States: another look at unionisation, schooling, sickness and unemployment using PSID data', *Journal of Labor Economics*, 3: 38–69.

Christensen, H.T. (1963) 'Child spacing analysis via record linkage: new data plus a summing up from earlier reports', *Marriage and Family Living*, 25: 272–80.

Clarke, R.V.G. and Cornish, D.B. (1972) *The Controlled Trial in Institutional Research: Paradigm or Pitfall for Penal Evaluators?*, Home Office Research Study No. 15, London: HMSO. Reprinted pp. 143–57 in R.V.G. Clarke and D.B. Cornish (eds) *Crime Control in Britain: A Review of Policy Research*, Albany NY: State University of New York Press, 1983.

Clarke, R.V.G. and Cornish, D.B. (eds) (1983) *Crime Control in Britain: A Review of Policy Research*, Albany NY: State University of New York Press.

Cleland, J. and Hobcraft, J. (eds) (1985) *Reproductive Change in Developing Countries: Insights from the World Fertility Survey*, Oxford: Oxford University Press.

Cleland, J. and Scott, C. (eds) (1987) *The World Fertility Survey: An Assessment*, Oxford: Oxford University Press.

Cochran, W.G. (1983) *Planning and Analysis of Observational Studies*, New York: Wiley.

Cohen, D.K. and Weiss, J.A. (1977) 'Social science and social policy schools and race', pp. 67–83 in C.H. Weiss (ed.) *Using Social Research in Public Policy Making*, Lexington MA: Lexington Books.

Coleman, J.S. (1961) *The Adolescent Society*, Glencoe IL: Free Press.

Coleman, J.S. (1964) 'Research chronicle: *The Adolescent Society*', pp. 184–211 in P.E. Hammond (ed.) *Sociologists at Work*, New York: Basic Books.

Coleman, J.S. (1970) 'Reply to Cain and Watts', *American Sociological Review*, 35: 242–9.

Coleman, J.S. *et al.* (1966) *Equality of Educational Opportunity*, Washington DC: US Government Printing Office.

Colledge, M. and Bartholomew, R. (1980) *A Study of the Long-Term Unemployed*, Sheffield: Manpower Services Commission.

Cook, J.D. *et al.* (1981) *The Experience of Work: A Compendium and Review of 249 Measurements and their Use*, New York: Academic Press.

Cook, T.D. and Campbell, D.T. (1979) *Quasi-Experimentation: Design and Analysis Issues for Field Settings*, Chicago: Rand McNally.

Cooper, H.M. (1998) *Synthesizing Research: A Guide for Literature Reviews*, Thousand Oaks: Sage.

Cooper, J. (1983) *The Creation of the British Social Services 1962–1974*, London: Heinemann.

Couper, M. *et al.* (eds) (1999) *Computer-Assisted Survey Information Collection*, New York: John Wiley.

Covello, V.T. (ed.) (1980) *Poverty and Public Policy: An Evaluation of Social Science Research*, Cambridge MA: Schenkman.

Cox, K.R. and Johnson, R.J. (1982) *Conflict, Politics and the Urban Scene*, Harlow: Longman.

Cragg, A. and Dawson, T. (1981) *Qualitative Research Among Homeworkers*, Research Paper No. 21, London: Department of Employment.

Cragg, A. and Dawson, T. (1984) *Unemployed Women: A Study of Attitudes and Experiences*, Research Paper No. 47, London: Department of Employment.

Craig, C. *et al.* (1985) *Pay in Small Firms: Women and Informal Payment Systems*, Research Paper No. 48, London: Department of Employment.

Craig, J. (1985) *A 1981 Socio-Economic Classification of Local and Health Authorities of Great Britain*, Studies on Medical and Population Subjects No. 48, London: HMSO.

Crain, R.L. and Mahard, R.E. (1983) 'The effect of research methodology on desegregation-achievement studies: a meta-analysis', *American Journal of Sociology*, 88: 839–54.

Crawford, E. and Perry, N. (eds) (1976) *Demands for Social Knowledge: The Role of Research Organisations*, London: Sage.

Cully, M. *et al.* (1998) *The 1998 Workplace Employee Relations Survey: First Findings*, London: Department of Trade and Industry.

Cully, M., Woodland, S., Reilly, A. and Dix, G. (1999) *Britain at Work: As Depicted by the 1998 Workplace Employee Relations Survey*, London: Routledge.

Cunningham, D.E. (1969) *Federal Support and Stimulation of Inter-disciplinary Research in Universities*, Washington, DC: US Department of Commerce, National Bureau of Standards, N70–21072.

Dale, A. and Egerton, M. (1997) *Highly Educated Women: Evidence from the National Child Development Study*, RS25, London: Department for Education and Employment.

Dale, A. and Marsh, C. (eds) (1993) *The 1991 Census User Guide*, London: HMSO.

Dalton, M. (1964) 'Preconceptions and methods in *Men Who Manage*', pp. 50–95 in P.E. Hammond (ed.) *Sociologists at Work*, New York: Basic Books.

Daniel, W.W. (1980) *Maternity Rights: The Experience of Women*, London: Policy Studies Institute.

Daniel, W.W. (1981) *Maternity Rights: The Experience of Employers*, London: Policy Studies Institute.

Daniel, W.W. (1986) *The Experiences of the Unemployed Flow*, London: Policy Studies Institute.

Daniel, W.W. and Millward, N. (1983) *Workplace Industrial Relations in Britain*, London: Heinemann.

Das Gupta, P. (1975) 'A method of computing period rates of spinsterhood and childlessness from census data applied to the United States', *Social Biology*, 22: 134–43.

Davies, C. (1980) 'Making sense of the census in Britain and the USA: the changing occupational classification of the position of nurses', *Sociological Review*, 28: 581–609.

Davis, J.A. (1977) *Cumulative Codebook for the 1972–1977 General Social Surveys*, Chicago: National Opinion Research Center.

de Boer, C. (1977) 'The polls: women at work', *Public Opinion Quarterly*, 41: 268–77.

Denham, A. and Garnett, M. (1998) *British Think-Tanks and the Climate of Opinion*, London: UCL Press.

Denzin, N.K. (1978a) *The Research Act: A Theoretical Introduction to Sociological Methods*, New York: McGraw-Hill.

Denzin, N.K. (1978b) *Sociological Methods: A Sourcebook*, New York: McGraw-Hill.

Denzin, N.K. and Lincoln, Y.S. (eds) (1994) *Handbook of Qualitative Research*, Thousand Oaks CA: Sage. Reprinted 1998 as 3 volumes: *The Landscape of Qualitative Research: Theories and Issues*, *Strategies of Qualitative Enquiry*, and *Collecting and Interpreting Qualitative Materials*.

Department of Employment (1983) 'Labour force survey changes', *Employment Gazette*, 91: 295–6.

Deutscher, I. (1972) 'Public and private opinions: social situations and multiple realities', pp. 323–40 in S.Z. Nagi and R.G. Corwin (eds) *The Social Contexts of Research*, New York: Wiley.

Dex, S. (1984a) *Women's Work Histories: An Analysis of the Women and Employment Survey*, Research Paper No. 46, London: Department of Employment.

Dex, S. (1984b) 'Work history analysis, women and large scale datasets', *Sociological Review*, 32: 637–61.

Dexter, L. (1970) *Elite and Specialized Interviewing*, Evanston IL: Northwestern University Press.

Dillman, D.A. (1978) *Mail and Telephone Surveys: The Design Method*, New York: Wiley.

Dilnot, A.W., Kay, J.A. and Morris, C.N. (1984) *The Reform of Social Security*, Oxford: Clarendon Press.

Ditton, J. (1977) *Part-Time Crime: An Ethnography of Fiddling and Pilferage*, London: Macmillan.

Dogan, M. (1993) 'Comparing the decline of nationalisms in western Europe: the generational dynamic', *International Social Science Journal*, 136: 177–98.

Dogan, M. (1998) 'The decline of traditional values in Western Europe: religion, nationalism, authority', *International Journal of Comparative Sociology*, 39: 77–90.

Donnison, D. and Soto, P. (1980) *The Good City: A Study of Urban Development and Policy in Britain*, London: Heinemann.

Donovan, P. (1995) 'The 'family cap': a popular but unproven method of welfare reform', *Family Planning Perspectives*, 27: 166–71.

Dooley, D. and Catalano, R. (1980) 'Economic change as a cause of behavioural disorder', *Psychological Bulletin*, 87: 450–68.

Douglas, J. (1976) *Investigative Social Research: Individual and Team Field Research*, Beverly Hills: Sage.

Drake, M., O'Brien, M. and Biebuyck, T. (1981) *Single and Homeless*, London: HMSO.

Drever, F. and Whitehead, M. (eds) (1997) *Health Inequalities: Decennial Supplement*, London: Stationery Office.

Duncan, G.J. (1984) *Years of Poverty, Years of Plenty: The Changing Economic Fortunes of American Workers and Families*, Ann Arbor: University of Michigan, Survey Research Center, Institute for Social Research.

Duncan, G.J. and Mathiowetz, N.A. (1984) *A Validation Study of Economic Survey Data*, Ann Arbor, Michigan: University of Michigan Institute for Social Research Survey Research Center.

Earl, P. (1983) *The Economic Imagination: Towards a Behavioural Analysis of Choice*, Armonk NY: M.E. Sharpe and Brighton: Harvester.

Eccles, M. and Freeman, R.B. (1982) 'What! Another minimum wage study?', *American Economic Review*, 72: 226–32.

Eckstein, H. (1975) 'Case study and theory in political science', pp. 79–137 in F. Greenstein and N. Polsby (eds) *The Handbook of Political Science: Strategies of Inquiry*, Reading MA: Addison-Wesley.

Edwards, P. and Scullion, H. (1984) 'Absenteeism and the control of work', *Sociological Review*, 32: 547–72.

Eichorn, D.H. *et al.* (eds) (1982) *Present and Past in Middle Life*, New York: Academic Press.

Einstein, A. (1936) 'Physics and reality', *Franklin Institute Journal*, 221: 349–82.

Elder, G.H. (ed.) (1985) *Life Course Dynamics: Trajectories and Transitions, 1968–1980*, Ithaca: Cornell University Press.

Elias, N. (1983) *The Court Society*, Oxford: Blackwell.

Elias, P. and Gregory, M. (1994) *The Changing Structure of Occupations and Earnings in Great Britain 1975–1990: An Analysis based on the NES Panel Dataset*, Research Series No. 27, Sheffield: Employment Department.

Englander, F. (1983) 'Helping ex-offenders enter the labour market', *Monthly Labour Review*, 106/7: 25–30.

Epstein, C.F. (1983) *Women in Law*, New York: Anchor/Doubleday.

Erikson, R. (1984) 'Social class of men, women and families', *Sociology*, 18: 500–14.

Erikson, R. and Goldthorpe, J.H. (1985) 'Are American rates of social mobility exceptionally high? New evidence on an old issue', *European Sociological Review*, 1: 1–22.

Erikson, R. and Goldthorpe, J.H. (1993) *The Constant Flux: A Study of Class Mobility in Industrial Societies*, Oxford: Clarendon Press.

Erikson, R., Goldthorpe, J.H. and Portocarero, L. (1979) 'Intergenerational class mobility in three Western European societies: England, France and Sweden', *British Journal of Sociology*, 30: 415–40.

Eurostat (1996) *European Community Household Panel: Survey Methodology and Implementation and Survey Questionnaires for Waves 1–3*, 2 vols, Luxembourg: Eurostat.

Fagin, L. and Little, M. (1984) *The Forsaken Families: The Effects of Unemployment on Family Life*, Harmondsworth: Penguin.

Faraday, A. and Plummer, K. (1979) 'Doing life histories', *Sociological Review*, 27: 773–98.

Farkas, G. (1977) 'Cohort, age, and period effects upon the employment of white females: evidence for 1957–1968', *Demography*, 14: 59–72.

Farrington, D.P. (1983) 'Randomised experiments on crime and justice', pp. 257–308 in M. Tonry and N. Morris (eds) *Crime and Justice: An Annual Review of Research*, vol. 4, Chicago: University of Chicago Press.

Feagin, J.R., Orum, A.M. and Sjoberg, G. (eds) (1991) *A Case for the Case Study*, Chapel Hill: University of North Carolina.

Featherman, D.L. and Hauser, R.M. (1978) *Opportunity and Change*, New York: Academic Press.

Ferber, R. and Hirsch, W.Z. (1979) 'Social experiments in economics', *Journal of Economics*, 11: 77–115.

Ferree, M.M. (1974) 'A woman for president? Changing responses 1958–1972', *Public Opinion Quarterly*, 38: 390–9.

Ferri, E. (ed.) (1993) *Life at 33*, London: National Children's Bureau.

Fevre, R. (1983) 'Cosmetic research: working for the United Kingdom Atomic Energy Authority', *Sociological Review*, 31: 39–55.

Fielding, N. (1981) *The National Front*, London: Routledge.

Fielding. N.G. and Lee, R.M. (1998) *Computer Analysis and Qualitative Research*, London: Sage.

Fields, G.S. and Mitchell, C.S. (1984) *Retirement, Pensions, and Social Security*, Cambridge MA: MIT Press.

Fields, G.S. and Mitchell, C.S. (1985) 'Estimating the effects of changing Social Security benefit formulas', *Monthly Labor Review*, 108, 7: 44–5.

Finch, J. (1987) 'The vignette technique in survey research', *Sociology*, 21: 105–14.

Fischer, C. (1982) *To Dwell Among Friends: Personal Networks in Town and City*, Chicago: University of Chicago Press.

Flaherty, D.H. (1979) *Privacy and Government Databanks: An International Perspective*, London: Mansell Scientific.

Flaim, P.O. and Hogue, C.R. (1985) 'Measuring labour force flows: a special conference examines the problems', *Monthly Labor Review*, 108, 7: 7–17.

Flanders, A. (1964) *The Fawley Productivity Agreements: A Case Study of Management and Collective Bargaining*, London: Faber & Faber.

Fogel, R.W. and Engerman, S.L. (1974) *Time on the Cross: The Economics of American Negro Slavery, and Evidence and Methods*, 2 vols, Boston: Little Brown and London: Wildwood House.

Fogelman, K. (ed.) (1976) *Britain's Sixteen-Year-Olds*, London: National Children's Bureau.

Fogelman, K. (ed.) (1983) *Growing up in Great Britain*, London: Macmillan.

Fogelman, K. and Wedge, P. (1981) 'The National Child Development Study – 1958 Cohort', pp. 30–43 in S.A. Mednick and A.E. Baert (eds) *Prospective Longitudinal Research*, Oxford: Oxford University Press.

Form, W.H. (1971) 'The sociology of social research', pp. 3–54 in R. O'Toole (ed.) *The Organisation, Management and Tactics of Social Research*, Cambridge MA: Schenkman.

Forth, J. *et al.*. (1997) *Family Friendly Working Arrangements in Britain*, Research Series No. 16, London: Department for Education and Employment.

Foster, J. (1974) *Class Struggle and the Industrial Revolution*, London: Weidenfeld & Nicolson.

Fowler, F.J. (1984) *Survey Research Methods*, Beverly Hills: Sage.

Freeman, H.E. *et al.* (eds) (1983) *Applied Sociology: Roles and Activities of Sociologists in Applied Settings*, San Francisco: Jossey Bass.

Freeman, R.B. and Medoff, J.L. (1982) 'Why does the rate of youth labour force activity differ across surveys?', pp. 75–114 in R.B. Freeman and D.A. Wise (eds) *The Youth Labor Market Problem*, Chicago: University of Chicago Press.

Freeman, R.B. and Wise, D.A. (eds) (1982) *The Youth Labor Market Problem: Its Nature, Causes and Consequences*, Chicago: University of Chicago Press.

Frey, J.F. (1983) *Survey Research by Telephone*, Beverly Hills: Sage.

Fruin, W.M. (1978) 'The Japanese company controversy', *Journal of Japanese Studies*, 4: 267–300.

Fruin, W.M. (1980) 'The family as firm and the firm as a family in Japan: the case of Kikkoman Shoyu Company Ltd', *Journal of Family History*, 5: 432–49.

Furet, F. and Ozouf, J. (1982) *Reading and Writing: Literacy in France from Calvin to Jules Ferry*, Cambridge: Cambridge University Press.

Gallie, D. (1978) *In Search of the New Working Class*, Cambridge: Cambridge University Press.

Gallie, D. (1984) *Social Inequality and Class Radicalism in France and Britain*, Cambridge: Cambridge University Press.

Gallie, D. *et al.* (eds) (1994) *Social Change and the Experience of Unemployment*, Oxford: Oxford University Press.

Galtung, J. (1967) *Theories and Methods of Social Research*, London: Allen & Unwin.

Galtung, J. (1990) 'Theory formation in social research: a plea for pluralism', pp. 96–112 in E. Oyen (ed.) *Comparative Methodology*, London: Sage.

Gamson, W.A. *et al.* (1982) *Encounters with Unjust Authority*, Homewood IL: Dorsey Press.

Ganzeboom, H.B.G. and Treiman, D.J. (1996) 'Internationally comparable measures of occupational status for the 1988 International Standard Classification of Occupations', *Social Science Research*, 25: 201–39.

Garofalo, J. and Hindelang, M.J. (1977) *An Introduction to the National Crime Survey*, Washington DC: US Department of Justice.

Garrett, E.M. (1996) 'The dawning of a new era? Women's work in England and Wales at the turn of the twentieth century', *Histoire Sociale/Social History*, 28, 56: 421–64.

Garrett, E.M. (1998) 'Was women's work bad for babies? A view from the 1911 Census of England and Wales', *Continuity and Change*, 13: 281–316.

Gauthier, A.H. (1996) 'The measured and unmeasured effects of welfare benefits on families: implications for Europe's demographic trends', pp. 295–331 in D. Coleman (ed.) *Europe's Population in the 1990s*, Oxford: Oxford University Press.

Genovese, M.A. (ed.) (1993) *Women as National Leaders*, Sage Focus Editions No. 153, Sage.

Gershuny, J. (1993) 'Post-industrial convergence in time allocation', *Futures*, 25: 578–86.

Gershuny, J. and Sullivan, O. (1998) 'The sociological uses of time-use diary analysis', *European Sociological Review*, 14: 69–85.

Gerson, K. (1985) *Hard Choices: How Women Decide about Work, Career and Motherhood*, Berkeley: University of California Press.

Gibbons, M. and Gummett, P. (1976) 'Recent changes in the administration of government research and development in Britain', *Public Administration*, 54 (Autumn): 247–66.

Gibbons, M. *et al.* (1994) *The New Production of Knowledge: The Dynamics of Science and Research in Contemporary Societies*, London: Sage.

Gieryn, T.F. (1983) 'Boundary work and the demarcation of science from non-science: strains and interests in professional ideologies of scientists', *American Sociological Review*, 48: 781–95.

Gilbert, N. (1997) 'Advocacy research and social policy', pp. 101–48 in M. Tonry (ed.) *Crime and Justice: A Review of Research*, vol. 22, Chicago: University of Chicago Press.

Gilbert, N. and Conte, R. (eds) (1995) *Artificial Societies: The Computer Simulation of Social Life*, London: UCL Press.

Gilbert, N. and Doran, J. (eds) (1993) *Simulating Societies: The Computer Simulation of Social Phenomena*, London: UCL Press.

Gilbert, N. and Mulkay, M. (1984) *Opening Pandora's Box: A Sociological Analysis of Scientists' Discourse*, Cambridge: Cambridge University Press.

Gilbert, N. and Troitzsch, K.G. (1999) *Simulation for the Social Scientist*, Buckingham: Open University Press.

Gilmartin, K.J. and Rossi, R.J. (eds) (1982) *Monitoring Educational Outcomes and Public Attitudes*, New York: Human Sciences Press.

Glaser, B.G. and Strauss, A.L. (1967) *The Discovery of Grounded Theory*, Chicago: Aldine.

Glasgow University Media Group (1976) *Bad News*, London: Routledge.

Glasgow University Media Group (1982) *Really Bad News*, London: Writers and Readers Publishing Cooperative Society.

Glass, G.V. *et al.* (1981) *Meta-Analysis in Social Research*, Beverly Hills: Sage.

Glenn, N.D. (1976) 'Cohort analysts' futile quest: statistical attempts to separate age, period and cohort effects', *American Sociological Review*, 41: 900–8.

Glenn, N.D. (1977) *Cohort Analysis*, Beverly Hills: Sage.

Glenn, N.D. (1981) 'The utility and logic of cohort analysis', *Journal of Applied Behavioural Science*, 17: 246–57.

Glenn, N.D. *et al.* (1978) 'The General Social Surveys: a symposium', *Contemporary Sociology*, 7: 532–49.

Goldstein, H. (1979) *The Design and Analysis of Longitudinal Studies: Their Role in the Measurement of Change*, New York: Academic Press.

Goldthorpe, J.H. (1983) 'Women and class analysis: in defence of the conventional view', *Sociology*, 17: 465–88.

Goldthorpe, J.H. (1984) 'Women and class analysis: a reply to the replies', *Sociology*, 18: 491–9.

Goldthorpe, J.H. *et al.* (1969) *The Affluent Worker in the Class Structure*, Cambridge: Cambridge University Press.

Goode, W.J. and Hatt, P.K. (1952) *Methods in Social Research*, New York: McGraw-Hill.

Gospel, H.F. and Littler, C.R. (eds) (1983) *Managerial Strategies and Industrial Relations*, London: Heinemann.

228    *Bibliography*

Gottfredson, M.R. (1984) *Victims of Crime: The Dimensions of Risk*, Home Office Research Study No. 81, London: HMSO.

Goyer, D.S. and Domschke, E. (1983) *The Handbook of National Population Censuses: Latin America and the Caribbean, North America, and Oceania*, Westport CT: Greenwood Press.

Grandjean, B.D. (1981) 'History and career in a bureaucratic labour market', *American Journal of Sociology*, 86: 1057–92.

Granovetter, M. (1984) 'Small is bountiful: labour markets and establishment size', *American Sociological Review*, 49: 323–34.

Greenbaum, T.L. (1998) *The Handbook for Focus Group Research*, London: Sage.

Gregg, P. and Machin, S. (1999) 'Child development and success or failure in the youth labour market', pp. 247–88 in D. Blanchflower and R. Freeman (eds) *Youth Employment and Joblessness in Advanced Countries*, Chicago: University of Chicago Press.

Gregory, M.B. and Jukes, R. (1998) 'The effect of unemployment on future earnings: low paid men in Britain 1984–94', pp. 165–84 in R. Asplund, P.J. Sloane and T. Ioannis (eds) *Low Pay and Earnings Mobility in Europe*, Cheltenham: Edward Elgar.

Gregory, M.B. and Thomson, A.W.J. (eds) (1990) *A Portrait of Pay, 1970–1982: An Analysis of the New Earnings Survey*, Oxford: Clarendon Press.

Griliches, Z. (1985) 'Data and econometricians – the uneasy alliance', *American Economic Review*, 75: 196–200.

Groves, R.M. and Kahn, R.L. (1979) *Surveys by Telephone: A National Comparison with Personal Interviews*, New York: Academic Press.

Gustman, A.L. (1984) 'Modelling individuals' behaviour: evaluation of a policymaker's tool', *Journal of Policy Analysis and Management*, 3: 191–205.

Guttentag, M. and Secord, P.F. (1983) *Too Many Women? The Sex Ratio Question*, Beverly Hills CA: Sage.

Hakim, C. (1979) *Occupational Segregation: A Comparative Study of the Degree and Pattern of the Differentiation between Men and Women's Work in Britain, the United States and Other Countries*, Research Paper No. 9, London: Department of Employment.

Hakim, C. (1980) 'Census reports as documentary evidence: the census commentaries 1801–1951', *Sociological Review*, 28: 551–80.

Hakim, C. (1982a) *Secondary Analysis in Social Research: A Guide to Data Sources and Methods with Examples*, London: Allen & Unwin.

Hakim, C. (1982b) 'The social consequences of high unemployment', *Journal of Social Policy*, 11: 433–67.

Hakim, C. (1983) 'Research based on administrative records', *Sociological Review*, 31: 489–519.

Hakim, C. (1985) *Employers' Use of Outwork: A Study Using the 1980 Workplace Industrial Relations Survey and the 1981 National Homeworking Survey*, Research Paper No. 44, London: Department of Employment.

Hakim, C. (1987) *Home-Based Work in Britain: A Report on the 1981 National Homeworking Survey and the DE Research Programme on Homework*, Research Paper No. 60, London: Department of Employment.

Hakim, C. (1991) 'Cross-national comparative research on the European Community: the EC Labour Force Surveys', *Work, Employment and Society*, 5: 101–17.

Hakim, C. (1996) *Key Issues in Women's Work: Female Heterogeneity and the Polarisation of Women's Employment*, London: Athlone.

Hakim, C. (1998) *Social Change and Innovation in the Labour Market: Evidence from the Census SARs on Occupational Segregation and Labour Mobility*, Oxford: Oxford University Press.

Hakim, C. (1999a) 'Models of the family, women's role and social policy: a new perspective from Preference Theory', *European Societies*, 1: 25–50.

Hakim, C. (1999b) 'Diversity and choice in the sexual contract: models for the 21st century', pp. 165– 79 in G. Dench (ed.) *Rewriting the Sexual Contract*, New York: Transaction Publishers.

Hakim, C. (2000) *Preference Theory: Work-Lifestyle Choices in the 21st Century*, Oxford: Oxford University Press.

Hammersley, M. (1984) 'Some reflections upon the macro-micro problem in the sociology of education', *Sociological Review*, 32: 316–24.

Hammersley, M. (1985) 'From ethnography to theory: a programme and paradigm in the sociology of education', *Sociology*, 19: 244–59.

Hammersley, M. (1997) 'Qualitative data archiving: some reflections on its prospects and problems', *Sociology*, 31: 131–42.

Hammond, P.E. (1964) *Sociologists at Work: Essays on the Craft of Social Research*, New York: Basic Books.

Hanson, R.H. (1978) *The Current Population Survey: Design and Methodology*, Technical Paper 40, Department of Commerce, Bureau of the Census, Washington: US Government Printing Office.

Hantrais, L. and Mangen, S. (eds) (1996) *Cross-National Research Methods in the Social Sciences*, London: Pinter.

Harbury, C.D. and Hitchens, D.M. (1979) *Inheritance and Wealth Inequality in Britain*, London: Allen & Unwin.

Hareven, T.K. (1982) *Family Time and Industrial Time*, New York: Cambridge University Press.

Harrop, M. (1980) 'Social research and market research: a critique of a critique', *Sociology*, 14: 277– 81.

Haug, M.R. (1971) 'Notes on the art of research management', pp. 198–210 in R. O'Toole (ed.) *The Organisation, Management and Tactics of Social Research*, Cambridge MA: Schenkman.

Hausman, J.A. and Wise, D.A. (eds) (1985) *Social Experimentation*, Chicago: University of Chicago Press.

Hechter, M. (ed.) (1983) *The Microfoundations of Macrosociology*, Philadelphia: Temple University Press.

Heclo, H. (1974) *Modern Social Politics in Britain and Sweden: From Relief to Income Maintenance*, New Haven CT: Yale University Press.

Heclo, H. and Wildavsky, A. (1981) *The Private Government of Public Money: Community and Policy inside British Politics*, 2nd ed., London: Macmillan.

Hedges, B.M. (1978) 'Sampling minority populations', pp. 244–61 in M. Wilson (ed.) *Social and Educational Research in Action*, London: Longman.

Heidenheimer, A., Heclo, H. and Adams, C. (1990) *Comparative Public Policy*, 3rd ed., New York: St Martin's Press.

Heller, T. (1982) *Women and Men as Leaders: In Business, Educational, and Social Service Organisations*, South Hadley MA: J.F. Bergin.

Hellevik, O. (1984) *Introduction to Causal Analysis: Exploring Survey Data by Crosstabulation*, London: Allen & Unwin.

Heron, J. (1996) *Co-operative Inquiry: Research into the Human Condition*, London: Sage.

Herriott, R.E. and Gross, N. (eds) (1979) *The Dynamics of Planned Educational Change*, Berkeley, CA: McCutchan.

Hershberg, T. (ed.) (1981) *Philadelphia*, New York: Oxford University Press.

Hill, M.S. and Corcoran, M. (1979) 'Unemployment among family men: a 10-year longitudinal study', *Monthly Labor Review*, 102, 11: 19–23.

Himmelweit, H.T. *et al.* (1981) *How Voters Decide: A Longitudinal Study of Political Attitudes and Voting Extending over Fifteen Years*, New York: Academic Press.

Hindelang, M.J. *et al.* (1979) 'Correlates of delinquency: the illusion of discrepancy between self-report and official measures', *American Sociological Review*, 44: 995–1014.

Hinds, P.S., Vogel, R.J. and Clarke-Steffen, L. (1997) 'The possibilities and pitfalls of doing a secondary analysis of a qualitative dataset', *Qualitative Health Research*, 7: 408–24.

Hirschi, T. and Gottfredson, M. (1983) 'Age and the explanation of crime', *American Journal of Sociology*, 89: 552–84.

Hirschi, T. and Selvin, H.C. (1973) *Principles of Survey Analysis: Delinquency Research*, New York: Free Press.

Hoaglin, D.C. *et al.*. (1982) *Data for Decisions: Information Strategies for Policymakers*, Cambridge MA: Abt Books.

Hodson, R. (1983) *Workers' Earnings and Corporate Economic Structure*, New York: Academic Press.

Hodson, R. (1984) 'Companies, industries, and the measurement of economic segmentation', *American Sociological Review*, 49: 335–48.

Hofferth, S.L. (1983) 'Childbearing decision-making and family well-being: a dynamic, sequential model', *American Sociological Review*, 48: 533–45.

Hofstede, G. (1980) *Culture's Consequences: International Differences in Work-Related Values*, Beverly Hills CA: Sage.

Hofstede, G. (1991) *Cultures and Organisations*, London: HarperCollins.

Hoinville, G. and Jowell, R. (1977) *Survey Research Practice*, London: Heinemann.

Holdaway, S. (1982) *Inside the British Police: A Force at Work*, Oxford: Blackwell.

Home Office (1991) *The Offenders' Tale: Janus Studies*, London: Home Office.

Home Office (1995) *Criminal Careers of those Born Between 1953 and 1973*, London: Home Office Statistical Bulletin No. 14/95.

Home Office (1999) *Reconvictions of Offenders Sentenced or Discharged from Prison in 1994, England and Wales*, London: Home Office Statistical Bulletin No. 5/99.

Hood, J.C. (1983) *Becoming a Two-Job Family*, New York: Praeger.

Hope, T. (1984) 'The first British Crime Survey: current and future research', *Home Office Research Bulletin*, 18: 12–15.

Hough, M. and Mayhew, P. (1985) *Taking Account of Crime: Key Findings from the 1984 British Crime Survey*, Home Office Research Study No. 85, London: HMSO.

Humphrey, R. (1985) 'How work roles influence perception: structural-cognitive processes and organisational behaviour', *American Sociological Review*, 50: 242–52.

Hunt, A. (1975) *Management Attitudes and Practices towards Women at Work*, London: HMSO.

Hunter, J.E. *et al.* (1982) *Meta-Analysis: Cumulating Research Findings across Studies*, Beverly Hills: Sage.

Husbands, C.T. (1983) *Racial Exclusionism and the City: The Urban Support of the National Front*, London: Allen & Unwin.

Hutchby, I. and Wooffitt, R. (1998) *Conversation Analysis: Principles and Applications*, Cambridge: Polity.

Hyman, H.H. (1967) *Survey Design and Analysis*, London: CollierMacmillan.

Hyman, H.H. (1972) *Secondary Analysis of Sample Surveys: Principles, Procedures and Potentialities*, New York: Wiley.

Hyman, H.H. and Wright, C.R. (1979) *Education's Lasting Influence on Values*, Chicago: University of Chicago Press.

Hyman, H.H., Wright, C.R. and Reed, J.S (1975) *The Enduring Effects of Education*, Chicago: University of Chicago Press.

Inglehart, R. (1977) *The Silent Revolution: Changing Values and Political Styles*, Princeton NJ: Princeton University Press.

Inglehart, R. (1990) *Culture Shift in Advanced Industrial Society*, Princeton NJ: Princeton University Press.

Inglehart, R. (1997) *Modernization and Postmodernization: Cultural, Economic, and Political Change in 43 Societies*, Princeton NJ: Princeton University Press.

Inglehart, R., Basañez, M. and Moreno, A. (1998) *Human Values and Beliefs: A Cross-Cultural Sourcebook – Political, Religious, Sexual, and Economic Norms in 43 Societies: Findings from the 1990–1993 World Values Survey*, Ann Arbor: University of Michigan Press.

Jack-Roller, The, and Snodgrass, J. (1982) *The Jack-Roller at Seventy: A Fifty-Year Follow-Up*, Lexington MA: Lexington Books.

Jagodzinski, W. (2001) *Religious and Moral Pluralism in Europe*, forthcoming.

Jahoda, M., Lazarsfeld, P.F. and Zeisel, H. (1972) *Marienthal: The Sociography of an Unemployed Community*, English ed., London: Tavistock.

Jefferys, M. and Sachs, H. (1983) *Rethinking General Practice: Dilemmas in Primary Medical Care*, London: Methuen.

Jennings, M.K. and Niemi, R.G. (1974) *The Political Character of Adolescence: The Influence of Families and Schools*, Princeton NJ: Princeton University Press.

Jennings, M.K. and Niemi, R.G. (1981) *Generations and Politics: A Panel Study of Young Adults and their Parents*, Princeton NJ: Princeton University Press.

Job, B.C. (1979) 'How likely are individuals to enter the labor force?', *Monthly Labor Review*, 102, 9: 28–34.

Johnson, J.D. and Tuttle, F. (1989) *Problems in Intercultural Research*, Newbury Park: Sage.

Johnson, J.M. (1975) *Doing Field Research*, London: CollierMacmillan, and New York: The Free Press.

Jones, C. (ed.) (1985) *Patterns of Social Policy: An Introduction to Comparative Analysis*, London: Tavistock.

Jones, E.L. (1983) 'The courtesy bias in South-East Asian surveys' pp. 253–60 in M. Bulmer and D.P. Warwick (eds) *Social Research in Developing Countries*, New York: John Wiley.

Joshi, H. (1984) *Women's Participation in Paid Work: Further Analysis of the Women and Employment Survey*, Research Paper No. 45, London: Department of Employment.

Joshi, H. and Paci, P. (1998) *Unequal Pay for Women and Men: Evidence from the British Birth Cohort Studies*, Cambridge MA: MIT Press.

Jowell, R. (1998) 'How comparative is comparative research?', *American Behavioural Scientist*, 42: 168–77.

Jowell, R. and Airey, C. (eds) (1984) *British Social Attitudes: The 1984 Report*, Aldershot, Hants: Gower.

Jowell, R. *et al.* (1998) *British and European Social Attitudes – the 15th Report: How Britain Differs*, Aldershot: Ashgate.

Kagan, R. (1978) *Regulatory Justice: Implementing a Wage-Price Freeze*, New York: Russell Sage Foundation.

Kalachek, E. (1978) 'Longitudinal labor market surveys: asking "how come", not "how many"', *Monthly Labor Review*, 101, 9: 8–14.

Kalleberg, A.L., Knoke, D., Marsden, P.V. and Spaeth, J.L. (1996) *Organizations in America: Analyzing their Structures and Human Resource Practices*, Thousand Oaks: Sage.

Kandiah, M.D. and Seldon, A. (1996) *Ideas and Think Tanks in Contemporary Britain*, 2 vols, London: Frank Cass.

Keller, U. (ed.) (1995) *Computer-Aided Qualitative Data Analysis: Theory, Methods and Practice*, London: Sage.

Kelman, H.C. (1967) 'Human use of human subjects: the problem of deception in social psychological experiments', *Psychological Bulletin*, 67: 1–11. Reprinted pp. 189–203 in J. Bynner and K.M. Stribley (eds) *Social Research: Principles and Procedures*, London: Longman, 1978.

Kemsley, W.F.F. *et al.* (1980) *Family Expenditure Survey Handbook*, London: HMSO.

Kessler, R.C. and Greenberg, D.F. (1981) *Linear Panel Analysis: Models of Quantitative Change*, New York: Academic Press.

Kessler-Harris, A. (1982) *Out to Work: A History of Wage-Earning Women in the United States*, London: Oxford University Press.

Kimberly, J.R. *et al.* (eds) (1980) *The Organisational Life Cycle: Issues in the Creation, Transformation and Decline of Organisations*, San Francisco: Jossey-Bass.

King, G., Keohane, R.O. and Verba, S. (1994) *Designing Social Enquiry: Scientific Inference in Qualitative Research*, Princeton NJ: Princeton University Press.

King, S. and Murray, K. (1996) 'Family and working lives survey: preliminary results', *Labour Market Trends*, 104: 115–19.

Klein, L. (1976) *A Social Scientist in Industry*, London: Gower.

Kogan, M. and Henkel, M. (1983) *Government and Research: The Rothschild Experiment in a Government Department*, London: Heinemann.

Kohn, M.L. (1969) *Class and Conformity: A Study in Values*, Homewood IL: Dorsey. 2nd edition, 1977, University of Chicago Press.

Kohn, M.L. (ed.) (1989) *Cross-National Research in Sociology*, Newbury Park: Sage.

Kohn, M.L. and Schooler, C. (1983) *Work and Personality: An Inquiry into the Impact of Social Stratification*, Norwood NJ: Ablex.

Kollock, P., Blumstein, P. and Schwartz, P. (1985) 'Sex and power in interaction: conversational privileges and duties', *American Sociological Review*, 50: 34–46.

Komarovsky, M. (ed.) (1975) *Sociology and Public Policy: The Case of the Presidential Commissions*, New York: Elsevier.

Krausz, E. (ed.) (1983) *Studies of Israeli Society, Vol. 2: The Sociology of the Kibbutz*, New Brunswick: Transaction Books.

Krausz, E. and Miller, S.H. (1974) *Social Research Design*, London: Longman.

Krueger, R.A. (1994) *Focus Groups: A Practical Guide for Applied Research*, London: Sage.

Kuechler, M. (1998) 'The survey method: an indispensable tool for social science research everywhere?', *American Behavioural Scientist*, 42: 178–200.

Lacey, C. (1970) *Hightown Grammar: The School as a Social System*, Manchester: Manchester University Press.

Lacey, C. (1976) 'Problems of sociological fieldwork: a review of the methodology of *Hightown Grammar*', pp. 63–88 in M. Shipman (ed.) *The Organisation and Impact of Social Research*, London: Routledge. Reprinted pp. 160–88 in M. Wilson (ed.) *Social and Educational Research in Action*, London: Longman, 1978.

Lattimore, P.K. and Witte, A.D. (1985) 'Programs to aid ex-offenders: we don't know that nothing works', *Monthly Labor Review*, 108, 4: 46–50.

Lavin, D.E. *et al.* (1981) *Right versus Privilege: The Open Admissions Experiment at the City University of New York*, New York: Free Press.

Lawton, R. (ed.) (1978) *The Census and Social Structure: An Interpretative Guide to the 19th Century Censuses for England and Wales*, London: FrankCass.

Lazarsfeld, P.F. and Reitz, J.G. (1975) *An Introduction to Applied Sociology*, New York: Elsevier.

Lazarsfeld, P.F., Sewell, W. and Wilensky, H.L. (eds) (1967) *The Uses of Sociology*, New York: Basic Books.

Leach, J.W. and Leach, E. (eds) (1983) *The Kula: New Perspectives in Massim Exchange*, Cambridge and New York: Cambridge University Press.

Leggatt, T. (1974) 'Management style and economic success in industry', pp. 185–205 in T. Leggatt (ed.) *Sociological Theory and Survey Research*, London: Sage.

Lein, L. (1984) *Families without Villains: American Families in an Era of Change*, Lexington MA: D.C. Heath & Co.

Lester, D. (1983) *Why People Kill Themselves: A 1980s Summary of Research Findings on Suicidal Behaviour*, 2nd ed., Springfield IL: Charles C. Thomas.

Levi, M. (1981) *The Phantom Capitalists: The Organisation and Control of Long-Firm Fraud*, London: Heinemann.

Lieberson, S. (1981) *A Piece of the Pie: Black and White Immigrants Since 1880*, Berkeley CA: University of California Press.

Lieberson, S. (1985) *Making it Count: The Improvement of Social Research and Theory*, Berkeley: University of California Press.

Lieberson, S. and Hansen, L.K. (1974) 'National development, mother tongue diversity, and the comparative study of nations', *American Sociological Review*, 39: 523–41.

Lievesley, D. and Waterton, J. (1985) 'Measuring individual attitude change', pp. 177–94 in R. Jowell and S. Witherspoon (eds) *British Social Attitudes: The 1985 Report*, Aldershot, Hants: Gower.

Light, R.J. and Pillemer, D.B. (1984) *Summing Up: The Science of Reviewing Research*, Cambridge MA: Harvard University Press.

Lightfoot, S.L. (1983) *The Good High School: Portraits of Character and Culture*, New York: Basic Books.

Lindblom, C.E. and Cohen, D.K. (1979) *Usable Knowledge*, New Haven CT: Yale University Press.

Lipset, S.M. (1964) 'The biography of a research project: *Union Democracy*', pp. 96–120 in P.E. Hammond (ed.) *Sociologists at Work*, New York: Basic Books.

Lipset, S.M. and Schneider, W. (1983) *The Confidence Gap: Business, Labor, and Government in the Public Mind*, New York: Free Press.

Lipset, S.M. *et al.* (1956) *Union Democracy*, Glencoe IL: Free Press. Reprinted Garden City: Doubleday Anchor Books, 1962.

Littler, C.R. (1982) *The Development of the Labour Process in Capitalist Societies: A Comparative Study of the Transformation of Work Organisation in Britain, Japan and the USA*, London: Heinemann.

Lloyd, C.B. and Niemi, B.T. (1979) *The Economics of Sex Differentials*, New York: Columbia University Press.

Lloyd, J. (1985) *Understanding the Miners' Strike*, London: Fabian Society.

Luker, K. (1984) *Abortion and the Politics of Motherhood*, Berkeley CA: University of California Press.

Lundberg, S. (1985) 'The added worker effect', *Journal of Labor Economics*, 3: 11–37.

Luszki, M.B. (1957) 'Team research in social science: major consequences of a growing trend', *Human Organisation*, 16: 21–4.

Luszki, M.B. (1958) *Interdisciplinary Team Research: Methods and Problems*, New York: New York University Press.

Lynd, R.S. and Lynd, H.M. (1929) *Middletown: A Study in Modern American Culture*, New York: Harcourt Brace Jovanovich.

Mackie, T. and Rose, R. (1982) *The International Almanac of Electoral History*, London: Macmillan.

Maital, S. (1982) *Minds, Markets, and Money: Psychological Foundations of Economic Behaviour*, New York: Basic Books.

Majchrzak, A. (1984) *Methods for Policy Research*, Beverly Hills: Sage.

Marín, G. and Marín, B.V. (1991) *Research With Hispanic Populations*, Newbury Park: Sage.

Marmot, M.G. and Wilkinson, R.G. (eds) (1999) *The Social Determinants of Health*, Oxford: Oxford University Press.

Marsh, C. (1982) *The Survey Method: The Contribution of Surveys to Sociological Explanation*, London: Allen & Unwin.

Marsh, C. (1984) 'Informants, respondents and citizens', pp. 206–27 in M. Bulmer (ed.) *Essays on the History of British Social Research*, Cambridge: Cambridge University Press.

Marshall, G. *et al.* (1991) *Social Class in Modern Britain*, London: Hutchinson.

Martin, J. and Butcher, B. (1982) 'The quality of proxy information – some results from a large-scale study', *The Statistician*, 31: 293–319.

Martin, J. and Roberts, C. (1984a) *Women and Employment: A Lifetime Perspective*, London: HMSO.

Martin, J. and Roberts, C. (1984b) *Women and Employment: Technical Report*, London: Office of Population Censuses and Surveys.

Martin, R. and Wallace, J.G. (1985) *Working Women in Recession: Employment, Redundancy and Unemployment*, Oxford: Oxford University Press.

Martin, S.E. (1980) *Breaking and Entering: Policewomen on Patrol*, Berkeley, CA: University of California Press.

Maunder, W.F. (ed.) (1974–85) *Reviews of United Kingdom Statistical Sources*, 17 vols, London: Heinemann and Oxford: Pergamon.

Mawby, R. (1979) *Policing the City*, Farnborough: Saxon House.

Mayhew, P. and Hough, M. (1982) 'The British Crime Survey', *Home Office Research Bulletin*, 14: 24–7.

McCann, K. *et al.* (1984) 'Telephone screening as a research technique', *Sociology*, 18: 393–402.

McClelland. D, (1961) *The Achieving Society*, Princeton NJ: Van Nostrand.

McCloskey, D.N. (1985) 'The loss function has been mislaid: the rhetoric of significance tests', *American Economic Review*, 75: 201–5.

McDill, E.L. and Rigsby, L.C. (1973) *Structure and Process in Secondary Schools: The Academic Impact of Educational Climates*, Baltimore: Johns Hopkins.

McGovern, J.R. (1982) *Anatomy of a Lynching: The Killing of Claude Neal*, Baton Rouge: Louisiana State University Press.

McGrath, J.E.P., Martin, J. and Kulka, R.A. (1982) *Judgement Calls in Research*, Beverly Hills: Sage.

McKnight, A., Elias, P. and Wilson, R. (1998) *Low Pay and the National Insurance System: A Statistical Picture*, Research Discussion Series, Manchester: Equal Opportunities Commission.

McRae, D. and Whittington, D. (1997) *Expert Advice for Policy Choice: Analysis and Discourse*, Washington DC: Georgetown University Press.

Mednick, S.A. and Baert, A.E. (eds) (1981) *Prospective Longitudinal Research: An Empirical Basis for the Primary Prevention of Psychosocial Disorders*, Oxford: Oxford University Press.

Melkas, H. and Anker, R. (1998) *Gender Equality and Occupational Segregation in Nordic Labour Markets*, Geneva: International Labour Office.

Merton, R.K. (1982) *Social Research and the Practising Professions*, Cambridge MA: Abt Books.

Metz, D.L. (1981) *Running Hot: Structure and Stress in Ambulance Work*, Cambridge MA: Abt Books.

Miers, S. and Kopytoff, I. (eds) (1977) *Slavery in Africa: Historical and Anthropological Perspectives*, Madison: University of Wisconsin Press.

Miles, M.B. and Huberman, A.M. (1994) *Qualitative Data Analysis*, Beverly Hills: Sage.

Milgram, S. (1963) 'Behavioural study of obedience', *Journal of Abnormal and Social Psychology*, 67: 371–8. Reprinted pp. 218–37 in M. Wilson (ed.) *Social and Educational Research in Action*, London: Longman, 1978.

Miller, D.C. (1992) *Handbook of Research Design and Social Measurement*, 5th ed., London: Sage.

Miller, W.L. (1983) *The Survey Method in the Social and Political Sciences: Achievements, Failures, Prospects*, Baltimore: Johns Hopkins.

Millward, N., Bryson, A. and Forth, J. (2000) *All Change At Work?*, London: Routledge.

Millward, N., Stevens, M., Smart, D. and Hawes, W.R. (1992) *Workplace Industrial Relations in Transition: The ED/ESRC/PSI/ACAS Survey*, Aldershot: Dartmouth.

Milner, D. (1983) *Children and Race*, London: Sage.

Mirlees-Black, C., Budd, T., Partridge, S. and Mayhew, P. (1998) *The 1998 British Crime Survey*, London: Home Office Statistical Bulletin No. 21/98.

Mitchell, D. (1991) *Income Transfers in Ten Welfare States*, Aldershot: Avebury.

Mitchell, J.C. (1983) 'Case and situation analysis', *Sociological Review*, 31: 187–211.

Moore, B. (1966) *Social Origins of Dictatorship and Democracy: Lord and Peasant in the Making of the Modern World*, Boston: Beacon.

Moore, D.P. (1984) 'Evaluating in-role and out-of-role performers', *Academy of Management Journal*, 27: 603–18.

Moore, S.F. (1983) *Law as Process: An Anthropological Approach*, London: Routledge.

Morgan, D.L. (ed.) (1993) *Successful Focus Groups*, Newbury Park CA: Sage.

Morgan, D.L. (1997) *Focus Groups as Qualitative Research*, London: Sage.

Morgan, D.L. and Krueger, R.A. (1998) *Focus Group Kit*, 6 vols, London: Sage.

Morrison, D.E. and Henkel, R.E. (1970) *The Significance Test Controversy – A Reader*, Chicago: Aldine.

Moser, C.A. and Kalton, G. (1971) *Survey Methods in Social Investigation*, 2nd ed., London: Heinemann.

Mott, F.L. (ed.) (1978) *Women, Work and Family*, Lexington MA: Lexington Books.

Mott, F.L. (ed.) (1982) *The Employment Revolution: Young American Women of the 1970s*, Cambridge MA: MIT Press.

Moylan, S., Millar, J. and Davies, B. (1984) *For Richer, for Poorer? DHSS Cohort*, DHSS Social Research Branch Research Report No. 11, London: HMSO.

Moyser, G. and Wagstaffe, M. (eds) (1987) *Research Methods for Elite Studies*, London: Allen & Unwin.

Mueller, C.F. (1982) *The Economics of Labor Migration: A Behavioural Analysis*, New York: Academic Press.

Murphy, J. (1985) 'Does the difference schools make, make a difference?', *British Journal of Sociology*, 36: 106–16.

Myers, J.L. (1966) *Fundamentals of Experimental Design*, Boston: Allyn & Bacon.

Nagi, S.Z. and Corwin, R.G. (eds) (1972) *The Social Contexts of Research*, New York: Wiley.

Namenwirth, J.Z., *et al.* (1981) 'Organisations have opinions: a redefinition of publics', *Public Opinion Quarterly*, 45: 463–76.

Naoi, A. and Schooler, C. (1985) 'Occupational conditions and psychological functioning in Japan', *American Journal of Sociology*, 90: 729–44.

Narendranathan, W., Nickell, S. and Stern, J. (1985) 'Unemployment benefits revisited', *Economic Journal*, 95: 307–29.

Nathan, R.P. (1988) *Social Science in Government: Uses and Misuses*, New York: Basic Books.

Nazroo, J.Y., Edwards, A.C. and Brown, G.W. (1997) 'Gender differences in the onset of depression following a shared life event: a study of couples', *Psychological Medicine*, 27: 9–19.

Ni Bhrolchain, M. and Timaeus, I.M. (1985) 'A general approach to the machine handling of event history data', *Social Science Information*, 24: 161–88.

Nicholson, W. and Wright, S.R. (1977) 'Participants' understanding of treatment in policy experimentation', *Evaluation Quarterly*, 1: 171–86.

Norris, G.M. (1978) 'Unemployment, subemployment and personal characteristics', *Sociological Review*, 26: 89–108 and 327–47.

O'Barr, W.M., Spain, D.H. and Tessler, M.A. (1973) *Survey Research in Africa: Its Applications and Limits*, Evanston: Northwestern University Press.

OECD (1978) *Multi-Purpose Household Surveys in Developing Countries*, Paris: OECD Development Centre.

OECD (1994) *The OECD Jobs Study*, Paris: OECD.

OECD (1995) *Literacy, Economy and Society: Results of the First International Adult Literacy Survey*, Paris: OECD.

OECD (1997) *Literacy Skills for the Knowledge Society: Further Results from the International Adult Literacy Survey*, Paris: OECD.

Olsen, M.E. and Micklin, M. (eds) (1981) *Handbook of Applied Sociology*, New York: Praeger.

ONS (1998) *Review of the ONS Longitudinal Study 1998*, ONS Occasional Paper No. 1, London: ONS.

ONS (1999) *Tracking People*, London: ONS.

Oppenheim, A.N. (1992) *Questionnaire Design, Interviewing and Attitude Measurement*, London: Pinter.

Orlans, H. (1972) *The Nonprofit Research Institute*, New York: McGraw-Hill.

Orlans, H. (1973) *Contracting for Knowledge*, San Francisco: Jossey-Bass.

Orne, M.T. (1962) 'On the social psychology of the psychological experiment with particular reference to demand characteristics and their implications', *American Psychologist*, 17: 776–83. Reprinted pp. 205–16 in N.K. Denzin (ed.) *Sociological Methods: A Sourcebook*, New York: McGraw Hill, 1978.

Osterman, P. (1980) *Getting Started: The Youth Labor Market*, Cambridge MA: MIT Press.

Osterman, P. (1982) 'Employment structures within firms', *British Journal of Industrial Relations*, 20: 349–61.

O'Toole, R. (1971) *The Organisation, Management and Tactics of Social Research*, Cambridge MA: Schenkman.

Oyen, E. (ed.) (1990) *Comparative Methodology: Theory and Practice of International Social Research*, London: Sage.

Pahl, J. (1983) 'The allocation of money and the structuring of inequality within marriage', *Sociological Review*, 31: 237–62.

Parcel, T.L. and Mueller, C.W. (1983a) 'Occupational differentiation, prestige, and socioeconomic status', *Work and Occupations*, 10: 49–80.

Parcel, T.L. and Mueller, C.W. (1983b) *Ascription and Labour Markets: Race and Sex Differences in Earnings*, New York: Academic Press.

Parker, J. and Dugmore, K. (1976) *Colour and the Allocation of GLC Housing: The Report of the GLC Lettings Survey 1974–75*, Research Report No. 21, London: Greater London Council.

Parnes, H.S. (1975) 'The National Longitudinal Surveys: new vistas for labour market research', *American Economic Review*, 65: 244–9.

Parnes, H.S. (ed.) (1981) *Work and Retirement: A Longitudinal Study of Men*, Cambridge MA: MIT Press.

Patton, M.Q. (1990) *Qualitative Evaluation and Research Methods*, Beverly Hills: Sage.

Payne, G. (1979) 'Social research and market research', *Sociology*, 13: 307–13.

Peil, M. (1982) *Social Science Research Methods: An African Handbook*, London: Hodder & Stoughton.

Percy, A. (1998) *Ethnicity and Victimisation: Findings from the 1996 British Crime Survey*, Home Office Statistical Bulletin No. 6/98, London: Home Office.

Phelps Brown, E.H. (1968a) *Report of the Committee of Inquiry into Certain Matters Concerning Labour in Building and Civil Engineering*, Cmnd 3714, London: HMSO.

Phelps Brown, E.H. (1968b) *Report on the Committee of Inquiry: Research Supplement*, Cmnd 3714–1, London: HMSO.

Phillips, D.P. (1983) 'The impact of mass media violence on US homicides', *American Sociological Review*, 48: 560–8.

Pilling, D. (1990) *Escape from Disadvantage*, London: Falmer.

Pinder, J. (ed.) (1981) *Fifty Years of Political and Economic Planning: Looking Forward 1931– 1981*, London: Heinemann.

Platt, J. (1976) *Realities of Social Research: An Empirical Study of British Sociologists*, London: Chatto & Windus.

Platt, J. (1981a) 'Evidence and proof in documentary research', *Sociological Review*, 29: 31–66.

Platt, J. (1981b) 'On interviewing one's peers', *British Journal of Sociology*, 32: 75–91.

Platt, S. and Kreitman, N. (1985) 'Parasuicide and unemployment among men in Edinburgh 1968– 1982', *Psychological Medicine*, 15: 113–23.

Plummer, K. (1983) *Documents of Life: An Introduction to the Problems and Literature of a Humanistic Method*, London: Allen & Unwin.

Prandy, K., Stewart, A. and Blackburn, R.M. (1982) *White-Collar Work*, London: Macmillan.

Przeworski, A. and Teune, H. (1970) *The Logic of Comparative Social Inquiry*, New York: Wiley.

Psacharopoulos, G. (1981) 'Lifetime profiles of earnings and employment: a survey', *Social Science Information*, 20: 743–85.

Punch, M. (1979) *Policing the Inner City: A Study of Amsterdam's Warmoesstraat*, Hamden CT: Archon Books.

Ragin, C.C. (1987) *The Comparative Method: Moving Beyond Qualitative and Quantitative Strategies*, Berkeley: University of California Press.

Ragin, C.C. (ed.) (1991) *Issues and Alternatives in Comparative Social Research*, Leiden: Brill.

Ragin, C.C. *et al.* (1984) 'Assessing discrimination: a Boolean approach', *American Sociological Review*, 49: 221–34.

Reif, K. and Inglehart, R. (eds) (1991) *Eurobarometer: The Dynamics of European Public Opinion*, London: Macmillan.

Reinharz, S. (1992) *Feminist Methods in Social Research*, New York: Oxford University Press.

Reskin, B. and Padavic, I. (1994) *Women and Men at Work*, Thousand Oaks: Pine Forge Press.

Reuss-Ianni, E. (1983) *Two Cultures of Policing: Street Cops and Management Cops*, New Brunswick NJ: Transaction Books.

Rexroat, C. and Shehan, C. (1984) 'Expected versus actual work roles of women', *American Sociological Review*, 49: 349–58.

Rindfuss, R.R. *et al.* (1984) 'The transition to motherhood: the intersection of structural and temporal dimensions', *American Sociological Review*, 49: 359–72.

Ritchie, J. and Wilson, P. (1979) *Social Security Claimants: A survey amongst the* customers of a local social security office carried out on behalf of the DHSS, London: OPCS.

Robins, P.K. *et al.* (ed.) (1980) *A Guaranteed Annual Income: Evidence from a Social Experiment*, New York: Academic Press.

Robinson, R.V. (1984) 'Reproducing class relations in industrial capitalism', *American Sociological Review*, 49: 182–96.

Robinson, R.V. and Kelley, J. (1979) 'Class as conceived by Marx and Dahrendorf: effects on income inequality and politics in the United States and Great Britain', *American Sociological Review*, 44: 38–58.

Robinson, W.S. (1950) 'Ecological correlations and the behaviour of individuals', *American Sociological Review*, 15: 351–7.

Robson, C. (1993) *Real World Research*, Oxford: Blackwell.

Rockman, B. (1976) *Studying Elite Political Culture: Problems in Design and Interpretation*, Pittsburgh: University Center for International Studies.

Rogers, D. and Chung, N.H. (1983) *110 Livingston Street Revisited: Decentralisation in Action*, New York: New York University Press.

Rokkan, S. (ed.) (1968) *Comparative Research Across Cultures and Nations*, Paris: Mouton.

Roos, P.A. (1983) 'Marriage and women's occupational attainment in cross-cultural perspective', *American Sociological Review*, 48: 852–64.

Rose, D. (1997) *Constructing Classes*, University of Essex ESRC Research Centre.

Rose, E.J.B. *et al.* (1969) *Colour and Citizenship, A Report on British Race Relations*, Oxford: Oxford University Press.

Rose, M. (1999) 'Explaining and forecasting job satisfaction: the contribution of occupational profiling', Future of Work Working Paper, Bath: University of Bath.

Rose, R. (1976) 'Disciplined research and undisciplined problems', *Inter-national Social Science Journal*, 28: 99–121.

Rosen, B. and Jerdee, T.H. (1975) 'Effects of employee's sex and threatening versus pleading appeals on managerial evaluations of grievances', *Journal of Applied Psychology*, 60: 442–5.

Rosenbaum, J.E. (1984) *Career Mobility in a Corporate Hierarchy*, New York: Academic Press.

Rosenberg, M. (1968) *The Logic of Survey Analysis*, New York: Basic Books.

Rosenthal, R. (1976) *Experiments Effects in Behavioural Research*, Enlarged edition, New York: Irvington.

Rosenthal, R. (1984) *Meta-Analytic Procedures for Social Research*, Beverly Hills: Sage.

Rosenthal, R. and Jacobson, L. (1968) *Pygmalion in the Classroom*, New York: Holt, Rinehart & Winston.

Rosenthal, R. and Rubin, D.B. (1978) 'Interpersonal expectancy effects: the first 345 studies', *Behavioural and Brain Sciences*, 3: 377–86.

Rosenthal, R. and Rubin, D.B. (1980) 'Summarising 345 studies of inter-personal expectancy effects', pp. 79–95 in R. Rosenthal (ed.) *New Directions for Method-ology of Social and Behavioural Science No.5: Quantitative Assessment of Research Domains*, San Francisco: Jossey-Bass.

Rosner, M. (1982) *Democracy, Equality and Change: The Kibbutz and Social Theory*, Darby PA: Norwood Editions.

Ross, C.E. and Mirowsky, J. (1984) 'Socially-desirable response and acquiescence in a cross-cultural survey of mental health', *Journal of Health and Social Behaviour*, 25: 189–97.

Ross, H.L. and Sawhill, I.V. (1975) *Time of Transition: The Growth of Families Headed by Women*, Washington DC: Urban Institute.

Rossi, P.H. (1971) 'Observations on the organisation of social research', pp. 151–72 in R. O'Toole (ed.) *The Organisation, Management and Tactics of Social Research*, Cambridge MA: Schenkman.

Rossi, P.H. (1980) 'The Presidential address: the challenge and opportunities of applied social research', *American Sociological Review*, 45: 889–904.

Rossi, P.H. (1987) 'No good applied social research goes unpunished', *Society*, 25: 73–79.

Rossi, P. and Freeman, H.E. (1999) *Evaluation: A Systematic Approach*, London: Sage.

Rossi, P.H., Berk, R.A. and Lenihan, K.J. (1980) *Money, Work, and Crime: Experimental Evidence*, New York: Academic Press.

Rossi, P.H. *et al.* (1974) 'Measuring household social standing', *Social Science Research*, 3: 169–90.

Rossi, P.H. *et al.* (1983a) *Victims of the Environment*, New York: Plenum Publishing.

Rossi, P.H. *et al.* (eds) (1983b) *Handbook of Survey Research*, New York: Academic Press.

Rossi, R.J. *et al.* (1976) *Methodology of the Project TALENT 11–year Follow-up Study*, Palo Alto CA: American Institutes for Research.

Roth, J.A. (1966) 'Hired hand research', *American Sociologist*, 1: 190–6. Reprinted pp. 392–406 in N.K. Denzin (ed.) *Sociological Methods: A Sourcebook*, New York: McGraw-Hill, 1978.

Royal Commission on the Distribution of Income and Wealth (1975–1980) *Reports, Evidence and Background Papers*, London: HMSO.

Rubery, J. and Fagan, C. (1993) *Occupational Segregation of Women and Men in the European Community*, Social Europe Supplement 3/93, Luxembourg: OOPEC.

Rubinstein, W.D. (1981) *Men of Property: The Very Wealthy in Britain since the Industrial Revolution*, London: Croom Helm.

Ruhm, C. (1998) 'The economic consequences of parental leave mandates: lessons from Europe', *Quarterly Journal of Economics*, 113: 285–318.

Runciman, W.C. (1983) *A Treatise on Social Theory, Vol. I: The Methodology of Social Theory*, Cambridge: Cambridge University Press.

Runyan, W.M. (1982) *Life Histories and Psychobiography: Explorations in Theory and Method*, New York: Oxford University Press.

Rutter, M. (1981) 'Longitudinal studies: a psychiatric perspective', pp. 326–36 in S.A. Mednick and A.E. Baert (eds) *Prospective Longitudinal Studies*, Oxford: Oxford University Press.

Rutter, M. *et al.* (1979) *Fifteen Thousand Hours: Secondary Schools and Their Effects on Children*, London: Open Books.

Ryder, N.B. (1965) 'The cohort as a concept in the study of social change', *American Sociological Review*, 30: 843–61. Reprinted pp. 138–67, 324–7 in M. Bulmer (ed.) *Sociological Research Methods*, London: Macmillan, 1977.

Salaff, J.W. (1981) *Working Daughters of Hong Kong: Filial Piety or Power in the Family?*, Cambridge: Cambridge University Press.

Saris, W.E. (1991) *Computer-Assisted Interviewing*, Newbury Park: Sage.

Saunders, C. and Marsden, D. (1981) *Pay Inequalities in the European Communities*, London: Butterworth.

Saunders, P. (1997) 'Social mobility in Britain: an empirical evaluation of two competing explanations', *Sociology*, 31: 261–88.

Saxe, L. and Fine, M. (1981) *Social Experiments: Methods for Design and Evaluation*, Beverly Hills: Sage.

Sayer, A. (1984, 1992) *Method in Social Science: A Realist Approach*, London: Hutchinson.

Scase, R. and Goffee, R. (1980) *The Real World of the Small Business Owner*, London: Croom Helm.

Schaie, K.W. (ed.) (1983) *Longitudinal Studies of Adult Psychological Development*, New York: Guilford Press.

Schelling, T.C. (1978) *Micromotives and Macrobehaviour*, New York: Norton.

Scott, J., Braun, M. and Alwin, D. (1998) 'Partner, parent, worker: family and gender roles', pp. 19–37 in R. Jowell *et al.* (eds) *British and European Social Attitudes – the 15th Report: How Britain Differs*, Aldershot: Ashgate.

Scott, R.A. and Shore, A.R. (1979) *Why Sociology Does Not Apply: A Study of the Use of Sociology in Public Policy*, New York: Elsevier.

Semin, G.R. and Manstead, A.S.R. (1983) *The Accountability of Conduct: A Social Psychological Analysis*, New York: Academic Press.

Sen, A. (1981) *Poverty and Famines: An Essay on Entitlement and Deprivation*, Oxford: Oxford University Press.

Sewell, W.H. and Hauser, R.M. (1975) *Education, Occupation and Earnings: Achievement in the Early Career*, New York: Academic Press.

Shapiro, D. and Mott, F.L. (1983) 'Effects of selected variables on work hours of young women', *Monthly Labor Review*, 106, 7: 31–4.

Shaw, C.R. (1966) *The Jack-Roller*, 2nd ed., Phoenix: Phoenix.

Shaw, L.B. (1985) 'Determinants of the increasing work attachment of married women', *Work and Occupations*, 12: 41–57.

Sherman, L.W. and Berk, R.A. (1984), 'The specific deterrent effects of arrest for domestic assault', *American Sociological Review*, 49: 261–72.

Sieber, S.D. (1973) 'The integration of fieldwork and survey methods', *American Journal of Sociology*, 78: 1335–59.

Siebert, W.S. and Sloane, P.J. (1981) 'The measurement of sex and marital status discrimination at the workplace', *Economica*, 48: No. 190: 125–41.

Siemiatycki, J. (1979) 'A comparison of mail, telephone and home interview strategies for household health surveys', *American Journal of Public Health*, 69: 238–45.

Silverman, D. (1993) *Interpreting Qualitative Data: Methods for Analyzing Talk, Text and Interaction*, London: Sage.

Simon, R.J. (1985) *Public Opinion and the Immigrant: Print Media Coverage 1880–1980*, Lexington MA: Lexington Books.

Simons, H. (ed.) (1980) *Towards a Science of the Singular: Essays about Case Study in Educational Research and Evaluation*, Occasional Publication No. 10, Norwich: Centre for Applied Research in Education.

Simpson, I.H. *et al.* (1982) 'Occupational recruitment, retention, and labour force cohort representation', *American Journal of Sociology*, 87: 1287–313.

Sklair, L. (1999a) 'Globalization', pp. 321–45 in S. Taylor (ed.) *Sociology: Issues and Debates*, London: Macmillan.

Sklair, L. (1999b) 'Global system theory and the *Fortune* global 500', *International Journal of Politics, Culture and Society*, 12: 435–50.

Sklair, L. (2000) *The Making of a Transnational Capitalist Class*, Oxford: Blackwell.

Skocpol, T. (1979) *States and Social Revolutions: A Comparative Analysis of France, Russia and China*, Cambridge: Cambridge University Press.

Slomczynski, K.M., Miller, J. and Kohn, M.L. (1981) 'Stratification, work and values: A Polish–United States comparison', *American Sociological Review*, 46: 720–44.

Small, S. (1983) *Police and People in London, Vol II: A Group of Young Black People*, London: Policy Studies Institute.

Smeeding, T., O'Higgins, M. and Rainwater, L. (1985a) *An Introduction to the Luxembourg Income Study*, Working Paper No. 1, Luxembourg: LIS-CEPS Institute.

Smeeding, T., O'Higgins, M. and Rainwater, L. (1985b) *Poverty in Major Industrialised Countries*, Working Paper No. 2, Luxembourg: LIS-CEPS Institute.

Smeeding, T., O'Higgins, M. and Rainwater, L. (eds) (1990) *Poverty, Inequality and Income Distribution in Comparative Perspective*, London: Harvester Wheatsheaf.

Smelser, N. (1976) *Comparative Methods in the Social Sciences*, Englewood Cliffs NJ: Prentice-Hall.

Smelser, N.J. (1980) 'Biography, the structure of explanation, and the evaluation of theory in sociology', pp. 23–30 in H.M. Blalock (ed.) *Sociological Theory and Research: A Critical Appraisal*, New York: Free Press and London: CollierMacmillan.

Smith, D. (1982) *Conflict and Compromise, Class Formation in English Society 1830–1914*, London: Routledge.

Smith, D.H. and Inkeles, A. (1966) 'The Om scale: a comparative social psychological measure of individual modernity', *Sociometry*, 26: 353–77.

Smith, D.J. (1981) *Unemployment and Racial Minority Groups*, London: Policy Studies Institute.

Smith, D.J. (1983a) *Police and People in London, Vol. I: A Survey of Londoners*, London: Policy Studies Institute.

Smith, D.J. (1983b) *Police and People in London, Vol. III: A Survey of Police Officers*, London: Policy Studies Institute.

Smith, D.J. and Gray, J. (1983) *Police and People in London, Vol. IV The Police in Action*, London: Policy Studies Institute.

Smith, H.W. (1975) *Strategies of Social Research: The Methodological Imagination*, Englewood Cliffs NJ: Prentice-Hall.

Smith, J.P. and Thomas, D. (1998) 'On the road: marriage and mobility in Malaysia', *Journal of Human Resources*, 33: 805–29.

Smith, S.J. (1985) 'Revised worklife tables reflect 1979–80 experience', *Monthly Labor Review*, 108, 8: 23–30.

Southgate, P. (1984) 'Crime and attitude surveys as an aid to policing', *Home Office Research Bulletin*, No. 18: 16–18.

Spain, D.S. and Bianchi, S.M. (1996) *Balancing Act*, New York: Russell Sage Foundation.

Spenner, K.I. (1983) 'Deciphering Prometheus: temporal change in the skill level of work', *American Sociological Review*, 48: 824–37.

Sproat, K.V. *et al.* (1985) *The National Longitudinal Surveys of Labor Market*

*Experience: An Annotated Bibliography of Research*, Lexington MA: Lexington Books.

Stacey, M. (1960) *Tradition and Change: A Study of Banbury*, Oxford: Oxford University Press.

Stacey, M. (1969) *Methods of Social Research*, Oxford: Pergamon.

Stacey, M. *et al.* (1975) *Power, Persistence and Change: A Second Study of Banbury*, London: Routledge.

Statistics Netherlands (1992) *The Socio-Economic Panel Survey: Content, Design and Organisation*, Voorburg/Heerlen: Netherlands Central Bureau of Statistics, Statistics of Income and Consumption Branch.

Steele, S.F. *et al.* (1999) *Solution-Centred Sociology: Addressing Problems Through Applied Sociology*, Thousand Oaks: Sage.

Stevens, P. and Willis, C.F. (1979) *Race, Crime and Arrests*, Home Office Research Study No. 58, London: HMSO.

Stewart, D.W. (1984) *Secondary Research: Information Sources and Methods*, Beverly Hills: Sage.

Stewart, D.W. and Shamdasani, P.N. (1990) *Focus Groups: Theory and Practice*, Newbury Park: Sage.

Stolzenberg, R.M. and Relles, D.A. (1997) 'Tools for intuition about sample selection bias and its correction', *American Sociological Review*, 62: 494–507.

Stolzenberg, R.M. and Waite, L.J. (1977) 'Age, fertility expectations and plans for employment', *American Sociological Review*, 42: 769–83.

Storey, D.J. (1994) *Understanding the Small Business Sector*, London: Routledge.

Stouffer, S.A. (1950) 'Some observations on study design', *American Journal of Sociology*, 55: 355–61.

St Pierre, R.G. (ed.) (1983) *Management and Organisation of Program Evaluation*, San Francisco: Jossey-Bass.

Strong, P.M. and Davis, A.G. (1977) 'Roles, role formats and medical encounters: a cross-cultural analysis of staff–client relationships in children's clinics', *Sociological Review*, 25: 775–800.

Sudman, S. (1976) *Applied Sampling*, New York: Academic Press.

Sykes, R.E. and Brent, E.E. (1983) *Policing: A Social Behaviourist Perspective*, New Brunswick, NJ: Rutgers University Press.

Szalai, A. *et al.* (eds) (1972) *The Use of Time*, The Hague: Mouton.

Szekelyi, M. and Tardos, R. (1993) 'Attitudes that make a difference: expectancies and economic progress', Discussion papers of the Institute for Research on Poverty, University of Wisconsin.

Szreter, S. (1996) *Fertility, Class and Gender in Britain 1860–1940*, Cambridge: Cambridge University Press.

Tajfel, H. (ed.) (1984) *The Social Dimension: European Developments in Social Psychology*, 2 vols, Cambridge: Cambridge University Press.

Tallman, I. *et al.* (1974) 'SIMCAR: A game simulation method for cross-national family research', *Social Science Information*, 13: 121–44.

Tallman, I. *et al.* (1983) *Adolescent Socialisation in Cross-Cultural Perspective*, New York: Academic Press.

Tanur, J.M. (1983) 'Methods for large-scale surveys and experiments', pp. 1–71 in S. Leinhardt (ed.) *Sociological Methodology 1983–1984*, San Francisco: Jossey-Bass.

Taub, R.P. *et al.* (1984) *Paths of Neighbourhood Change: Race and Crime in Urban America*, Chicago: University of Chicago Press.

Taylor, C.L. (ed.) (1980) *Indicator Systems for Political, Economic, and Social Analysis*, Cambridge MA: Oelgeschlager, Gunn & Ham.

Taylor, C.L. and Jodice, D.A. (1983) *World Handbook of Political and Social Indicators*, 3rd ed., 2 vols, New Haven CT: Yale University Press.

Taylor, M. (ed.) (1998) *British Household Panel Survey User Manual*, Colchester: University of Essex.

Terkel, S. (1974) *Working: People Talk about What They Do All Day and How They Feel about What They Do*, New York: Pantheon.

Thomas, P. (1985) *The Aims and Outcomes of Social Policy Research*, London: Croom Helm.

Thompson, B. *et al.* (1981) 'Longitudinal studies in Aberdeen, Scotland', pp. 60–76 in S.A. Mednick and A.E. Baert (eds) *Prospective Longitudinal Research*, Oxford: Oxford University Press.

Thompson, D. (1981) 'The ethics of social experimentation: the case of DIME', *Public Policy*, 29: 369–98.

Thompson, P. (1975) *The Edwardians: The Remaking of British Society*, London: Weidenfeld & Nicolson.

Thornberry, T.P. and Christenson, R.L. (1984) 'Unemployment and criminal involvement: an investigation of reciprocal causal structures', *American Sociological Review*, 49: 398–411.

Thornberry, T.P. and Farnworth, M. (1982) 'Social correlates of criminal involvement: further evidence on the relationship between social status and criminal behaviour', *American Sociological Review*, 47: 505–18.

Todd, J.E. and Dodd, T. (1985) *Children's Dental Health in the United Kingdom 1983*, London: HMSO.

Tomlinson, S. (1983) *Ethnic Minorities in British Schools: A Review of the Literature 1960–82*, London: Heinemann.

Torode, B. (1984) *The Extra-Ordinary in Ordinary Language: Social Order in the Talk of Teachers*, Rotterdam: Konteksten.

Tourangeau, R. and Smith, A.W. (1985) 'Finding subgroups for surveys', *Public Opinion Quarterly*, 49: 351–65.

Townsend, P. (1979) *Poverty in the United Kingdom*, London: Allen Lane.

Traugott, M.W. and Clubb, J.M. (1976) 'Machine-readable data production by the federal government', *American Behavioural Scientist*, 19: 387–408.

Treiman, D.J. (1977) *Occupational Prestige in Comparative Perspective*, New York: Academic Press.

Tuma, N.B. and Hannan, M.T. (1979) 'Approaches to the censoring problem in analysis of event histories', pp. 209–40 in K.F. Schuessler (ed.) *Sociological Methodology*, San Francisco: Jossey-Bass.

Tuma, N.B. Hannan, M.T. and Groeneveld, L.P. (1979) 'Dynamic analysis of event histories', *American Journal of Sociology*, 84: 820–54.

Udy, S.H. (1964) 'Cross-cultural analysis: a case study', pp. 161–83 in *Sociologists at Work* (ed.) P.E. Hammond, New York: Basic Books.

Useem, M. (1976) 'State production of social knowledge: patterns in government financing of academic social research', *American Sociological Review*, 41: 613–29.

Van Dijk, J. *et al.* (1990) *Experience of Crime Across the World: Key Findings of the 1989 International Crime Survey*, Deventer: Kluwer.

Van Dijk, J. *et al.* (1993) *Criminal Victimisation in the Industrialised World: Key Findings of the 1989 and 1992 International Crime Surveys*, Directorate for Crime Prevention, Ministry of Justice, PO Box 20301, NL-2500 EH, The Hague, Netherlands.

Van Dijk, J. *et al.* (1998) *Criminal Victimisation in Eleven Industrialised Countries*, Directorate for Crime Prevention, Ministry of Justice, PO Box 20301, NL-2500 EH, The Hague, Netherlands.

Van Maanen, J. (ed.) (1979) 'Qualitative methodology: a symposium', *Administrative Science Quarterly*, 24: 519–702. Reprinted as *Qualitative Methodology*, Beverly Hills: Sage, 1983.

Veevers, J.E. (1973) 'Voluntarily childless wives: an exploratory study', *Sociology and Social Research*, 57: 356–66.

Voorhees-Rosen, D.J. and Rosen, D.H. (1981) 'Shetland: the effects of rapid social change on mental health (Scotland)', pp. 178–88 in S.A. Mednick and A.E. Baert (eds) *Prospective Longitudinal Research*, Oxford: Oxford University Press.

Waite, L.J. and Stolzenburg, R.M. (1976) 'Intended childbearing and labor force participation of young women: insights from nonrecursive models' *American Sociological Review*, 41: 235–52.

Waldfogel, J. (1998) 'The family gap for young women in the United States and Britain: Can maternity leave make a difference?', *Journal of Labor Economics*, 16: 505–45.

Waldfogel, J. (1999) 'The impact of the Family and Medical Leave Act', *Journal of Policy Analysis and Management*, 18: 281–302.

Walker, M.A. (ed.) (1981) *Crime Statistics*, Oxford: Pergamon.

Walker, M.A. (1983) 'Some problems in interpreting statistics relating to crime', *Journal of the Royal Statistical Society*, Series A, 146: 281–93.

Walker, M.A. (1985) 'Statistical anomalies in comparing the sentencing of males and females', *Sociology*, 19: 446–51.

Walker, R. (ed.) (1985) *Applied Qualitative Research*, Aldershot, Hants: Gower.

Wall, W.D. and Williams, H.L. (1970) *Longitudinal Studies and the Social Sciences*, London: Heinemann.

Walsh, E.J. (1982) 'Prestige, work satisfaction and alienation: comparisons among garbagemen, professors, and other work groups', *Work and Occupations*, 9: 475–96.

Walton, J. (1966a) 'Substance and artifact: the current status of research on community power structure', *American Journal of Sociology*, 71: 430–8.

Walton, J. (1966b) 'Discipline, method and community power: a note on the sociology of knowledge', *American Sociological Review*, 31: 684–9.

Warwick, D.P. and Lininger, C.A. (1975) *The Sample Survey: Theory and Practice*, New York: McGraw-Hill.

Warwick, D.P. and Osherson, S. (eds) (1973) *Comparative Research Methods*, Englewood Cliffs NJ: Prentice-Hall.

Wasserman, I.M. (1984) 'Imitation and suicide: a re-examination of the Werther effect', *American Sociological Review*, 49: 427–36.

Webb, E.J. *et al.* (1966) *Unobtrusive Measures: Non-Reactive Research in the Social Sciences*, Chicago: Rand McNally.

Webber, R.J. and Craig, J. (1978) *A Socio-Economic Classification of Local Authorities in Great Britain*, OPCS Studies on Medical and Population Subjects No. 35, London: HMSO.

Weber, R.P. (1990) *Basic Content Analysis*, Newbury Park: Sage.

Weiss, C.H. (ed.) (1977) *Using Social Research in Public Policy Making*, Lexington MA: Lexington Books.

Weiss, C.H. (1983) 'Ideology, interests and information: the basis of policy positions', pp. 213–45 in D. Callahan and B. Jennings (eds) *Ethics, the Social Sciences and Policy Analysis*, London: Plenum Press.

West, D.J. (1969) *Present Conduct and Future Delinquency*, London: Heinemann.

West, D.J. and Farrington, D.P. (1973) *Who Becomes Delinquent?*, London: Heinemann.

West, D.J. and Farrington, D.P. (1977) *The Delinquent Way of Life*, London: Heinemann.

Westie, F.R. (1957) 'Towards closer relations between theory and research: a procedure and an example', *American Sociological Review*, 22: 149–54.

White, M. (1983) *Long-Term Unemployment and Labour Markets*, London: Policy Studies Institute.

Whitfield, K. and Strauss, G. (eds) (1998) *Researching the World of Work: Strategies and Methods in Studying Industrial Relations*, Ithaca: ILR Press.

Whyte, M.K. (1978) *The Status of Women in Preindustrial Societies*, Princeton NJ: Princeton University Press.

Whyte, W.F. (1955) *Street Corner Society: The Social Structure of an Italian Slum*, 2nd ed., Chicago and London: University of Chicago Press, re-printed 3rd ed., 1981.

Whyte, W.F. (1982) 'Social inventions for solving human problems', *American Sociological Review*, 47: 1–13.

Wiersma, G.E. (1983) *Cohabitation: An Alternative to Marriage?*, The Hague: Kluwer Academic.

Williams, C.L. (1989) *Gender Differences at Work: Women and Men in Nontraditional Occupations*, Berkeley: University of California Press.

Williams, C.L. (ed.) (1993) *Doing Women's Work: Men in Nontraditional Occupations*, Newbury Park CA and London: Sage.

Willigan, J.D. and Lynch, K.A. (1982) *Sources and Methods of Historical Demography*, New York: Academic Press.

Wilson, J.Q. (ed.) (1983) *Crime and Public Policy*, San Francisco: ICS Press/ Transaction Press.

Wolfgang, M.E. *et al.* (1972) *Delinquency in a Birth Cohort*, Chicago: University of Chicago Press.

Wolfgang, M.E. *et al.* (1985) *From Boy to Man – From Delinquency to Crime: Follow-up to the Philadelphia Birth Cohort of 1945*, Chicago: University of Chicago Press.

Wrench, J. and Lee, G. (1982) 'Piecework and industrial accidents: two contemporary case studies', *Sociology*, 16: 512–25.

Wright, E.O. (1985) *Classes*, London: Verso.

Wright, E.O. (1997) *Class Counts: Comparative Studies in Class Analysis*, Cambridge: Cambridge University Press.

Wright, J.D. *et al.* (1979) *After the Clean-Up: Long Range Effects of Natural Disasters*, Beverly Hills: Sage.

Wright, J.D., Rossi, P.H. and Daly, K. (1983) *Under the Gun: Weapons, Crime and Violence in America*, Hawthorne NY: Aldine.

Wrigley, E.A. (ed.) (1972) *Nineteenth Century Society: Essays in the Use of Quantitative Methods for the Study of Social Data*, Cambridge: Cambridge University Press.

Wrong, D.H. (1961) 'The over socialised conception of man in modern sociology', *American Sociological Review*, 26: 184–93.

Yin, R.K. (1993) *Applications of Case Study Research*, Newbury Park: Sage.

Yin, R.K. (1994) *Case Study Research: Design and Methods*, Beverly Hills: Sage.

Zeisel, H. (1982) 'Disagreement over the evaluation of a controlled experiment', *American Journal of Sociology*, 88: 378–96.

Zeisel, H. (1985) *Say it With Figures*, London: Harper & Row.

# Author index

# Subject index